# PATRIOTISM AND NATIONALISM

## Their Psychological Foundations

# PATRIOTISM
# AND NATIONALISM

## Their Psychological Foundations

BY LEONARD W. DOOB

*New Haven and London, Yale University Press, 1964*

Copyright © 1964 by Yale University.
Designed by Crimilda Pontes,
set in Caledonia type,
and printed in the United States of America by
Connecticut Printers, Inc., Hartford, Conn.
All rights reserved. This book may not be
reproduced, in whole or in part, in any form
(except by reviewers for the public press),
without written permission from the publishers.

Library of Congress catalog card number: 64–20915

*To Princess Mary de Rachewiltz and Professor Josef Schwarz,*
*Two friends in South Tyrol.*
*Each in a unique and different way*
*Embodies the deeper virtues and perplexities of patriotism*
*And evokes envy and respect.*
*They have been witting and unwitting mentors in this venture—*
*Let them hear an expression of profound gratitude and affection:*
*Servus, ciao, Grüss Gott*

# CONTENTS

# PREFACE

A few years ago I planned, as I wrote in my application to Yale University and to the John Simeon Guggenheim Memorial Foundation, to "test and refine conclusions" I had derived from research in Africa by collecting data in a European area involving conflict between two cultures. I chose South Tyrol in northern Italy for reasons besides its incredible beauty and attractiveness. I know German reasonably well, I could understand people without help from an interpreter. Just as Africans have been affected by outside cultures, those of Arabs and Europeans, so the Tyroleans must also have been influenced, I thought, by strangers, the Italians.

The brilliant analogy turned out to be a trifle false. The German-speaking people of South Tyrol have not been appreciably affected by contacts with Italians for many centuries or by being politically a part of Italy for more than four decades. But one influence is incontrovertible: the policies and the presence of Italians have increased Tyrolean patriotism. Patriotism and not acculturation very quickly became the subject of my inquiry. Then the step from patriotism to nationalism was unavoidable.

Unfortunately or not, I am a psychologist permeated with a long-enduring interest in anthropology and sociology. I cannot, as a result, consider a region or a problem in its own right. I painfully goad myself to search for similarities between the research of the moment and some wider universe—and this proclivity I consider neither praiseworthy nor conceited, but iniquitous and accursed. Quickly, I felt in South Tyrol, these people are not unique. What they say concerning their right to the land, for example, I heard Afrikaners and Zulu maintain in Natal in 1955: we were here first; not they. Or the close connection between love of national customs and a church, I recalled from the summer of 1940, pervades a community of pious, jolly Scots Catholics in Nova Scotia. And did I not similarly wonder, five years before that, in a small town in Mississippi, whether people speak the truth to a stranger when they wish to display the attractive features of their way of life?

I was unable, it became apparent in South Tyrol, to confine myself to Tyroleans. They had to serve as the inspiration for a general treatise which might embody not only my own impressions and research in Africa, Jamaica, and elsewhere but also, more importantly, the insights of sagacious, patient scholars. As ever, I groped to achieve a significant system of classification as a step toward analysis and principles. This book is the outcome.

Primarily my aim is to view, in a preliminary manner, patriotism and nationalism as they function inside patriots and nationalists. How do people feel when they discharge these roles, and why do they feel that way? Obviously I do not maintain that other modes of analysis—history, political science, journalism, literature—are less important; they are different. I have employed a psychological or behavioral approach because, as I have been unsubtly hinting, I am powerless to do otherwise and because I think, not unexpectedly, that such an approach really has been more or less neglected. So be it, then: South Tyrol is not the world but it is part of it; and usually a single good case provides more than intuition about the general phenomenon it would illustrate.

A writer, especially one who has happily worked outside his own country, incurs many debts whose number seems staggering when, with the task of writing completed, he tries honestly to acknowledge them. I spare no adverbs. The dedication singles out the two people who have been particularly influential and generous. My wife, Eveline Bates Doob, and Prince Boris de Rachewiltz have struggled unfailingly, often thanklessly, and perhaps successfully to prevent me from overlooking the viewpoint of Italy and of Italians. Dr. Roberto Biscardo, Dr. Fritz Ebner, and Dr. Rainer Seberich graciously permitted me to work in the schools of South Tyrol; and a similar courtesy was extended in North Tyrol by Dr. Alois Burtscher, Dr. Herbert Rainer, and Dr. Gottfried Reitinger. Margaret M. Nagle valiantly combed the amorphous literature and has been a cheerful, cheering critic; I am indebted to the Concilium on International Studies at Yale University for her services. Jane G. Olejarczyk conscientiously converted a manuscript into printer's copy which Jane V. Olson of the Press then prudently polished and sagaciously improved. I am deeply grateful to Yale University and the John Simeon Guggenheim Memorial Foundation. They did approve and support the plan mentioned in the first sentence of this Preface. I have not been faithful to that plan, I admit without blush or regret, and I rather imagine that they, like me, are not surprised.

L. W. D.

*New Haven, Connecticut*
*November 1963*

# 1. Analysis, Definitions, Methods, and Other Very Exciting Preliminaries

Nationalism is unquestionably one of the most important problems, if not the most important one, of this century. Surely it would be in better taste not to utter such a flat, modest conviction in the opening sentence of a book. Still whenever a writer voluntarily subjects himself to the joyful misery that writing entails he must feel that his theme merits a very high rating. It seems better, consequently, to make the statement unabashedly than to be coy or cunning. Convincing evidence in support of the claim, moreover, is unfortunately close at hand: nationalism—as well as patriotism —is related to war, and war is actually and potentially so destructive that it bestows pervasive significance upon any related topic.

Moans about nationalism are as pointless as complaints about disease or mortality. Fine feelings expressed verbally either in a crude or subtle manner do not alter nonverbal facts. Such phenomena must first be understood before they can be affected or controlled. Of course, of course, the semi-sophisticated must impatiently say, whoever believes otherwise? The banal reminder, alas, is not superfluous in the midst of the stream of spoken and printed attacks upon nationalism which appear almost whenever there is freedom of speech and press. And then, too, not only abuse but sometimes also praise is heaped upon nationalism, which is then viewed as the inevitable culmination of patriotism or God's will. Here, it must be disclosed, no sides are taken, or at least not deliberately. The purpose of this book is the understanding of the psychological foundation of nationalism, especially that of patriotism, through patient analysis. Guidance, control, persuasion come later, and then only after a dash of value judgment has been added.

1

And so the writer, miraculously, has required only two introductory paragraphs to purge himself of bias. His conscience is as clear as ever it can be. Let him plunge into the task at hand.

There are various analytic approaches to nationalism, since the topic challenges many learned disciplines. Foremost is the historian, who recounts either minutely or sweepingly the incidents in the development of one or more countries from a particular point in time at which nationalism is claimed to have been either absent or weak to another at which it became very strong or overpowering. In the strict tradition of his craft, this type of scholar emerges with an ordering of detailed events whose very concreteness suggests their singularity. Thus the growth of nationalism in Bolivia has depended upon a rather unique set of circumstances which cannot possibly have been replicated entirely in some other land such as modern Egypt. After he or his colleagues have surveyed nationalism in a number of countries, an historian may summon the intellectual courage to seek general trends in the developmental patterns; details may be singular but, on a higher level of abstraction, they can be grasped as illustrative of a unifying principle. The man producing unification may have been Bolivar in one nation and Nasser in another, and the life histories and the deeds of the two may also have been most diverse; but the two leaders, the induced conclusion states, possessed organizing skill and enough mystique to attract followers, and eventually they both were enthroned as heroes in their lands.

An historical account of nationalism in one or more countries may or may not relate aspects of this phenomenon to a set of specified economic, political, social, or geographical factors. The other social sciences, however, almost always deliberately seek to show that some $X$ associated with nationalism depends upon or varies with some $Y$ or set of $Y$'s. Immediately, it must be noted, much of the literature in those disciplines is admittedly historical too, again with a difference: the growth of one institution is singled out for special emphasis. Consider how policy and behavioral sciences generally deal with nationalism in countries outside the West. Political scientists stress almost exclusively the changes in government and the factors producing and affected by those changes. Economists in their turn concentrate upon the economic changes (preferably, according to the academic fashion of the day, quantitative ones) which allegedly occur before nations can function in the modern world of the United Nations and before they can participate in international trade; for them, nationalism is, more often than not, one of the noneconomic factors affecting economic events. Sociologists and anthropologists move a step or two away from historical analysis and offer the description and analysis of societies which, in the light of some definition, can be considered nationalistic.

The animal of nationalism is so large that a political scientist can focus upon the organization and structure of a nation-state or upon its political parties, an economist upon a country's natural resources or its international trade, a sociologist upon the origins and ideologies of the ruling elite, an anthropologist upon the changes in social organization demanded and produced by nationhood—and all of them may be discussing some section of the same elephant. Although insights from such sources are accepted with grateful acclaim, they are nevertheless not the subject of the present approach. For just as social science disciplines assume but do not systematically focus upon the human beings whose existence obviously is presupposed, so their analyses of nationalism omit or deal only incidentally with the people who live within the nation and who therefore reflect and affect, in varying degrees, their country's development and problems. Without claiming superiority or denying inferiority, this treatise would timidly concentrate upon the psychological foundations of nationalism within all the nationals of a country.

The mere assertion that there are psychological foundations of nationalism may elicit skepticism and disbelief. If the historical development of Bolivia and Egypt are uniquely different, then what reasonable ground exists for believing that Bolivians and Egyptians, who have lived under diverse nationalistic regimes, are psychologically similar? Naturally it is easy to say that the people are different; their languages, for example, are unrelated and so, to the extent that language affects behavior—and to some extent it does—they themselves must differ. Such diversities can easily be discerned and emphasized, but it is much more difficult and likewise important to discover and dissect the underlying similarities.

The foundations of nationalism, then, must be more or less universal for a relatively simple reason: the possession and exercise of similar potentialities and skills require similar attributes. Whether you live in Bolivia or Egypt or, for that matter, in Siberia or Buganda, most though not all relevant aspects of your behavior must be virtually identical if you are successfully to ride a bicycle. The machine's requirements are the critical factors that very definitely restrict the range of variations. Although nationalism is a bit more complicated than a bicycle, it also demands certain kinds of behavior and outlaws others.

The metaphor of the bicycle, however, is applicable to nationalism only by making a basic assumption: the nationalism to which people adapt and which they and their leaders create is everywhere similar, just as all bicycles are very much alike. Is this so? At issue is the tedious question of definition, a question which must therefore be at least tentatively settled forthwith.

### Definitions

Whoever writes about nationalism unveils a private definition in his introductory remarks; hence the literature on the subject is crowded with formal definitions. The following three may or may not be typical, but at least they stem from writers belonging to different disciplines:

> An ideological commitment to the pursuit of the unity, independence, and interests of a people who conceive of themselves as forming a community [Fallers, 1961, p. 677].
>
> A consciousness, on the part of individuals or groups, of membership in a nation, or of a desire to forward the strength, liberty, or prosperity of a nation, whether one's own or another [Royal Institute, 1939, p. xviii].
>
> A condition of mind in which loyalty to the ideal or to the fact of one's national state is superior to all other loyalties and of which pride in one's nationality and belief in its intrinsic excellence and its "mission" are integral parts [Hayes, 1937, p. 6].

Three points in the definitions may be effortlessly observed. They contain language, firstly, that is psychologically loaded:

"ideological commitment" and "people who conceive of themselves"; "a consciousness"; and "a condition of mind." In fact, some
writers, even though they are political scientists, agree with novel-
ists (Zangwill, 1917, pp. 37–39) that the distinctive attribute of a
nation is the feeling people have toward one another: "The sim-
plest statement that can be made about a nation is that it is a body
of people who feel that they are a nation; and it may be that when
all the fine-spun analysis is concluded this will be the ultimate
statement as well" (Emerson, 1960, p. 102). The acclaimed historian of nationalism quoted above notes that nationalism is used
in three other senses: to refer to the process of nation-building, to
the theory or ideal behind that process, and to the activities of
particular political parties. He stresses, nevertheless, the psychological element, because in his opinion "this is the nationalism
which in the twentieth century is most in evidence [and] which
colours thought and conditions action in political, social, and cultural spheres, in our domestic politics and in our foreign relations"
(Hayes, 1937, pp. 5–6).

Then, in the second place, definitions of nationalism revolve
around sociological or political concepts which themselves require
explication: "community," "nation," "national state," "nationality."
And, thirdly, they are not limited temporally, geographically, or
culturally: any group in the past, present, or future may be called
nationalistic if it satisfies the requirements that are set forth. This
means, therefore, that nationalism has been defined as (1) some
kind of psychological state (2) characterizing people in some sort
of group (3) anywhere, any time. Established social usage seems
sufficiently clear, or can thus be made to appear so.

Before using these three inductions as the bases for formal definitions, however, another trio of distinctions involving types of
human reactions must be distinguished. When people respond to a
stimulus pattern, they are affected inevitably by their antecedent
*predispositions,* which have been called central tendencies, traits,
feelings, beliefs, attitudes, response tendencies, etc. Then they
may make certain *demands* as a result of what they are perceiving
and of these predispositions. Finally, their demands may induce
them to take *action,* that is, they exhibit in consequence overt behavior.

In this analysis the predispositions, being subjective and internal, are referred to as *patriotism*. The concept is customarily used in precisely that sense; its most common definition, "love of country," is obviously subjective and psychological. *Nationalism* arises psychologically when patriotism leads to certain demands and possibly also to action. Nationalism is thus not a psychological term as such: the demands and the actions stem from a psychological state, patriotism, but the ensuing demands and actions are politically, socially, economically significant. Now, then, it is finally possible to unfurl two formal definitions reflecting these weighty matters as well as the gems salvaged from the literature:

> PATRIOTISM: the more or less conscious conviction of a person that his own welfare and that of the significant groups to which he belongs are dependent upon the preservation or expansion (or both) of the power and culture of his society.

> NATIONALISM: the set of more or less uniform demands (1) which people in a society share, (2) which arise from their patriotism, (3) for which justifications exist and can be readily expressed, (4) which incline them to make personal sacrifices in behalf of their government's aims, and (5) which may or may not lead to appropriate action.

These not so innocent definitions immediately raise two questions of fact. First, is patriotism universal? According to the definition, the answer is likely to be in the affirmative. People are always socialized in groups, one of which is certain to be recognized as a society with its own distinctive culture; they most certainly must come to associate their welfare and that of other groups to which they belong with that society. Patriotism may vary in degree; the traitor may be negatively patriotic; but zero patriotism does not seem probable.

Then, secondly, is nationalism also universal? Here the answer is *probably no*. For the patriotic conviction concerning the relation of welfare and country need not be accompanied by demands and actions. Potentially, however, patriotism can give rise to nationalism; if the beloved society is threatened, then preserving it can quickly become a national policy.

The two definitions are intended to have unlimited scope, so that reference can be made to patriotism or nationalism in the ancient or modern world and in nonliterate and literate societies. To designate a more definite universe of discourse, a modifying adjective can be added, such as classic, Western European, nineteenth-century, African, democratic, communist, or Christian. Or the patriotism and nationalism of a society may be examined piece by piece in terms of geographical regions, social strata, or political organizations. *National* either as an adjective (as distinguished from *nationalist* or *nationalistic*) or as a noun will be used without prejudice or psychological overtones simply to refer to any phenomenon associated with a nation, including the inhabitants.

Regrettably the definitions announced above contain words and phrases requiring elaboration. The patriot is said to be "conscious" because, having been made aware of his love of country, he can appreciate the fact that other people share his convictions; but he is only "more or less" conscious since, presumably, unconscious factors always play some role in behavior. The concept of "conviction" also carries psychological overtones: the national has ideals and beliefs concerning his country, himself, and the relation between the two. "Welfare" conveys the importance of patriotism: the person believes that his most valued goals are somehow connected with, or "dependent" upon, his country. In the words of one extremely astute analyst, he gives his "supreme" or "final" loyalty not to "the family, the tribe, the city, [or] the manor" but to his state or nation (King, 1935, pp. 1–2). Thus the state and not some other group possesses "sovereignty" from the psychological viewpoint (Swanson, 1960, p. 20).

The groups considered significant within the nation vary from society to society and from person to person, but they undoubtedly include the family and the equivalent of the church. The presence in the definition of a key concept from political science, "power," would emphasize that people are to some degree aware of the state's function in this respect. "Culture" suggests broadly the social heritage and the system of interlocking habits which people acquire during socialization and which both in fact and in fantasy they share with one another. And likewise "society" would indicate that the formal and informal organizations in which people are embedded—the social structure, the groups, the classes—function within the state.

The definition of nationalism, if we may now proceed to that concept, does not indicate the exact nature of the demands people make, for this is a substantive matter which depends on the historical context. Their general content, however, is specified when their origin is attributed to people's patriotism; hence those demands pertain to "the preservation or expansion (or both) of the power and culture" of people's own society. Although patriotism may be an individual matter, nationalism is most definitely social: people must "share" the demands. Noteworthy is the distinction between "preservation" and "expansion." Most nonliterate societies as well as the smaller and more "conservative" nations today are deeply interested in retaining most of the culture and power they already possess. The imperialistic expansion of some nations at the expense of others, on the other hand, is stressed by communist writers: "Imperialism is the period of an increasing oppression of the nations of the world by a handful of 'great' nations" (Lenin and Zinoviev, 1931); the bourgeoisie "has made barbarian and semi-barbarian countries dependent on the civilized ones, nations of peasants on nations of bourgeois, the East on the West" (Marx and Engels, 1930). The definition implicitly notes that expansionist demands flow from the desire to preserve and strengthen an existing nation by extending its influence; but the wish to preserve need not be accompanied by expansionist demands.

A few additional observations about the definition of nationalism must be briefly made. The assumption is stated that "justifications" accompany nationalist demands. Their nature, however, is not immediately specified but is discussed at length in subsequent chapters. The phrase "appropriate action" calls attention to the fact that action may or may not result from the demands; when there is action, it is "appropriate" in the sense that it represents an attempt to achieve those wishes. The range of ensuing activity that is motivated by patriotism is obviously very great. Thus the appropriate action for patriotic people living under a tyrant is to rebel. But before the rebellion they may simply engage in conspiratorial activity. Or they may seek temporary peace by rationalizing the status quo. In any case, the definition suggests, they stand ready to make personal sacrifices so that their government can be preserved or expanded: secondary drives within them are so strong that under some circumstances or in some situations their goal involves satisfactions to be attained only in collaboration with their contemporaries.

## Levels

The nature and scope of patriotism and nationalism have now been broadly suggested. They can be approached—and hopefully measured—on three different levels. First, in the manner of anthropology and sociology, attention can be focused upon the general tendencies in the society, such as customs, culture traits, folkways, etc., which indicate that a significant section of the population has absorbed certain traditions and hence can be jointly characterized. On this level, it is possible to speak of a "government" having a "nationalistic" policy or of executing some policy for "nationalistic" reasons. It seems wiser and more realistic, however, to presume that not an abstraction but identifiable officials of that government—with or without support from their followers, yet functioning within a society possessing its own more or less singular social structure—are convinced that their welfare or that of their country is definitely dependent upon preserving or expanding its power and culture, so dependent in fact that the policy or action is considered desirable or necessary.

The concept of "national interest" sounds very psychological since people of course have interests. In fact, though, the interests of a nation cannot be located with dispatch. Perhaps in this context the phrase suggests that a small elite in the country wants or does not want a policy or action; or else that over a long period of time everybody will be affected favorably or unfavorably by some measure. To a certain degree, therefore, the concept of national interest is based upon personification and as such is an important component of nationalism, yet it is not a psychological process. Similarly reference is made to "collective security" when what is meant is not necessarily the personal security of every citizen at the moment but the relation of the armies or the economies of various states to one another. Collective security is thus conceivable without personal security, and vice versa, although ordinarily some relation between the two exists.

Then, on a second level, an effort is made to detect or determine modal behavior exhibited under specified circumstances. Emphasized, for example, is the role that people more or less consistently perform in connection with a particular status. Under what conditions, the question here is, do people govern themselves by the convictions that form a part of their patriotism; just when and why do they make national demands or act nationalistically? Again, and with the same vagueness, attention is called to the conditions under which a country or a foreign office behaves nationalistically.

Finally, one particular modal tendency in the society can become the object of research, viz. the way in which the observed uniformities, or some of them, are organized within people and expressed by them. The terms here are not precise and are often abused—"modal personality," "national character," "basic personality"—but they serve the laudable function of seeking to relate discernible tendencies within many people to their personalities. Here is a psychological problem in a strict, narrow sense.

On any one of the three levels concerned with modal tendencies, the problem of individual differences has to be generally ignored. Although assuredly people differ with respect to age, sex, education, and the numerous groups to which they belong, research may be concentrated upon the responses of "normal" adults. Even the deviants, however, are likely to be influenced by the norms; they may be rebelling against such standards, or eventually they will wish or be forced to conform. Modal tendencies within a society, including those pertaining to nationalism, are of psychological significance simply because they indicate conformity. Nonconformity is important when it gives rise to detectable changes in the conformity-producing norms.

It is perfectly true, moreover, that group differences with respect to patriotism and nationalism may have enormous political and social significance within a society. The leaders of a nation, for example, influence the opinions and feelings of followers; in some instances it is the nationalism of the elite and not of the vast body of citizens that determines foreign policy and the country's reputation in international affairs. This gap between elite and masses can be slight (the Nazi hierarchy and a majority of Germans) or great (the prime minister or president and most Africans in the newly independent countries of that continent). In this book such intranational differences are not gainsaid but assumed. The contention is advanced, nevertheless, that the premier and the peasant, regardless of the social distance between them, regardless of the way in which they discharge their roles in the society, and regardless of the social and political structure of the nation, can be included within the same psychological frame of reference: each has convictions, each makes demands, each tries to carry out actions that are similar in form but vary in content when he is stirred by patriotism or nationalism.

The analyst, regardless of the level at which he operates, is always faced with a complication arising from the fact that frequently social processes interact over time. It may be seriously contended, for example, that patriotism strengthens nationalism and vice versa: at a given moment and under certain conditions, people's patriotic predispositions encourage their leaders to make nationalistic demands and engage in nationalistic activities, those demands and activities reinforce the patriotism, the still stronger patriotism permits greater demands and more intense activity, etc. A Spiraled Explanation (capitalized for painless reference in future chapters) must be invoked. The same situation exists in connection with a variety of other phenomena, such as race prejudice (Myrdal, 1944, pp. 1065–70) and acculturation (Doob, 1960a, pp. 19, 66–70). During a particular period of time, it is difficult if not impossible to distinguish cause from effect; and the question of which process was the initial cause in the past must usually remain unanswered.

A final gasp about this psychological approach: more than verbal baptizing, it is hoped, is occurring when patriotism and nationalism are analyzed psychologically. Immediately, it can be presumed, for example, that the predisposition now defined as patriotism operates within people when it serves some useful purpose for them (motivation); that they may be influenced by patriotism when they would apprehend the external world (perception); that they must slowly or suddenly learn its components (reinforcement); and that they may unlearn it (extinction). Critically important questions connected with extinction from a political standpoint also become evident: Under what conditions is patriotism likely to be weakened? Can nationalism give way to internationalism? In addition, since aspects of patriotism and nationalism resemble race or ethnic prejudice psychologically, it becomes possible to use the vast knowledge which exists in that field and which has been comprehensively and eclectically summarized in a single volume (Allport, 1954). For prejudice, according to modern usage, involves unfavorable attitudes toward outgroupers; and obviously patriotism also contains similar attitudinal components regarding other nationals.

## Measurement

A word about measurement, for the procuring of precise data is one of the surest ways to puncture loose, unprecise generalizations. The discussion here is of a preliminary sort, for references to methods appear throughout the book. It must be immediately presumed that nationalism, like virtually every phenomenon subject to scrutiny, is not likely to be either present or absent but, if not absent, then to be present in some degree. That which varies is the strength of patriotism as well as the demands and the actions to which such patriotism gives rise. The degree of patriotism may be related to the demands and the actions: the stronger the patriotism, the greater the probability that demands and actions will arise. That relation, however, is not a perfect one: staunch patriots can be content with what they have.

The strength of patriotism can be considered a function of the patriot's conviction that his welfare or that of his group depends upon the preservation or expansion of the power and culture of the society. At one end of such a continuum, he states and truly and deeply regrets that he has but one life to lose for his country; at the other, virtually a zero point, he has little or no interest in his country. More specifically, the two points can be qualitatively described:

*Strong patriotism:* the person feels that his welfare is intimately connected with the nation's power and culture; hence he subjugates many of his own important needs to the demands of the state. He is often affected by these patriotic feelings; he is conscious of his nationality; he seeks and finds evidence for his country's distinctiveness and aspirations; he joyfully identifies himself as a citizen of the country; he plans his life in a way which in his opinion best promotes the common weal. Of all his group loyalties, he is convinced that the allegiance to his country is the most compelling. The state is supreme, and should be so.

*Weak patriotism:* the person feels that his welfare is much more intimately and importantly connected with other groups than the nation; the power and culture of that nation may be of some concern to him but only as a matter of curiosity or as a target for hostility; when he obeys the state, he does so unwillingly or begrudgingly. He is rarely conscious of his nationality; he does not boast about his country or find evidence for its distinctiveness, and in fact may be quite ignorant concerning that alleged attribute; he considers himself primarily a member of the other groups to which he belongs, he may even stress the cosmopolitan aspects of his beliefs and behavior; and he plans his life in terms of non-national ideals. Allegiance to his country, in brief, has an exceedingly low priority. The state exists to serve people; it may be unavoidably important, but so are other institutions.

Like many other concepts in social science, that of patriotism is considered here to be both realistic and inferential. Realistically, most nationals would reveal, in varying degree, the presence of the predispositions mentioned above if they could be induced to consider themselves very carefully and deliberately and then to express their feelings and thoughts freely and completely. Ordinarily they stand relatively mute and do not spontaneously declaim their convictions or chant patriotically. When asked directly and bluntly, however, whether or not they share a sentiment related to patriotism or nationalism which someone else, a compatriot or an investigator, lays before them, they can indicate their assent or dissent with dispatch. Differently expressed: they are able more readily to recognize than to recall the components of their own patriotism. In addition, just as the partial view of the social-class structure possessed by people in each stratum requires a detached observer to collect data from all strata and then later to conceptualize them (Davis et al., 1941, pp. 59–83), so the components of patriotism cannot be totally ascertained by empirical research alone. You discover a great deal about patriotism and nationalism from talking with people, from listening to them, and from asking them direct questions; eventually, however, you yourself must assemble the pieces if you would view the picture as a whole.

This methodological query leads to a helpful hypothesis: the more readily or easily people respond spontaneously in a manner related to patriotism, the stronger and the more important to them their patriotic predispositions are likely to be. For strong and important response tendencies must be so frequently exercised and must lead so inevitably to satisfaction that the likelihood of evoking them under a large number of circumstances is increased. The deeply involved patriot lives by his creed; he seeks out and is offered opportunities to express his devotion. In contrast, a person immersed in his own affairs finds gratification in other groups and less often directs his attention, or has it directed, toward the nation in which he lives. The speed and the manner in which he responds to the suggestion that he report "what comes into your mind when you think of your country" can provide a sensitive index to, or at least preliminary insight into the strength and content of his patriotism.

The direct approach to patriotism is to ask people a question or a series of questions concerning their country. "Which country in the world gives you the best chance of leading the kind of life you would like to lead?" In 1948, the following percentage of people in samples from each of the indicated countries named their own country in replying to that question: 96 United States, 83 Australia, 51 Britain, 50 Norway, 45 urban Mexico, 43 France, 36 Italy, 31 Netherlands, and 30 West Germany (Buchanan and Cantril, 1953, p. 30). The question reveals something about people's patriotism of course, but the information is probably very limited. For one thing the time of the survey, shortly after the war, affected the replies; this must account for the low percentages among the Europeans, particularly in West Germany. Then, even if people replied conscientiously, they must have been considering "the kind of life" they would like to lead in fantasy without necessarily considering all concrete details: the most popular alternative country in all instances was the United States, which was noted for its economic prosperity. That such a question measured some fairly central disposition, however, is suggested by the relatively high agreement between the ranks of the countries as indicated above and their ranks with respect to other feelings ascertained during the same survey and also by objective measures. The feelings involved "security" as determined by the replies to four other questions and by the perceived flexibility of the social-class structure; the objective measures were the per capita income, the per capita food supply, and the living space as estimated from the population density (ibid., p. 35).

New subjective indices of patriotism and nationalism clearly need to be devised. Several will be subsequently suggested in the chapters which follow. Here one challenge for research methodology can be quickly mentioned. It may be that those with strong attitudes have or think they have well organized relations among their various beliefs and feelings; for them patriotism or nationalism is a philosophy or Weltanschauung from which they are able to discern interconnections among apparently discrete bits of behavior. Love of country in their case is not a Sunday phenomenon that is turned on for some occasions and off most of the time; rather it dominates their actions incessantly, and they are aware that this is so. But how can such a subtle, subjective state of affairs be validly tested?

The reader, the very patient reader, may at this point writhe, utter complaints concerning the verbal twists of this chapter, and then exclaim that too little attention is being paid to the actual behavior of people and nations. The unapologetic reply is that, while of course behavior is important and of ultimate concern, a knowledge of predispositions can furnish in advance a clue to future action. It is critical, for example, to estimate the strength of unexpressed patriotism because that predisposition is capable ultimately of affecting behavior. At the same time, the admission must be made, no prediction is possible only from a knowledge of predispositions. Whether or not patriotism leads to nationalistic demands and then results in nationalistic action depends both upon the strength of those predispositions and upon people's conceptualization of the consequences likely to occur from expressing themselves or engaging in appropriate action.

Let the reader try once more: cannot the strength of nationalism be measured by determining the extent to which the stated objectives of a nation are obtained? No, that measure reflects not only psychological factors involving the strength of people's convictions concerning their country's aims and their own welfare but also the actual resources and manpower of the government's disposal. In fact, objective indices, however inviting and useful, are similarly ambiguous or perilous. The readiness of nationals to modify existing practices by accepting innovations from other nations, for example, might be utilized as a negative index of nationalism. Such an assumption quickly leads an investigator into the quicksand of social change, a very tricky problem in its own right. In this writer's opinion, one, only one, point seems reasonably clear in the literature on that subject: the acceptance, modification, and relinquishment of any cultural form, whether nationalistic or not, depends upon the form itself as well as upon the culture. If this is so, the criterion of change must be viewed as highly relevant to the task of measuring the strength of nationalism, but not conclusive.

Or, common sense suggests, strongly patriotic people willingly support the policies of their government and are even eager to make the sacrifices demanded by their leaders. Do they also then both joyfully and honestly pay taxes? Tax-paying cannot be an infallible index since behavior seldom follows a simple cause-and-effect sequence; information is needed in each instance concerning the traditions associated with the collection of taxes, the modes of enforcing legal decrees, the nature and size of the tax, etc.— and the "et cetera" here is by no means perfunctory. Is not the existence of a high protective tariff a symptom of nationalism? Probably yes, at least for those believing that the purpose of the measure is to fortify the national economy. Their nationalism, however, is shared with most people in the country only if the latter are aware of the higher price they must pay for the protected goods and are eager to do so.

Another tempting approach is the survey of objective materials. Analyses have been made of the media of communication through which patriotism is engendered or reinforced. A classical book on

French nationalism, for example, presents a very adequate account of the contents of the French press and of the textbooks once employed in French schools. It is said, for example, that "over five-sixths of Frenchmen . . . are exposed to the strongly nationalist curriculum of primary education and not to the broader and more humanitarian training of later education" (Hayes, 1930, p. 50). There is of course a strong presumption that such exposure was successful to some degree, but probably there was also some kind of discrepancy between the media and the responses of the audience; unknown, in another word, is the effectiveness of the exposure. Here is the first example of a phenomenon which occurs so frequently in connection with efforts to understand patriotism and nationalism psychologically that yet another stereotyped, capitalized, expressive, bold phrase must be created: Risky Stimulus Inference. Such an Inference is one about people's reactions which cannot be precise and which requires validation because it is made exclusively on the basis of knowing only the external conditions confronting them. Usually no alternative other than running a risk of this sort is available if the analyst wishes to come at least close to the psychological problem at hand, but he undoubtedly never quite lands there.

It is possible to avoid the difficulties associated with measuring patriotism and nationalism psychologically by abandoning the task altogether. After all, what counts is the decision of the elite—why not concentrate upon them if the nationalism of a nation is to be understood? Such a view has merit in the study of government and international relations. Eventually, however, the ugly, nasty psychological questions reappear. Since leaders are people, how can their behavior be analyzed? Are they not also influenced by ordinary citizens? Do they not epitomize, though somewhat uniquely, national trends? Psychology enters any social science, if only to play a minor role; here it is being deliberately pushed onto the center of the stage.

## Types of Nations

The description of nationalism and of the patriotism from which its characteristic demands spring has been sufficiently abstract so that both terms, it is hoped, are potentially useful in any kind of society. There are obviously important differences between societies that must give rise to variations in the content, if not the form, of patriotism and nationalism. The nationalistic demands and activities of a tribe in central Australia are not the same as those of the Irish, though both love their country and are willing to defend it. For this reason three types of nations can be distinguished but, as is true of virtually all typologies, the distinctions between them must not be considered absolute. For convenience non-neological labels are provided:

*Traditional nations:* nonliterate, nonindustrialized societies, formerly referred to as primitive or savage, including most but not all of the countries now often called "underdeveloped." "Traditional" suggests that patriotism, nationalism, or any doctrine is not likely to be self-consciously formulated but to be accepted unquestioningly from the social heritage. Whether the loyalty of people in such a society is directed to a supreme leader per se, to a leader as a symbol of his nation, or to some combination of these is an empirical question and not a matter of definition. The term here would also recall the fact that all modern nations have evolved from various kinds of nonliterate groups at some time in the past.

*Insular nations:* literate, rural societies or communities where technology and urban influences are relatively unimportant. The Basques fall into this category, and so to a certain extent do the French Canadians. In the modern world, such nations are cultural enclaves; somehow they insulate themselves from the peoples surrounding them.

*Modern nations:* contemporary nations that are dependent upon industrialization and, to a certain extent, upon international trade. The nationalism associated with these countries in the nineteenth and twentieth centuries stemmed from the French Revolution, which, in the opinion of one historian, produced the following doctrine not only in France but also in other European countries, notably Germany and Italy: "the cult of liberty, the aspiration toward nationhood one and invincible, the longing for a national cohesion and a new national spirit, the idea of a state rooted in popular consent and enthusiasm and supported by the active participation of the people." Then within a decade there was a marked change: "The tyrant to be fought was no longer the domestic oppressor but the foreign enemy; the liberty worshipped was not so much individual freedom from a strong, authoritarian government but national independence and power" (Kohn, 1962, p. 1).

In addition to the nationalism associated with these different types of nations, one other phenomenon must be mentioned: *internationalism*. When governments delegate some of their power or some of their sovereignty to an international body, characteristic changes in the demands and the predispositions of some people in that state must take place.

The order in which the four terms have been introduced, indeed the terms themselves, would neither suggest nor preclude the possibility of an evolutionary development from the traditional nation to internationalism. Here is an issue happily beyond, way beyond, the scope of this book. No, the distinctions are required only in order to suggest that patriotism and nationalism appear under differing political, social, economic, and historical circumstances. A given nation, moreover, may contain societies of more than one type. In the United States, some Indian tribes still represent a form of the traditional nation; there are insular communities in mountain areas of the South; the country as a whole is modern; a very small segment is international in its outlook.

For other than psychological purposes, different distinctions may be fruitfully introduced, but usually they pertain to the precise goals sought by the state. Thus a sharp line is drawn between "the oppressed and competing nationalities of the nineteenth century and . . . the superpowers of the mid-twentieth century," since the scope and aim of certain European countries shifted quantitatively, perhaps even qualitatively, in less than a century. The same writer, however, notes that even these two expressions of nationalism have "one thing in common," which is that the nation is "the ultimate point of reference for political loyalties and actions" (Morgenthau, 1948, pp. 268–69). This "one thing" is sufficient to equate the two kinds of nationalism psychologically: whether the state seeks independence or the conquest of the world is an important distinction politically and morally, but either goal requires citizens whose patriotism and demands differ not in form but in detailed content. According to another historian (Shafer, 1955, pp. 5, 60), although modern nationalism may be quite unique, "loyalty, patriotism, and national consciousness are ingredients [which] preceded it in time"; and "sentiments akin to nationalism are possibly as old and as prevalent as man and society." It seems reasonable, in short, to bring together in a single analysis all kinds of social and political organizations and to examine their common psychological core.

The question of whether patriotism is the same or similar in traditional, insular, and modern societies is largely but not completely an empirical one. Certainly the conviction that there is a significant conviction between personal or group welfare and the government or state varies from nation to nation. In a traditional society, patriotism and nationalism are usually oriented toward preservation, although sometimes people or their leaders seek to extend their power or to establish international alliances. Generally insular societies emphasize preservation, but preservation may be attainable, in the opinion of the inhabitants, only through expanding power or by securing independence. Modern nations are also characterized by the demand for political independence (that is, either for continuing or acquiring it), which in turn is based on another conviction, viz. that nationals directly or through their leaders should manage their own affairs. People supporting internationalism are convinced that not all their personal welfare is linked to the nation, but that some or much of it is dependent upon an international organization; national sovereignty appears less important. In spite of such variability, however, it is still possible to maintain that the nature of the components of patriotism and nationalism does not appreciably fluctuate. Whether the conviction stresses preservation or expansion, people connect their welfare with the nation. Nothing sensational or radical is thus being defended; it is like saying that the concept of "intelligence" can be employed to describe behavior or people in any society and that therefore a man can be called stupid or smart, on different standards, whether he lives in Aden, America, or Austria.

*Purview*

The evidence offered in this book comes from three sources. First, there is the general scholarly literature on patriotism and nationalism which is part of social science. Although often the generalizations seem based upon insufficient evidence, they reflect the distilled wisdom and experience of scholars. Then, secondly, priority is given to concrete, empirical studies. Unfortunately, few of these exist.

Thirdly, considerable attention is paid to the patriotism and nationalism of South Tyrol for a completely fortuitous reason: the writer has collected data there and believes that the Tyroleans can serve—no better, but certainly no worse, than any other single area of the world—as a relevant case history. There are about 250,000 people who call themselves South Tyroleans and who live in the South Tyrol (Alto Adige in Italian); elsewhere this brief summary of the situation has appeared:

> After World War I the region of South Tyrol, which covers an Alpine area of 2,857 square miles from the top of the Brenner Pass to within 16 miles of Trent, was transferred by the Allies from Austria to Italy. At the time roughly 87 per cent of the inhabitants were German-speaking, 9 per cent Italians, and 4 per cent Ladins. During the last forty years [particularly in the Mussolini era], large numbers of Italians have moved into the South Tyrol while, according to available estimates, the German- and Ladin-speaking populations have increased only slightly. At the moment, therefore, about one-third of the population is Italian, almost all of whom live in the capital city of Bolzano (Bozen) and in the other large towns. By and large the relations between Italians and South Tyroleans (as the two groups generally call themselves) are hostile or evasive; from time to time, especially during the summer of 1961 [but continuing sporadically through 1963, as this account is being revised], electric power lines and, to a much lesser degree, public buildings [have been dynamited by a small group of patriotic terrorists receiving material aid and encouragement from irredentist Austrians]. South Tyroleans are Catholics and have their own political party. Above all else, they seek to retain their language and cultural identity, and appear thus far to have almost completely succeeded in doing so. Their proclaimed political goal is "autonomy" within the Italian Republic, which they define culturally as a diminution of Italian influence and politically as a greater degree of self-government than that permitted by what they consider to be Italy's deceitful interpretation of the 1946 Treaty of Paris.

> Presumably nonofficial groups in Austria, however, seek the reunification of South Tyrol with North and East Tyrol under the Austrian Republic. In the autumn of 1960 and again in 1961 Austria referred the claims of the South Tyroleans to the United Nations; negotiations between Italy and Austria and also [through 1963] between South Tyrolean and Italian officials have been taking place; but a lasting solution to the conflict seems to be neither imminent nor probable [Doob, 1962, pp. 172–73].

In a few instances data were also obtained in North Tyrol (whose capital is Innsbruck), the Austrian province from which the insular nation of South Tyrol was separated.

In addition, a simple, trite, literary device is frequently and unabashedly employed to enliven and to illustrate the exposition: statements enclosed in *single* quotation marks are fictions derived intuitively from the literature and from this writer's experience in various nations. Everyman, Every Patriot, Every National would thus indicate his point of view. That view of course requires but will not receive here substantiation because adequate data simply have not been discovered. Beware, therefore, of the sentences clothed in single quotation marks; they are timid hypotheses melodramatically expressed.

This chapter can be summarized and the remainder of the book foreshadowed by considering with some care the accompanying diagram which seeks to offer at a glance the high points of the analysis. The diagram is a modification of one previously employed to try to indicate all the factors which play a role in communication (Doob, 1961, p. 11) and can be invoked here because so much of patriotism and nationalism depend upon communication; yet modifications are necessary in order to elaborate upon people's reactions to their country. The beginning (at the top of the diagram), as is true on any psychological level, refers to the stimuli in the outside world which repeatedly and ultimately cause people to respond (Chapter 2). These stimuli reach nationals through certain Media of Communication, which is thus the second point on the diagram (Chapter 3). Then reactions occur, three aspects of which must be analyzed in some detail (Chapters

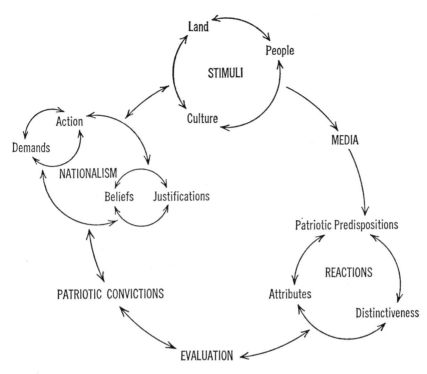

4 and 5). People do more than react—they also evaluate (Chapter 6). What emerge are the convictions of patriots concerning their own welfare and that of the significant groups to which they belong (Chapter 7). The path then leads to demands and actions, the hallmarks of nationalism (Chapter 8), and to the justifications therefor (Chapter 9). The justifications themselves, being important as a reflection of nationalism, are examined in some detail (Chapters 10 and 11) and then are illustrated in an interlude on war and peace aims (Chapter 12). The analysis ends where it started, viz. at the stimuli; but the second time around an attempt is made to discover the patterns that facilitate patriotism and nationalism (Chapter 13), with specific reference to the role performed by the enemy or foreigner (Chapter 14) and to internationalism (Chapter 15). The arrows in the diagram suggest very tentatively the probable interactions between the variables; only one variable, Media, functions in a single direction.

And now to work.

## 2. The Ingredients

A basic contention of this book is that, although the content of the demands behind nationalism and the nature of national actions vary, the patriotism from which they spring has certain ingredients that are roughly everywhere the same. People in the north may love a barren tundra and those near the equator a grassy savanna, but they both are emotionally attached to the land on which they live. Those in one nation identify themselves with people having brown skins, those in another with compatriots having white skins, but both have distinctive attitudes toward the people in their midst. And patriots in one country are willing to make sacrifices in behalf of a special kind of cereal, a semiannual festival, the virtue of bravery, and a dress of many colors, whereas those elsewhere are enthusiastic about meat, the church, thoroughness, and fur collars; but both revere a way of life, a culture. Land, people, and culture are the basic stimulus patterns or referents of patriotism; it is they that give rise to, and then become the essential components of, "national consciousness" or whatever the psychological ingredients of patriotism are called. In discussing this trinity of stimuli, it is neither possible nor desirable to avoid making frequent references to people's responses, if only because a stimulus becomes psychologically relevant when it evokes a response.

The problem of designating the stimuli of a milieu is an ancient and honorable one for which no completely satisfactory solution has been found. Long ago, for example, it was pointed out that the physical and social environments are not equivalent to the psychological environment. They become that environment only when they affect the behavior of the people under scrutiny. The people in turn need not be conscious of them in all respects; the wall behind a person belongs to a person's "momentary environment" even though he is not aware of it for the time being (Lewin,

24

1936, pp. 18–19). With such a viewpoint, a group of investigators once spent a year investigating the "psychological ecology" of a Midwestern community with a population of slightly over 700. At the outset they noted that the community had "a limitless number of parts," which included "such varied features . . . as the weather vane on the Courthouse, the town constable, the upper social class, Delaware Street, the Methodist Church, the Old Settlers' Picnic, auctions, the Negro residents, the Culver family, the Stop-for-Pedestrians signs, weddings, the volunteer fire department, a school tax of 9 mills, May Day, the North precinct, Mrs. Arla Grainger, a bonded indebtedness of $8,500, the *Midwest Weekly,* and the prevailing southwest wind" (Barker and Wright, 1955, p. 45). Careful, very careful observation indicated that these stimuli were socially structured and that people actually participated in only a limited number of the situations available to them. When 107 varieties of "community behavior settings" were ranked with respect to time spent therein, the site most closely related to patriotism and nationalism, "government and school offices," was eighth (ibid., p. 105).

What does such a survey accomplish? For one time period within a particular community it provides an accurate account of people's movements. It does not indicate how they reacted, how they felt about the "settings" in which they found themselves. Without this information there is no way of knowing why they drifted in and out of some settings more frequently than others. Indeed one moment at a ceremonial may have affected the participants more deeply or intensely than hours in "trafficways" (defined as "traveling between behavior settings"). Even with a knowledge of psychological space or of the entire psychological environment, in short, a Risky Stimulus Inference is still necessary to comprehend how the people themselves react to, conceptualize, and evaluate that space or that environment in which they perforce or voluntarily live. These reactions, conceptualizations, and evaluations, for better or worse, are being here scrutinized.

### Land

The initial referent of patriotism must be the land on which people live. Any randomly selected definition of nation usually features this attribute at the outset: "a group of persons born in a community having certain geographical boundaries and . . ." (Dingwall, 1946, p. 9). Psychologically, too, land is basic, since the goal or consequence of much early activity by infants and children is the exploration of ever wider areas of space. At first this space is confined to the child's own body, to his mother, and to the immediate surroundings. As he becomes reasonably familiar with his family's dwelling, he extends his vision and other senses to the neighborhood and eventually—and eventually, to what? Eventually to the entire land, the country, the nation. The description, it must be quickly stated, sounds and is deceptively simple. Actually, as will be indicated later on, solid evidence does not exist for assuming that the experiencing of space progresses in such tidily expanding circles of contact. At some point the sequence of body-mother-room-house-neighborhood-town-county-province-region-country-continent-hemisphere-world-universe is probably interrupted, and a leap is made from a circumscribed area to one farther afield. Before completing the exploration of his own region or acquiring some sort of familiarity with it, the child or the adult may journey elsewhere in his country or abroad. In addition, symbols begin to replace actual experience. But the land remains a concrete reality: here the home is located, here a living is earned, here the web of human relationship exists, here death eventually occurs. To purify an area in honor of a god, such as the island of Delos for Apollo, the Athenians "not uncommonly" removed the two most realistic symbols of human habitation: they prohibited births and burials on the sacred soil (Laidlaw, 1933, pp. 67–68).

Gradually as they mature, therefore, people come to designate some physical portion of the earth's surface as their country. It is true that the land itself is usually too large to be perceived at a glance the way a vase or a cow can be grasped, but tangible symbols are at hand which can be apprehended and understood. There are fixed boundaries indicated by concrete barriers such as rivers, seas, mountains, and forests. Artificial frontiers are made meaningful by gates, police and customs officers, signs, and flags; and the distinctive color on maps causes the abstractions of latitude and longitude to appear real. You know where your country begins and ends. In addition, various adjectives are in common use within each society to designate the land considered to be outside the perceived boundaries of the mother country: foreign, alien, overseas, external, strange, enemy, etc.

Some segment of the land, furthermore, is perceived again and again until it comes to signify or represent the whole. Any physical or natural feature can serve that function. There is the terrain itself: mountains, hills, plains, rivers, lakes, and indeed the very horizon. On the terrain are plants, trees, and animals. Then over time there are changes that are cyclical or progressive. Repetition of the seasons and of the weather becomes evident. During longer periods of time, growth, aging, erosion, and death occur. The variety is clearly almost infinite, but some features are selected as being noteworthy and are inextricably associated with the land. You can describe your country, or certainly the place where you were born, or where you now live: is it flat, sandy, rocky, fertile, cold, beautiful?

The importance of the land is suggested by the fact that "property rights," which usually include privileges and obligations with respect to the land or its products, are among the universal institutions of mankind (Murdock, 1945, p. 124). Even nomadic groups probably have some sense of territoriality. Although the Siriono in Bolivia have "no prescribed territories," they obviously recognize the land through which they roam: one band does not hunt in the neighborhood of another whose hunting trails are thus respected; and, to avoid contact with other groups, they retreat farther into the jungle (Holmberg, 1950, pp. 51–52, 62–63). All sections of a nation are not and cannot be valued equally—a distant area may appear relatively strange and even unimportant—but in some significant sense people connect the land with themselves and their welfare.

Obviously the land and its special features evoke strong emotional responses when they have been associated with a people's way of life, for then they realistically represent the important values of the society. A Comanche chief thus addressed American officials in 1867:

> You said that you wanted to put us on a reservation, to build us houses and make us medicine lodges. I do not want them.

I was born upon the prairie, where the wind blew free and there was nothing to break the light of the sun. I was born where there were no enclosures and everything drew a free breath. I want to die there and not within walls . . . why do you ask us to leave the rivers, and the sun, and the wind and live in houses? Do not ask us to give up the buffalo for the sheep [Wallace and Hoebel, 1952, p. 283].

## People

When patriots think of their country, they often have other people in mind. For inescapably associated with the routine of living are members of one's family, neighborhood, and nation. It is they who transmit and enforce the rules of the society, it is they who come to stand for home and country, and so it is they who can function as the stimuli that evoke feelings of membership and the corresponding patriotic predispositions. 'Whenever I recognize a member of my tribe on the streets of this town,' Africans who have migrated from their traditional homesites to urban areas say in effect, 'I get homesick.'

No subtle taxonomy is needed to designate the kinds of people who evoke patriotic responses. Almost always a distinction is drawn, by citizens and social scientists alike, between in-and outgroupers, between compatriots and foreigners, between countrymen and aliens. The following customs, classifications, or institutions exist everywhere and suggest the variety of human relationships that are evaluated, regulated, and hence perceived: age-grading, community organization, cooperative labor, education, etiquette, gift-giving, government, greetings, hospitality, inheritance rules, kin groups, penal sanctions, personal names, law, modesty concerning natural functions, population policy, property rights, residence rules, sexual restrictions, status differentiation, trade, visiting, weaning (Murdock, 1945, p. 124). Perhaps the most frequent differentiation of all is that between leaders and followers.

These distinctions immediately raise problems, only a few of which will be mentioned in passing at this point, and then to emphasize the importance of people as stimuli. First, is there really a sharp, qualitative distinction between compatriots and foreigners? At first a continuum seems evident: the number of people who can evoke the response of countryman and hence of some aspect of the nation simply increases as more and more groups are perceived or grasped. Parents are part of the immediate family, the immediate family is included among relatives, relatives are members of the same community, the community belongs to the region, and the process continues until some large group like the nation is reached. Again the same question that was raised concerning the perception of the land must be repeated here: Does the learning process really push people through such neatly constructed concentric circles? At some point in time, the extension must be discontinued: those on the other side of the national boundaries are probably never considered to belong to the ingroup, although temporary or permanent alliances between nations can very well bring them, for the purposes at hand, within the magic circle. The outgroupers, moreover, probably also fall along a continuum of eligibility as potential ingroupers: the nationals of one foreign country are considered similar or simpatico, those from another, bizarre or barbarous. The notion of a continuum from parents to nation and then among foreigners, however, undoubtedly oversimplifies some of the changing relationships among people. Ordinarily a child must consider himself a member of his parents' group, but on occasion he joins his siblings or other peers to wage war against them. At any rate, as stimuli people constantly remind us of the groups to which they and we belong, including their nationalities.

The very relativity of their status and attributes indicates the importance of leaders as stimuli that can arouse partiotic predispositions. Clearly the respect they evoke from their followers and the degree to which they are identified with the nation fluctuate from country to country and vary within a single country from one period to the next. During medieval times, the allegiance of Europeans, for example, tended to be toward the particular leaders they served in the smaller political units to which they belonged; but now loyalty to a large nation-state persists almost but not quite completely regardless of who its leaders at a given moment happen to be. Or during a war people are more likely to feel dependent upon and hence respectful toward their own leaders, who, consequently, as communicators stand a better chance of being persuasive or instantly obeyed.

It must be evident that people can be variously viewed. If you want a partner at the other end of a seesaw, you note your friend's weight or his distance along the board from the fulcrum. You may also react to him as a potential partner in a hunting expedition or a business venture. Or you may consider him a compatriot or a foreigner. In that last role he is making you aware of your nationality and of his. The human attributes likely to be perceived will be considered at some length in Chapter 4 and throughout the rest of the book.

### Culture

The land and its people are the stimuli, the concrete realities, of patriotism and nationalism. In all probability, however, as already stressed, no person ever directly experiences all aspects of his nonhuman and human surroundings, although he is likely to feel convinced that somehow he grasps them. How in fact is such a conviction acquired? After some initial experiences and after acquiring some facility in his native language, the child is able to short-circuit the learning process and to extend his knowledge not through actual contact but through symbolic extension. He does not have to meet all people in his area, in his country, in the world, to be able to believe that they have heads and eyes and feet; on the basis of what he has experienced he infers, assumes, feels that everyone anywhere has these attributes. What he rarely observes, in short, are the land and its people as such; instead he is confronted with or notes segments or symbols of those stimuli. These segments or symbols are traditional within his society and are summarized, quickly and securely, in the concept of culture.

On the land people are confronted with stimuli that are the product of human labor and ingenuity, the cultural artifacts existing in any society. These range from homes and public buildings to paths or roads and purely symbolic monuments. They include patternings of such structures: settlements, villages, cities. Human efforts to dominate or regulate the physical environment are also part of culture: the mode of cultivating fields and of tending herds (at least in societies possessing agriculture and domesticated animals); dams, levees, and bridges; transportation media; and other machines, tools, and instruments. In effect, any artifact can be singled out. The cataloguing of the possibilities may be endless, but every person in a society effortlessly recognizes the identifying features of his milieu. 'That building, that tower, that street, that way of stacking hay in fields, all these mean home and country.'

Care must be exercised not to make reckless or careless Risky Stimulus Inferences from the presence of cultural artifacts in a nation. Everywhere in the South Tyrol, for example, small shrines are visible: near houses, on roads, in fields, atop mountains, etc. Usually they are carved in a style which clearly distinguishes them from similar objects in Italy and therefore they possess the potentiality of reminding people of their nationality. But do they? Can it be inferred that they serve as a medium which reinforces patriotism? In fact, they are so much a part of the landscape that, it must be guessed, their nationalistic, if not their deeply pious religious, message usually goes unnoticed. Even Catholic priests who tip their hats or quickly bow their heads as they pass by and likewise their owners or guardians who lovingly and carefully tend them and often bedeck them with flowers may not note, when their attention is directed to them, their patriotic significance. The presence of these religious objects reflects people's piety, of course, but their precise psychological role for the present generation cannot easily be specified.

The uniqueness of a person can be directly observed; more frequently, however, that uniqueness is unnoticed and attention is concentrated upon the numerous social elements or customs which each individual shares with his contemporaries and constantly displays. The beginning is speech, which serves as the vehicle for expressing and receiving the conventional language of the society. Significance is also attached to nonspeech sounds such as grunts and sobs. The appearance of the human body conveys information concerning the person: the condition of his muscles and his skin can indicate his age and occupation, and other symbols are added culturally. The skin itself, for example, may be scarred or tattooed; the earlobes or the nasal septum may be pierced; a tooth or finger may be removed—and thus national membership or status is communicated. The body is also less irrevocably changed, although customarily such changes are retained just as tenaciously: any anatomical section, especially the face, can be loaded with cosmetics; coiffure is manipulated intricately or blatantly; and clothes are ruthlessly and ingeniously devised to be not only protective but also decorative, enticing, and comfortable. Ornaments and insignia may encumber the body and serve similar functions. Finally, a bodily movement is interpreted in accordance with prevailing custom, as a quick reference to gait or etiquette is sufficient to document.

In addition, the collective activities of people and the tools and instruments which they employ are regulated by custom and hence can be perceived as components of the nation. Here, too, the range is great. There are actions that sustain life directly and indirectly: the ways in which food and drink are obtained, the techniques for carrying on trade. And there are other actions that nourish the human spirit: religion, education, art. The universal and almost infinitely plastic needs of people everywhere, in brief, give rise to an almost infinite series of communications (Doob, 1961, pp. 56–145).

The responses to be evoked by cultural stimuli are usually unequivocal. Most often such unequivocality is achieved by labels attached to the land and its people. The labels are constantly perceived and then themselves become the prevailing responses. The most prominent symbol performing these stimulus-response functions is the name of the country. Then there are collective nouns enabling people to refer to themselves as if they were a single organism or entity operating in complete harmony and unison: people, folk, fellow citizens, public, electorate, generation, race. The addition of the possessive "our" to these words as well as to almost any noun referring to the land and its people quickly provides the same collective connotation: "our people," "our generation," "our natural resources," "our music." Eventually the nation as a word and concept is considered to be an organism functioning like a particular person, and so references are made to "the national will," "national destiny," "public interest," "public opinion," "the country's welfare," "Volksgeist," "Volksseele." At this point the mode of expression grows very, very personal: 'Our country is too proud to fight,' 'Our country has been insulted,' 'Our country goes to war,' 'Our country seeks independence,' 'Our country has a right to . . .' Such personification (Hayes, 1937, p. 17) may also be given a literal twist, and then a hero (Joan of Arc), a mythical figure (John Bull), a cartoon (Uncle Sam), comes to represent or in fact to be the country in people's thought. The concept of the nation, through verbalizations and slightly extended symbols, in short, acquires a superorganic sacredness of its own. To cast even a verbal slur upon it or its name or other symbol is blasphemy, hence taboo, and quickly and decisively punishable.

After the name of the country and other symbols therefor have been thoroughly learned and reinforced, they are capable of evoking many specific and general responses. Specific responses include those referring to the land and its people in all conceivable respects. General responses are less easy to describe. The recollection of the flag, another concrete symbol, or something as fleeting as a national song may on some occasions be the internal response. Generally, however, unless challenged or provoked, people's reactions are likely to reflect feelings to a greater degree than content: the name of their country is heard and they feel happy or proud. For that name to function effectively, in short, there need be no explicit awareness of the referents of land and people.

And so it seems hardly necessary to stress the fact that many of the verbal expressions representing the country or its people usually become little more than clichés. At one point in the past people may have comprehended their exact meaning and have been induced to seek future goals after being thereby reminded of what their ancestors or they themselves once experienced. But over time —for new generations and for people as they mature—the words devolve into vocal vibrations evoking favorable, though diffuse, responses. The text of the national anthem, after being memorized, probably possesses no more intellectual content than the melody it accompanies. On occasion, when there is a national or personal crisis or when the individual is in an unusual context (such as visiting a foreign country), however, the name, the national symbol, the anthem can elicit deeply emotional and even specific responses.

The ready appearance of the "correct" verbal response usually signifies the existence of patriotism or nationalism. Ordinary men and women in the newly liberated countries of Africa and Asia often continue to think of themselves as members of a traditional society (or tribe) and not of the nation-state. Their political socialization has progressed when they respond rapidly to the question, "What are you?", or its equivalent with the approved political label. They should say, "I am a Nigerian," "I am a Senegalese," "I am a Kenyan," instead of, respectively, "I am an Ibo," "I am a Wolof," "I am a Luo."

The other symbols besides the name which represent a nation obviously also evoke a wide variety of responses among the nationals who use them. But they are likely to be unequivocal in one respect: they arouse that name, which then serves to mediate many of the responses attached to them. Risky Stimulus Inferences from such symbols, however, are often too easily assayed. Thus in a conventional manual it is asserted that "the national flag is the symbol of what a nation has done, what it aspires to do, and what, in practice, it idealizes"; for Rumania, for example, "the blue in the flag represents the sky, the gold the country's wealth, and the red the nation's bravery" (Smith and Taylor, 1946, pp. 36, 127). It is to be doubted that all Rumanians have ever been acquainted with the meanings of these three colors or that, among those who once were given the information in school, this precise information is frequently elicited by the flag. Probably Rumanians recognize their flag merely because it is distinctive and because it provokes certain emotions.

Distinctive names are likewise attached to outstanding features of the physical environment and to significant customs, and thus facilitate communication. You and I are arranging to meet at the top of a particular hill. Our arrangements can be concluded more rapidly if the hill has a name: "We shall see each other at the top of Old Green Hill." In the absence of a name known to both of us, we would have to describe the location in some detail. Such names quickly become associated with the region and the country, and thus are part of the patriotic predisposition. The outsider just sees a hill there, the patriot names it and may therefore personalize it. The name, furthermore, facilitates the storing of details: you remember the experiences you had on Old Green Hill, you know that its colors in autumn are generally more intense than those on its neighbors, you believe that its top peak now suffers from more erosion than it did when you were a child. Such labels may be cozy nicknames or part of the local dialect or the national language; they are embedded, consequently, in people's patriotism.

The nationals of a country also have names to refer to outsiders. These names may be very specific in a geographical sense and they can serve objectively to distinguish outgroupers. We call them French or German, and the terms are simply translations of the word which Frenchmen and Germans use to describe themselves. General words are usually accompanied by negative connotations: foreigners, strangers, barbarians. And then there are the very specific words of opprobrium, some of which are too impolite to mention in this respectable treatise, too many of which the reader already knows, and all of which help the cause of Evil. An even richer thesaurus is usually employed to designate and characterize the entire culture or various culture traits of one or more outside nations.

Innumerable referents in a nation, furthermore, cannot be perceived directly because they no longer exist; perception must be indirect on the basis of artifacts and verbal symbols. People are reminded, or remind themselves, of the way the land once looked, of buildings that used to be inhabited and were then torn down or sacked, and of people who have long been dead. Patriotism always includes some reference to the past in order, for example, to justify a claim to the land or to assert that all nationals are descended from a common ancestor (Delaisi, 1925, p. 166). Among the ancestors or predecessors who receive homage and thus help to keep the present day nation united are heroes. These great men of long ago may be completely legendary or, more likely, they have had legends attached to them. They include the founders of the country and leaders who have been particularly outstanding in the fields of religion, fighting, or governing. Often, too, there are folk heroes, ordinary men—and women—whose status in the society was once not high but whose accomplishments are now considered to have been extraordinary. Great Men cannot be dismissed too quickly; more homage will be respectfully paid to their role in nationalism later on in this book.

This chapter on the stimulus components of patriotism and nationalism cannot end without calling attention again to the arrows
at the top of the Diagram in the previous chapter. They would
suggest that the land as viewed scientifically is affected by people
and also affects them: resources provide opportunities, and then
the inhabitants alter the land. Culture plays a similar role. Finally,
there is reciprocity between people and their culture: those with a
rich culture, however richness be defined, may achieve even
greater riches, and their achievements can become the culture of
new generations. A very fancy, pleasant Spiral.

# 3. The Media of Communication

An adequate analysis of patriotism and nationalism does not require a lengthy discussion of the various media of communication and their peculiarities. Some media oblige the communicator to be present as the audience is reached (speech, drama, clothes) and others do not (print, tape, money). The actual site at which a communication is received can affect its influence (Doob, 1961, pp. 57, 123). The critical point to be emphasized here is that almost all the media, regardless of location, very frequently and prominently contain patriotic and nationalistic materials and appeals and therefore, in the painful jargon of some social scientists, keep patriotism and nationalism dramatically "salient." For the important goals of a society and the approved regulations determining the ways they can be reached are taught and retaught through the media of communication. Such goals are remotely or directly associated with people's land, countrymen, and culture as well as with foreign countries, foreigners, and alien cultures.

## Pervasiveness

The significant role of the media in establishing and reinforcing patriotism can be indicated in two complementary ways. First, patriotic communications follow each national literally from birth to death. At the outset a child is given a name which may be, often must be "typical" of the names prevalent in his society or his cultural area; thereafter he is labeled and thus is always reminded, however dimly, of membership in the nation. As he moves through some kind of rite de passage and is welcomed to manhood, he is made to appreciate the obligations he has to his nation's leaders and to the country which they head. In a modern nation he usually is required to perform military service for some period of time;

and professional warriors can be expected constantly to stress the
national ideals he may be called upon to defend. His own children
belong not only to him but also to the state, a fact that is brought
to his attention as he registers their birth or somehow acknowl-
edges their existence before a central authority. In death he is
sometimes surrounded by patriotic paraphernalia: his body may
be wrapped in his country's flag, a military or civic band may accompany the cortege, the obituary somehow stresses what he has
contributed to his country, and obviously he is buried in accordance with the rituals current in his society. The person so sketchily
and glibly described has been a male, but with slight variations a
female could be similarly depicted: patriotism, with or without
nationalism, is present and strengthened on almost every significant occasion and so is unwittingly and often unconsciously absorbed as part of everyday existence.

Then, secondly, it is actually almost impossible to find a medium of mass communication that is without some patriotic or nationalistic message. In schools pupils are taught by word of mouth
or by textbook about the glories of the past, the opportunities of
the present, and the destiny of the future. News that circulates
through travelers, rumor, or the modern mass media selectively
features events of interest to the nationals who constitute the audience. Usually there is some connection between the convictions
and goals of nationalism on the one hand and the content and direction of religion on the other; for example, Sunday sermons
may extol a people's culture, their nationality, and religious beliefs simultaneously (Miner, 1939, pp. 113–14). Holidays and festivals occur at regular or irregular intervals. Monuments, tablets,
even signs remind people of their past by commemorating historical personages and events. Church bells sound when there is a
national holiday or a national victory. In fact, daily life is saturated with objects which on occasion remind people of their nationality: the mode of cultivating their fields, the style of house in
which they live, the utilization of the rooms inside (for example,
do they customarily sleep in the living room, do they eat together
in the kitchen?), the particular conventionalized phrases with
which they greet one another, the clothing they wear, and the
type of grave in which they are buried and the kind of memorial

upon it. In rural areas of the South Tyrol, the traditional material that is used to bind the pickets of a fence to each other and to their poles is plant fiber or any pliant twig; more recently wire has been substituted, an innovation sometimes interpreted by older people as a symptom not only of the modern world but of Italian modernity, which is thus accused of violating Tyrolean culture is still another way. Even fibers, twigs, and wire, consequently, can evoke patriotic predispositions.

## Importance

For decades the interacting relation between the growth of nations and the media of communication has been pointed out both qualitatively (McDougall, 1920, pp. 181–85) and quantitatively (King, 1935, pp. 11–12). According to one investigator, political power depends upon the collection, the storing, and the dissemination of information concerning both the state and its citizens. The information includes more than that involved in "the mere exchange of goods and services"; assimilation and unity within a country are promoted, he asserts, "if the ability to communicate over wide ranges of subjects is spreading faster among men than is necessitated by their working together directly and by the limited direct communication which this entails" (Deutsch, 1953, pp. 49, 99). Such an approach seeks to transcend descriptive history by providing indices for the two sets of variables, nationhood and the media, but it is necessarily limited in two respects: the pattern of relationships is somewhat singular for each society; and, like all correlations, this one cannot specify the causal sequence that is involved.

It is not difficult, however, to visualize in some detail the role of the media of communication in a nation-state. From the standpoint of leaders, government must clearly communicate—the young must be socialized so that they become patriotic; many, certainly the most important, edicts of governments must be obeyed and, before there can be obedience, the contents of those edicts must be transmitted; and in general only a government whose actions are comprehended to some degree is able to command popular support. The citizens of a country must realize how interdependent they are, and therefore their government must be "visible" in a tangible manner (Wallerstein, 1961, p. 91): they appreciate its authority and strength whenever they observe its police or soldiers; they come to apprehend its distinctive traditions and modes of behaving; and they learn the sentences that demonstrate the identification of their welfare with the state. Even the most authoritarian government cannot function effectively without taking people and their needs into account—there must be upward communication so that officials can become acquainted with those needs. Run-of-the-mill citizens are compelled to communicate with one another if they are to develop a consciousness of themselves as members of the same society. Then in democratic or neodemocratic societies political parties or factions employ similar communications to recruit their own more specialized followings.

The role of the media is important in any society, but its precise nature varies of course with the kind of nation being served. The media in traditional nations probably differ from those of insular and modern nations in a number of ways. First, in the former there are few if any specialized communicators, men whose primary function is to communicate or receive communications. The communities are generally smaller, the chances for misunderstandings are perhaps slighter. Secondly, the media to preserve communications over time are scarce, especially in the absence of writing; as a result, although substitutes may have been developed, great reliance is placed, by and large, upon the oral transmission of information both within the society at a given moment and over generations. The content of communications, thirdly, is usually more limited in traditional than in modern societies; in fact, it has been suggested (Wilson and Wilson, 1945, pp. 28, 40) that contacts there and hence the ensuing communications are comparatively less extensive and more intensive. In such societies, moreover, most communications are transmitted in face-to-face situations. As a result of the intimate contacts and the high value placed upon stratification, there may be a stronger inclination than in modern nations to judge the validity or goodness of a communication by its source or by the communicator rather than by the content. And finally, as many observers have reported again and again, "no voices need to be raised to defend the traditional ways because no other ways are on the agenda" (Lerner, 1958, pp. 141–42).

As nations move away from traditional forms, the media of communication become more numerous and begin to affect markedly the rate of societal growth. The elite who are the political leaders employ the media to achieve independence for their country and then afterwards to reeducate their followers. For they, having come—in the words of one hypothesis—"to sense the possibility of an orderly and law-directed world" (Pye, 1962, p. 188), act upon their new conviction and seek to change the society and its people by deeds, law, and communications.

In Africa, for example, various kinds of political, social, and educational organizations were established, especially following World War II, through which a few people learned the values of the outside world and thus came to seek more vigorously their own independence. After breaking political ties with the metropolitan powers, African leaders have sought to weaken the identification of tribesmen with traditional societies and instead to focus their loyalties upon the nascent nation-states. Special communications have been required to try to prevent internal disunity: as a result of the removal of the common enemy, the colonial power, there has been a tendency everywhere—and not just in the Congo —for groups and individuals to assert their own interests, which previously they had submerged in the common struggle (Wallerstein, 1961, p. 87).

In this situation, too, children must be differently socialized; adults—if possible—must be resocialized, which generally means a shift away from loyalty to the tribe in the direction of patriotism focused upon the new nation-state. Opposition must often be both physically and symbolically garroted, lest the elite lose its new power and the country its new orientation—or at least so the elite often believe. For these reasons, politics "is not sharply differentiated from the spheres of social and personal relations," and the single party in control tends "to take on a world view and represent a way of life" (Pye, 1962, pp. 16–18).

During the same stage, moreover, modern advertising either appears or becomes much more important. It seeks to introduce the mechanical comforts and the distracting diversities of the new way of life and so, in brief, to help maximize discontent with old ways. Governments develop professional communicators who have positions and eventually departments of their own; and often these technicians seek primarily to perpetuate the political party in power. At this historical juncture, too, literacy increases, because more children go to school and because more adults are trained formally or informally. The contents of the mass media are quite unsubtle. Villains from the past and the opposition in the present are attacked. At its level of sophistication the audience looks for black-and-white rather than grey distinctions.

In modern societies that are strongly nationalistic, the flow from the mass media continues in greater volume. All kinds of professional and technical communicators develop: journalists, commentators, public relations counsellors, ghost writers, artists, etc. The competition for the attention of people grows so keen that suddenly the trend away from the face-to-face contacts characteristic of traditional and insular nations is reversed, and the need for such contacts increases. And so the telephone transmits the voice of one person to another, and the airplane moves the communicator quickly from place to place so that he can be directly observed and heard as he communicates. In addition and more importantly, many, perhaps most, people tend to be effectively reached not directly through the mass media but through informal leaders who themselves have been influenced by those media and then transmit what they have learned to people valuing their opinions (Katz and Lazarsfeld, 1955). Of course features of the communication network remain unchanged as nationalism and the economy of the society change. Some media continue to be used only for very specific purposes, such as the siren and whistle which convey communications pertaining to time or danger. Certain patterns of communication are employed on very specialized occasions (the political oration), others much more extensively (a proverb, a cliché).

Both in theory and practice the prevailing beliefs and convictions of a society can be perpetuated only when they are featured in those media which reach the very young. Theory indicates the

significance of early influence, and practice suggests that any nation places great emphasis upon teaching the "correct" patriotic
ideas from the outset. In the modern state, for example, parents
deliberately impose their views and attitudes through symbols
and other media in the home, less deliberately through casual,
day-by-day references to the country and outgroupers. Schools
operated by the state have usually been established or strengthened by strongly inclined nationalist leaders, since they are "the
basic and the most reliable agencies of nationalist propaganda
among the Masses" (Hayes, 1937, p. 86). Then both in and outside schools there are organizations of youth in which the glories
of the past are intertwined with demands for future sacrifices. By
the time the child is ready to assume adult responsibilities, he is
acquainted, however sketchily and inaccurately, with his country's importance, history, songs, flag, holidays, etc.; he has at least
verbal knowledge concerning his own national responsibilities;
and he himself has had some experience as a nascent patriot.

## Groups

A moment ago it was suggested that many people in modern
society are reached not directly by the media of communication
but indirectly through the leaders of the groups to which they belong. In fact, according to some analysts, a knowledge of such
groups is perhaps more helpful in understanding and predicting
behavior than is the formulation of general principles or an investigation of central personality traits (Sarbin, 1954). For so much
of what occurs depends upon the influences of the moment, and
those influences are exerted through groups, generally small
groups. Each group, it is clear, has its own somewhat unique rules
and regulations, each demands and obtains particular forms of
behavior. Nothing more is being asserted than the banal but critical fact that the family, the clique, and the association are important determinants of attitude and behavior. And so it must
smoothly follow that small meaningful groups receive and transmit
many communications with patriotic and nationalistic themes.

In the modern day, groups have served as the medium for
nationalism in two ways. First, leaders who express nationalistic

demands and guide nationalistic activities have usually banded together in some kind of organization; almost never does a lone voice cry out to people to unite for the sake of their country. Then patriots and superpatriots have associations through which they strengthen their own national loyalties and seek to indoctrinate others. Usually the military, in order to bolster the morale of the country they must defend and of the men within their own ranks, and also in order to remain in power, actively propagate the patriotic faith.

A pair of distinctions may be helpful in understanding these groups. In the first place, the reinforcement of patriotism or nationalism may be a primary objective or just an incidental one; when it is a primary objective, other functions may be simultaneously served. Membership in the American Legion, for example, provides men with recreation and with an opportunity to mingle socially with other veterans from most of the social levels of a community; belonging to a more exclusive organization, such as the historical society, is likely to be a gratifying symbol of social prestige (Warner et al., 1949, pp. 92–93). In contrast, some athletic clubs in Europe, though dedicated almost exclusively to a sport such as "football," promote on occasion the cause of nationalism: they meet teams from other countries in contests that arouse national feelings, or their members are reminded that the game helps to develop "national character."

Then, secondly, the patriotic or nationalistic content of the group's communications may be broad or constricted. The broad type features the cultural distinctiveness of an area or prepares its members along general educational lines so that they will be, for example, better-informed citizens. The specific message stresses the need to achieve a concrete goal for the country, such as increased armaments.

To comprehend patriotism and nationalism fully, therefore, it is necessary to observe in detail how the media of communication function not in general but within important groups of a society. Here is a task to be discharged by analyzing the particular groups at hand; once again, singularity precludes generalizations other than the following broad rubrics to guide understanding. First, the history and present functioning of the group must be described by collecting the bare facts concerning its formation, growth or decline, rules, and accomplishments. Then the effects of the group upon its members are observed. Generalizations can be made concerning the kinds of persons (viewed sociologically or psychologically) who join and do not join; the circumstances under which members are influenced by the standards of the group; and the changes in them which occur or do not occur as a result of their membership. Often this last point is difficult to explore with any precision, not only because a control group of equivalent nonmembers may not be available but also because observation or measurement may be impossible or subject to error. The outside consequences must likewise be noted: to what extent do members utilize in other situations the experience they have obtained from being members; in what respects does the group as a whole affect outsiders or perhaps the rules and customs of the society?

Finally, it is necessary to mention that groups in a society may be strengthened when they are associated with patriotism or nationalistic media of communication. In the South Tyrol, as in many Catholic countries, most festivals are basically religious and consequently focus upon a special church service. Before and especially after that service, however, the "worldly" aspects of the holy day are enjoyed and the symbols of nationalism appear. A band in native costume leads a religious procession into the church and then contributes its music to the celebration of the mass. The decorations on the roads in the neighborhood of the church display the national colors and emblems. Amid the completely secular events during the day—the trading, dancing, drinking, and love-making—people chat and exchange views on politics, which almost always include some unfavorable reference to the Italians, who are said to be oppressing or ruining the nation. Often in Western countries an official or unofficial religion is proclaimed (Royal Institute, 1939, p. 18), so that religion and nationalism become legally entwined.

### Content

Patriotic, nationalistic communications resemble other types of communications in many respects. Many of them are not premeditated but are transmitted unintentionally. Polite, even perfunctory references to the nation's ideals appear as part of a customary ritual or on ceremonial occasions. Children in schools mechanically pledge allegiance to the flag without necessarily or frequently considering the meaning of the words they have memorized. In modern countries of the West, allusions in speeches to the national destiny are often considered mere rhetoric, very desirable but again without formal meaning or commitment. This state of affairs exists during so-called normal times when people and their society are relatively peaceful. Very self-conscious and deliberate appeals to nationalism, however, are sounded during a crisis or in behalf of a program of expansion that calls for sacrifices. Then the flag takes on some of the symbolic and deeply emotional significance associated with totems in traditional societies. The unintentional nature of communication under "normal" conditions is made possible, again, by previous heavy reinforcements so that people conform without much reflection and behave in the respectable, approved manner. Where such reinforcement is lacking—for example, in the developing nationalism of the underdeveloped countries—patriotic communications are more likely to be carefully planned and transmitted. Adults there resemble children in older nations; their learning of the new national anthem, for example, is so recent that it continues to have emotional and even intellectual significance.

Likewise, as is true of communication in general and as frequent references in this book to Risky Stimulus Inferences suggest, there is almost always some discrepancy between the apparent goals of patriotic and nationalistic communications and the actual reaction of the audience. Even those responding in the desired way may have diverse reasons for doing so. It would be a mistake, however, to discount a communication just because it does not achieve its apparent goal. For some other goal may be attained; and it is difficult to anticipate in advance the precise consequences of any communication over time. What is ineffective now may eventually become influential. In addition, the expression of the communicator at the very least reveals something about him and his aspirations. Thus children in a very small French community were once required to learn the following admonitions, among others, which appeared in their civics textbook: "The French nation has a body formed by the soil and the men who live on it; a soul formed by the history, language, tradition, and symbols"; (2) "A good citizen . . . respects the law, pays his taxes loyally, accepts the military obligation, and defends his *patrie* when it is threatened"; (3) "Politics should not be an excuse for furthering private interests and above all it should not unleash our passions" (Wylie, 1958, pp. 206–07). Now certainly it cannot be assumed that the children, no matter how letter-perfect their memorization had been, either understood or believed the statements as they recited them in school or that they followed their implications when they grew up. So magnificently sweeping a Risky Stimulus Inferences dare no man make. But they must have perceived the noble sentences, and they may have been subtly affected; hence the school assignments could have contributed, along with thousands of other communications, to the mystique with which Frenchmen often view their country.

In actual content, nationalistic communications can refer to any aspect of the land and its people, and they pose as statements of fact or as declarations of duty and responsibility. Their variety is literally without end. In the South Tyrol, for example, red appears on the Tyrolean flag and in some traditional dress, with the result that one writer claims it has become itself an important medium: "The color red expresses the unity of the land and continues to express our feeling of belonging together" (Ilg, 1955, p. 219).

A later chapter—the thirteenth—is devoted to the conditions facilitating nationalism. Here a small portion of that discussion must be anticipated by suggesting that, in spite of diversity in content, patriotic communications in successful nations always stress certain points: an account of the society's development from the past, a statement concerning its functioning in the present, and a declaration pertaining to its future actions and policies. The pieces may be scattered but together they form a rather coherent view of the society over time which is pitched at such a level that it is intelligible to virtually every person. This does not mean that all members of the nation can effortlessly recite its history or mythology, passionately declaim its present greatness and contributions, or eloquently assert the ambitions and ideals it possesses concerning its future destiny. Those details, if not subject to direct recall, are recognizable, so that each person is able to feel, however dimly, some connection between the particular communication he hears on the one hand and the total picture he believes to exist on the other; and he is thus convinced that he and his contemporaries share a common origin and history.

National credos contain similar themes for a number of reasons. Every person himself experiences the flow of time and soon comes to realize the fact of death, which means, he deduces or observes, that people have preceded him in the past and that others will exist in the future when he is no longer alive. Somehow, therefore, there is a need to be provided with a history and with some outline of the future in order to explain and soften the sequence of events. Then, too, the individual would be loath to transform his own goals into social ones or to make sacrifices in behalf of the group unless he were provided with a comprehensive explanation that commands his respect and evokes some fear or awe within him. Comfort is gained from knowing that he is part of an endless stream that originated in the past, continues in the present, and will flow on indefinitely in the future.

The past recreated in myth or history for each nation is usually divided into certain chapters. The beginning of the earth and of life thereon is accounted for. Sometimes, as in the great religions of the West, the story of genesis involves not only the nation but also the earth and all the people or even the universe itself. Often, though, attention is concentrated upon the region and one's compatriots either because little else was known at the time the versions were created or because both the outside and outsiders appear unimportant and are thought not to require special explanation. Apparently, too, these beginnings are always unusual: the gods themselves or some heroic ancestors are credited with the great act, and the people or their surroundings at the primordial time are endowed with superhuman properties which ordinarily either no longer exist or else appear most infrequently (Tegnaeus, 1950, pp. 9–13, 179–81). As if to provide concrete verification for the account, solid objects from the past are exhibited and considered very sacred.

A nation must have, in brief, a rich heritage if people are to acquire the pride associated with patriotism and with their own country. This point is made forcefully in the following summary of what has been occurring in modern Africa:

> Perhaps the most important, and deeply felt, aspect of the nationalist answer to the myth of African barbarism is the new stress placed on the qualities of pre-European African societies: their achievements in such fields as the plastic arts, work in gold and bronze and ivory, music and dancing, folk story, and folk poetry; the complexity and depth of their religious beliefs and metaphysics; their conception of the community—as "consisting of the dead, the living, and the unborn"; their rational attitude to sexual relations and to the place of women in society—their delight in children and reverence for the aged; their view of education, as a process continuing through life; their dislike of autocracy, and their delicate political mechanisms for securing the expression and adjustment of different interests and wills [Hodgkin, 1956, p. 174].

And so in modern Africa, scholars and leaders are placing great stress upon the study of history. In the absence of written records, attention is directed to oral traditions and to the artifacts which archaeologists are encouraged to uncover. Africans are no different from any other people in thus emphasizing a heroic background. They happen only to be doing so a little later than some other countries and their efforts are well publicized in an era which trumpets almost any innovation.

Nationalism is so important to people that they seem also to require or demand especially sacred and concrete symbols to epitomize some of their beliefs, especially those concerning the past. Somewhere in a country, therefore, are shrines where the bodies of extraordinary ancestors are buried, where significant objects from the past are exhibited, or where people may come when they wish to pay homage to the past or seek spiritual guidance or sustenance for the future. In more sophisticated countries adults voluntarily wander through the halls of museums, which, though quite secular in comparison with shrines, usually serve very similar functions; and children may be marched there by their teachers so that they can have a firsthand view of their country's greatness. When a nation is relatively prosperous, when it has had a sufficiently long past, and when its scholars through chance or skill have been able to assemble an impressive collection, then the visitors in the museum are likely to be able to view virtually every aspect of the society's material culture and to appreciate some of its nonmaterial traits in selected periods of the past. Shrines and museums, it may also be noted, try to give the impression of being permanent institutions and thus to symbolize the continuity of the nation itself. Elsewhere in modern nations the names of heroes are carved in stone or engraved in bronze, so that memory of them will endure eternally.

Symbols that can be easily displayed and comprehended are also required. Literate countries, for example, have national anthems and nonliterate ones have characteristic melodies or rhythms: the intellectual content of most music is so vague and unstructured that people can easily learn to associate with it a wide variety of thoughts and feelings. The band starts to play or the drum sounds, and immediately there is evoked a host of hard-to-define emotions ranging from the mild pleasure of recognition to an overwhelming sense of devotion to the country.

In a completely artificial but intelligible manner, modern nations often select a flower to symbolize their unity: that plant may not grow in every field, but at least it is sufficiently common so that specimens can be displayed and admired. In sentimental terms too thick to be cut by logical analysis appears this story in a reader intended for third and fourth grade children in the South Tyrol concerning a national symbol:

> The Holy Virgin Mary sits in the sun. She is spinning wool from the snow-white small lamb which grazes in paradise. Once as she fell asleep while spinning and dreamed of the human race, a small tuft of wool dropped to the ground and remained suspended on a high boulder. People found it and called it edelweiss [Rosegger, 1960, p. 161].

With equal sentiment animals serve the same totem function, but their representations must often be stylized in order to appear distinctive; thus the eagle is a favorite animal for this purpose since, aside from its alleged qualities and behavior, it can be variously drawn or at least labeled so that its symbolic meaning remains apparent. Some of these animals—the British lion, the Russian bear, the French cock, the Chinese dragon—have acquired, in a stereotyped and hence predictable manner, the presumed personality traits of the nations they are supposed to symbolize.

More critical than music, flowers, animals, flags or any other objects that serve as symbols for the nation is the actual referent with which people connect their own welfare and that of the significant groups to which they belong. One writer believes that prior to the French Revolution people's loyalties were concentrated upon real people, such as a pope, an emperor, or a prince. Subsequently they have been compelled to identify themselves with only "a political idea": "A nation is, in the last analysis, just an idea and not really a terribly concrete one at that. No one has ever seen the General Will and few the Constitution" (Boveri, 1963, pp. 17–21). Obviously the alleged change has not been quite so sweeping, for some people even in a modern democracy associate their welfare not with an abstraction but with a very concrete leader or way of life. In any case, a nation's media of communication help to vivify the connection between welfare and referent. Perhaps the most dramatic and impressive vehicle is that of an oath: on occasion people are compelled to pledge their loyalty to their country. The oath itself may indicate the punishment for failing to keep the word thus communicated. God Himself is invoked as a witness, prosecution for perjury is possible, and the consequent fines and prison terms are specifically listed.

In addition, sanctions are usually attached to antinational communications. Actual deeds committed against one's country of course constitute treason, the traditional penalty for which is death, expulsion, or some other severe punishment. Likewise, hostile utterances against the state may fall into the treasonous category and receive harsh, if relatively less severe, treatment. In a modern state the taboo sentiments are either specified in laws and statutes or else they are so well known that they need not be codified. Incitement to revolution or open insurrection is obviously a crime, but you also may not attack one of your country's heroes verbally or act irreverently toward its symbols. It is unnecessary to try to imagine what happens to Americans who cast doubts upon the character of George Washington or any National Hero or who would spit or trample upon the Stars and Stripes. Subversion is another hideous offense, especially among teachers, textbook-writers, and those concerned with the mass media in general.

In a modern state some opposition by amateur and professional critics and by political opponents is tolerated—perhaps their existence is a real sign of political or emotional maturity—but these communications are not supposed to transgress certain not always well-defined limits beyond which they are considered unpatriotic, become unpopular, and hence lose some of their effectiveness. Even the cynicism of the sophisticated concerning the absolutism of patriotism and many of its modes of expression is replaced by silent, usually sincere seriousness in time of war. The severity of the punishment given antipatriotic communicators may reflect the strong patriotism of the majority or the uneasiness of a minority in power. Under such circumstances those matters may be attacked that are not thought to be sacrosanct. And yet, paradoxically, the sacrosanct ought to be strong enough to resist an attack.

Some of the leaders and most of the superpatriots of modern nations pursue a goal of complete isolation: they would transmit and reinforce only the values they hold to be good and true and exclude all others. For this reason students of modern nationalism list among its evils and abuses attributes such as exclusiveness and narrowness; and they assert that it places "a premium on uniformity" and seeks to increase "the docility of the masses" (Hayes, 1937, p. 258). Three comments are impossible to repress. First, the consequences thus alleged may be correctly identified; but are not such tendencies prevalent in any society, nationalistic or not, which would maintain itself? Evidence is needed, and such evidence is not easy to gather. Then if the charges are correct, are the attributes necessarily bad? Whoever says they are is possibly ethnocentric. And the postulated state of affairs may in fact never be completely achieved. In the twentieth century, dictators and patriots, we think or hope we now know, are pursuing a will-o'-the-wisp at a time when international communication is developing so rapidly and efficiently. True, most people behind whatever curtain is designated, including ones erected by the West, are not straining to become cosmopolitan and are in fact hearing very few of the international communications. But there are cracks produced by radio and television, science, and the exchange of peoples.

No more than passing reference is made to the endless topic of truth vs. falsity (phrased differently: education vs. propaganda) in the content of patriotic and nationalistic communications, and then really only to indicate awareness that the issue arises if nationalism is to be judged. Perhaps, when passions are high, truth is likely to be slighted; hence nationalism abounds in communications that are either deliberate fabrications or unintentional reflections of the communicator's decided biases. The exposure of such communications has occurred again and again, and indeed needs to be repeated, for humanistic if not for analytical purposes.

# 4. The Perception of Attributes

Nationals respond to their own land, their countrymen, and their culture as well as to foreign countries, foreigners, and foreign cultures; and these stimuli reach them through various media of communication. Any stimulus pattern has innumerable attributes capable of being observed and emphasized. In fact, one of the important contributions of science or art is to discover and, respectively, to measure or evaluate attributes hitherto unnoticed or unappreciated. The discussion at this point seeks to isolate those attributes of the land, people, and culture that are relevant to patriotism and nationalism. The molecular weight of the national flag is clearly an attribute which need not be considered as that symbol stirs men's souls in battle or in stress. 'I like this food, it tastes good, it helps my health, it looks appetizing . . .'—up to this point, the attributes being noted are unrelated to patriotism— 'and it is distinctly French.' The last attribute suggests that the reaction, including the other attributes being perceived, may be related to patriotism and nationalism, whether or not the devotee of the food is a Frenchman.

Consciously or unconsciously those attributes of stimulus patterns are perceived, reacted to, and possibly remembered which literally if tritely make living possible. For instead of succumbing to chaos people find some consistency in the external world. They and their contemporaries know what to expect; they are able to make value judgments; they respond in a way that satisfies their needs and aspirations. Patriotism arises when some aspect of the nation is associated frequently and importantly with these characteristic modes of apprehending the world.

What is apprehended at a given moment, in any context, is always a function of two interacting factors: the stimulus pattern evoking the experience and the person's own predispositions. Here it is said that patriotic predispositions represent remnants from the past which influence the present and the future. It may appear as if the analysis has been caught up in a bit of circular reasoning, as if patriotism were being explained in terms of patriotic dispositions. The time factor, however, permits a very graceful exit from the circle into the usual Spiral. Over the years nationals acquire a set of tendencies, the patriotic predispositions. Perception is affected by these predispositions and, as a result, patriotism grows stronger or weaker after each experience. Your patriotism makes you consider the girls of your region extremely beautiful —people from other lands with a different and equally ethnocentric sense of aesthetics may think them too fat or too thin, too vulgar or too shy—and each time you appreciate their extraordinary beauty your love of country increases.

The attributes of the land, the people, and the culture which are perceived in and outside a nation can now be briefly described. In each instance it must be presumed that both a stimulus and a patriotic predisposition interact. The attributes are arranged in the order of decreasing importance of the stimulus and of increasing importance of the predisposition.

## Composition and Physique

The appearance, the sound, the feel, the scent of the land, of its people, and sometimes even of their culture give rise to certain immediate perceptions requiring little or no reflection. 'That waterfall is high, not low'; 'That clothing has been manufactured domestically, it has not been imported'; 'That building is in keeping with prevailing architectural styles, it does not look foreign'— attributes such as these are quickly discerned and asserted. Patriots are likely to believe that the stimulus patterns themselves have the unique or typical attributes, and their knowledge and conviction are certain and unequivocal. In part they are correct since many sense qualities are directly derived from the stimuli out there. A purely objective scientist or even a deadly enemy would agree that a spot on the landscape is clearly a waterfall, not a geyser or a skyscraper. Predispositional or cultural factors operate when the waterfall is considered 'magnificent,' but its magnificence may or may not be connected with the splendor of the nation.

Can people actually identify the physical attributes of their nation? In the absence of concrete evidence, a reasonable hypothesis would be that their success depends upon the distinctiveness of the environment as they have experienced it. Unhesitatingly they recognize a photograph of their own home, of the street on which it is located, and perhaps of the view from their bedroom window, provided there are clear-cut cues for them to have perceived and to have learned. Someone from an Alpine area, when confronted with a scene from the Canadian Rockies or Tibet, can exclaim that 'this looks as if it might be my country,' obviously because tall mountains everywhere have some attributes in common; but such a person will not be perplexed or confused when seeing a picture taken on the Great Plains or the Siberian steppes.

A more interesting question is whether people of different nationalities can be distinguished exclusively on the basis of physical attributes. American college students, for example, have been asked to identify the race of faces in photographs. By and large, such research suggests that races differ with respect to their recognizability and that people's belief in their ability to distinguish between ethnic groups of similar skin color (Jews and Gentiles, Chinese and Japanese) far outstrips their actual performance (Allport, 1954, pp. 132–35). In real life accuracy is likely to be greater because other cues more reliable than physiognomy are usually present: clothing, coiffure, gestures, and speech.

The psychologically important fact, then, is not so much the accuracy of people's judgments concerning nationality as the confidence they show in their own attribution. For a generation social scientists in the West have been demonstrating that people are willing to identify a person's nationality and often also to appraise his character merely on the basis of the few stereotyped cues provided by his appearance or photograph. In one study, for example, a sample of Britons was shown ten photographs of Americans and asked to indicate whether each was an "American type" or not. Of the 716 persons who finally cooperated and hence composed the sample, 680 made one or more selections to indicate their idea of this type; thus 95 per cent believed they could provide such an identification from photographs alone. In addition, "very few of the respondents had any reservation or any questions about the use of the word 'types' to describe Americans" (Graham, 1954).

### Processes and Activities

The composition of a river and the physique of a person may give rise to immediate sense impressions, but frequently attention is paid to their attributes over a period of time and not at a given moment. 'That river is carrying gravel and topsoil down into the valley'; 'Our people must toil very hard to earn a living.' The actions of people upon the land are likely to be noted; a characteristic way of plowing fields, for example, is considered to be an attribute of a particular type of land and a reflection of a custom handed down to, and then followed by, its owner. Culture itself falls under this dynamic heading, inasmuch as recognizing an event or an instance of behavior as part of a traditional series from the past that will continue into the future presupposes a judgment transcending the stimulus pattern at hand.

### Traits

The land, its people, and their culture are thought to possess certain characteristic, rather consistent ways of reacting or behaving. Men and women postulate such traits after noting processes and activities over time, but they may believe they are perceiving them directly, in the manner of composition and physique. 'The sea is dangerous'; 'That man looks honest.' In addition, traits of this kind are often believed to be inherent and immutable. 'The stone is hard,' 'The land is fertile,' 'The building is cheerful,' 'The man is ambitious,' 'The woman is gentle'—that is their nature, their destiny, their fate. In modern nations, probably because of the diffused influence of biological science, social science, Marxism, and democratic ideology, laymen are less likely to trace traits to heredity, and instead they place responsibility upon early childhood training, which is thought to establish predispositions as rigid as those stemming from the genes.

The tendency to ascribe or not ascribe traits to people appears to be another universal basis for arriving at value judgments. Enough diversity resulting from age, sex, and genetic disposition exists everywhere for such discrimination to occur. Anthropologists are joined even by philosophers in detecting that proclivity. Of the three central categories composing a system of ethics, for example, one is called "judgments of moral worth" and is defined as the predicating of "moral goodness or badness of some attribute of a person's character, or his character as a whole" (Mandelbaum, 1955, p. 135). If such a judgment is to be passed, the attribute of the trait itself must first be perceived.

The traits ascribed to other people are particularly numerous, as a glance at the adjectives on any page of an unabridged dictionary can demonstrate. Still the labeling related to patriotism and nationalism—and to many other phenomena—occurs, it would appear, on only three rather clear-cut levels. First, human nature in general is characterized: basically people everywhere are the same because they are human beings and consequently similar traits must appear in every nation. The conviction that all men are inherently selfish, for example, can have immediate political consequences: the government must be stern, people must be motivated or compelled to help their fellows in times of emergency. Secondly, there are views concerning the traits of a nation. Again the problem of national character mentioned in Chapter 2 appears, but this time on a psychological rather than a factual level: what do people think of themselves and of those living in other countries? Finally, persons may be judged not merely as human beings and as members of a nation but as more or less unique personalities. While at any moment traits may be ascribed on all three bases, nationalists are probably prone to view people not as human or distinctive personalities but as nationals; or at least they emphasize or give precedence to such stereotyping. On that level, especially, people have preferences among traits, perhaps simply because they believe that their compatriots possess them. 'I approve of industriousness, and most of my countrymen are industrious; and even though I somewhat secretly admire nonchalant people, I know that such people, unlike my compatriots, never accomplish very much.'

An interesting psychological problem is the determination of the conditions under which traits are ascribed to people because of their nationality. One investigation, based upon adequately large samples of French, German, and American university students, provides a few preliminary clues. The task for the student was to "form impressions" of a hypothetical person on the basis of "a few facts" provided in a brief personality sketch. The nationality of the person in the sketch was specified as being French, German, or American; his profession was said to be that of businessman or college professor, or it was left unspecified; but in all other respects the descriptions were identical. The impressions of the students acting as subjects were obtained by instructing them to examine a list of trait names and to check those which "best characterized the person described." After checking the traits, they were asked to indicate the bases on which they had made their selections. In all three countries the sample was divided into two experimental subgroups: half the subjects were told in advance that they would rate people of three different nationalities and hence presumably they were inclined to compare the three; and the other half were asked simply to rate a single sketch (e.g. that of "an American businessman" or "a French professor"). Only two of the significant findings are relevant here. First, nationality was claimed as the basis for ascribing the personality traits more frequently by the subjects who rated three nationalities than by those who rated only a single nationality; and nationality was employed more readily when rating foreigners than it was when rating compatriots (Bruner and Perlmutter, 1957). In this situation, consequently, the stereotype concerning national traits played a more important role when three sketches, differing only with respect to nationality, were judged and compared than when a single sketch of specified nationality was judged. The subjects also presumably were, or thought they were, better acquainted with their own countrymen, and hence utilized nationality as a guide to a lesser degree than they did when judging outsiders. Stereotyping, in short, functioned more energetically in some contexts than in others.

At the risk of becoming ethnocentric, though at a very high and hence respectable level of conceptualization, it is amusing to wonder whether it is possible to locate personality traits which are

more or less universally noted and which, when they are present
to some degree, are everywhere held in high esteem. Two seem
promising candidates: intelligence and conscientiousness. First, as
tasks are performed and problems solved, some people are apparently able more quickly or efficiently than others to run through
the required performance or to find the solution. The intelligence in question need not be of the abstract sort so highly valued
in Western society; it may reflect simple ingenuity, dexterity, or
slyness. Then, a conscientious person is likely to carry out the task
at hand, even in the absence of external compulsion; such a trait
is undoubtedly useful everywhere.

Specific studies reveal that the actual traits ascribed to one's
own nation and to others naturally vary from person to person and
from time to time. In a survey of samples in eight Western countries in 1948, people were confronted with a dozen traits and were
asked to "select as many as you wish" which they believed could
be used to describe their compatriots and people in other nations.
The trait "intelligent," for example, was chosen by 50 per cent or
more of the informants from six of the nations to be applied to
compatriots, but only by 49 and 32 per cent of those, respectively,
in the samples from the Netherlands and Norway. Other traits frequently employed in a majority of the countries to describe compatriots were "hardworking," "brave," and "peace-loving." The
highest percentage calling the Russians "intelligent" was found
among the Australians, but that figure was only 16; the lowest, 4
per cent, came from the Norwegians (Buchanan and Cantril, 1953,
pp. 46–47). Clearly these respondents tended to select a flattering
adjective to describe themselves and to withhold it from Russians,
whose country they did not particularly like. One study among
American college students, however, suggests that the relation
may not be so simple: traits which the subjects disliked but which,
according to their view, characterized themselves they attributed
to countries "without much relation" to the preference for those
countries (Child and Doob, 1943).

For present purposes, the significant fact to be observed in
straightforward surveys is that people in Western nations are
willing to specify the traits they believe characterize their countrymen and the peoples of other nations. In the study of the eight

Western countries just cited, for example, the informants were offered a thirteenth alternative after the list of twelve traits, viz. "impossible to characterize." The highest percentage choosing that final alternative for their own country was only 8 in the case of the Netherlands and Norway. For stereotyping other countries, the corresponding mean percentage was also relatively low, 25. The highest figures were found in the German and Netherland samples: among the former, 49 per cent could not characterize France and 71 per cent China; among the latter the respective figures for the same countries were 46 and 54 per cent (Buchanan and Cantril, 1953, pp. 46–47).

In any case, regardless of the real facts in the situation, people believe there are sufficient observable data to justify conclusions concerning the traits they ascribe to their own nation and to foreign nations. One common basis for dichotomizing the peoples of the world is that of bargaining: some love, others hate to bargain. The bargainers do not have fixed prices; both buyers and sellers enjoy exercising their wits to arrive at what appears to each to be a fair price; trading is thus a sport. The nonbargainers, on the other hand, believe in the rule of law: they want to know where they stand, they prefer to have people mean what they say, trading is thus a matter-of-fact procedure. Almost any shop, any taxicab, any transaction can be thought to reveal the modal practice of a nation in this respect and hence to provide a solid basis in reality. Human behavior is so varied that it is probably fruitless to attempt to apply the kernel-of-truth hypothesis to stereotypes: a wisp of truth—any kind of truth—can be imagined in connection with most ascribed personality traits.

Some well-grounded insight into the traits likely to be observed in others, however, can be obtained by noting both the behavior and the traits people customarily esteem. One philosopher, concentrating as most philosophers do upon the problem of value, has collected concrete data, in the manner of an anthropologist, among the Hopi Indians. He visited their reservation on three occasions, conversed with them, studied their folktales, consulted the impressions of other investigators, and received detailed replies to a series of direct questions concerning their hopes, sources of pride and shame, worries, and fear. These people, he reports, have a "conception of the ideal man" who is "a good family man"; "agreeable in his social relations"; "not dangerous" in the sense that he is "peaceable" and hence "does not get drunk or into brawls"; "cooperative" in his community and especially with his relatives; "honest"; "modest"; "quiet and unobtrusive"; "cheerful"; "manly and brave" and yet "on the submissive side in social relations"; and—noble paragon—"a good worker" because he is "persistent, foresighted, and careful" (Brandt 1954, p. 138). If the Hopi can really be characterized in such detailed strokes, then it seems probable that they note whether their neighbor behaves himself in terms of those standards and whether he can be characterized as honest, modest, brave, etc.

Another approach, unfortunately impressionistic, suggests that Americans admire heroes who are "self-respecting, decent, honorable, with a sense of fair play." They have a "strong prejudice against the wise guy" and against "vanity or personal arrogance." They believe that "character is more important than brains" (Wecter, 1941, pp. 482–85). Americans who allegedly value heroes with these attributes must themselves wish to possess the traits and must observe their presence or absence in others.

### Development and Potentialities

Up to this point the discussion of traits has been relatively simple: central tendencies are ascribed to the land, its people, and their culture. Now there is a slight twist in perception as people note or postulate the temporal qualities of a particular trait. They do not simply in fact observe processes and activities over time, rather they become consciously aware of development from the past and of potentiality for the future. Development is stressed: 'That soil is fertile because we and our ancestors have always tilled it carefully'; 'Our courage springs from an old tradition.' Or potentiality: 'That land would make a good factory site'; 'We would be more prosperous if we were free.'

People possess, or think they possess, perspective: what is perceived now is the culmination of elaboration in the past. Every society, it has been noted in the previous chapter, has its own version of how its nationals and their institutions have come into existence and then subsequently developed. Here not the symbolic value of this history but its realistic necessity must be noted. A nation is a product of past events that have in fact occurred. Some of those events are remembered—or cannot be forgotten—and become part of the prevailing tradition. Changes take place even in the most stable societies: people grow old, natural resources become more or less scarce within the memory of those exploiting them. All men, consequently, cannot fail to believe that some change is inevitable and that they, too, have antecedents. Change and antecedents they seek to comprehend by invoking the standards they employ to judge the shifts they themselves have experienced.

The developmental attributes of the land and its people are apprehended for additional reasons. Although a real consciousness of history as such has allegedly existed in the Western world for less than two centuries (Kohn, 1962, p. 60), large numbers of scholars and scientists now deliberately investigate the past and continually emerge with new facts. A knowledge of history is certainly part of the curriculum in every formal educational system, though opinions may differ concerning the adequacy or veracity of the particular versions that are taught. The mass media, after they have devoted space or time to the breathless moment and the exciting future, delve into the past and offer "background" materials.

Nationalists whose country has not gained its independence are especially sensitive to the unrealized potentialities of their land and its people. 'Think of what we could do, think of what we could accomplish if we were free.' Development and potentiality can be simultaneously noted: development will continue into the future because of the potentialities that can presently be detected. It is pointless to identify your welfare with a state unless you think that nation has the potentiality of continuing, continuing in fact more gloriously than in the past or at least just as gloriously. 'Some day we shall be free,' it has been said by people seeking their independence; 'Some day we shall be more prosperous,' it is said almost everywhere—and the attributes suggesting such improvement in the future are observable now. The most famous and influential mode of analysis in the modern world is the Marxian one, which postulates the coming of socialism by assuming that capitalism has within it the "seeds," that is, the certain potentiality, of its own destruction.

## Symbolizing

It has been previously indicated that, in addition to land and people, culture exists as a set of complicated stimuli which can be perceived and that one of the most common and important cultural stimuli is the country's name. The argument can be made to leap forward: virtually any predisposition has been affected by culturally determined events in the past and therefore almost every perception is influenced by some cultural predisposition. Words in particular, as semanticists point out, have a tendency to stand between us and our environment. The land and its people are not, cannot, be apprehended naively or directly; some form of internal symbolizing intervenes. New perceptions, new events, are thus related to past experience, rendered more intelligible, and are less painfully learned and stored. Usually names perform this function and hence must be included among the perceived attributes of a stimulus.

Virtually all aspects of the land, its people, and the culture have symbolic labels which, when evoked, serve to emphasize some attributes and not others. Most societies have titles that are carefully attached to certain men and women occupying a specified status. If you know that the man is called a Paramount Chief, you can anticipate his behavior, you yourself must behave appropriately, and you are simultaneously reminded both of his position and of the social organization enabling him to perform the role of leader.

Especially critical for patriotism and nationalism is the name of the country which, as already noted, can be applied to a wide variety of stimulus patterns and situations. Their psychological components may seem unrelated to one another, as indeed is the case when patriotism is broken down into "numerous loyalties to specific objects" (Hunter, 1932, p. 26); but the verbal label or a fleeting pronominal equivalent (such as "we") places them all in a single category. Mountains and rivers, fruits and vegetables, folktales and operas, women and men, summer and winter—'what a variety our country has, and it is all ours.'

The process of stereotyping personality traits can now be conveniently summarized. First, there is the tendency to ascribe such traits to people: 'He is honest [dishonest].' From the ascribed trait a deduction is drawn: 'He is honest [dishonest] and therefore he will [will not] do this.' The trait may be ascribed as a result of a nationality symbol: 'He is a Swede, hence he is honest [dishonest], and therefore he will [will not] do this.' These processes in turn depend on two assumptions people have a tendency to make: first, they believe that traits are associated with nationality and, secondly, they are convinced that, when they are not explicitly provided with the information, they can make the identification, for example, merely by looking at a person or his photograph. The role of the nationality symbol is thus clearly quite crucial in judging people's behavior, and it probably functions similarly with respect to the land and the culture.

It would be interesting to know the referent of the country's symbolic name among children and adults. Surely, the temptation is to reply that the referent is the country itself. When someone says "The United States of America," he means the entire country, all 50 of the states. But does he? An adult, when challenged, undoubtedly will say just that, but do children? Or does the adult ordinarily contemplate all parts of the country with equal intensity as he hears or employs the name? Does not "America" mean for him the area in his immediate vicinity to which the rest of the nation is attached?

The German language seems to offer a unique opportunity to throw some light on this problem because of the ambiguity of a commonly used word, *Heimat*. That word by itself usually refers to birthplace but it can also mean, in different contexts, home, neighborhood, hometown, country of birth, nationality. If you meet a German-speaking person overseas and inquire in German about his Heimat, he will mention his country of origin: Germany, Austria, or some other nation where he was born or has lived most of his life. If you ask the same question in Germany, he is likely to mention a region or state: Bavaria, the Rhineland, Prussia, Saxony, etc. If you ask the question in Bavaria and you also indicate that you know he comes from there, he will probably name a town; and eventually he will specify a neighborhood but, if he is an adult, probably not his residence or the exact house of his birth. For most speakers of German, the word is saturated with sentiment and sentimentality, as this quotation from a very popular almanac in South Tyrol drippingly demonstrates:

> When we say this dear word "Heimat," then a warm wave passes over our hearts; in all our loneliness we are not completely alone and in all our sorrow we are not without comfort.
>
> What is Heimat?
>
> Heimat is first of all the mother earth who has given birth to our folk and race, who is the holy soil, and who gulps down God's clouds, sun, and storms so that together with their own mysterious strength they prepare the bread and wine which rest on our table and give us strength to lead a good life. . . .
>
> Heimat is landscape, but a landscape composed of divine drawings which the hand of the Master has sketched on the face of the earth; it is a piece of sculpture from the workshop of the Eternal Artist. . . .
>
> Heimat is mother earth. Heimat is landscape. Heimat is the landscape we have experienced. That means one that has been fought over, menaced, filled with the history of families, towns, and villages. Our Heimat is the Heimat of knights and heroes, of battles and victories, of legends and fairy tales. But more than all this, our Heimat is the land which has become fruitful through the sweat of our ancestors. For this Heimat our ancestors have fought and suffered, for this Heimat our fathers have died [Kirschweng, 1953].

In the spring of 1961, the writer conducted a study among 497 children in eight primary schools of South Tyrol and among 740 children in six primary schools of North Tyrol. (For convenience this study, after being introduced here, will hereafter be referred to as the Tyrolean Heimat Study.) The children were asked by their teachers to write a brief composition on the following question: "What do you like and what do you not like about your Heimat?" ("Was gefällt dir in deiner Heimat gut und was nicht?") The question is obviously open-ended: the children could write what they wished, and they could choose to mention both their likes and their dislikes or to ignore one set of feelings. They were not told that an American was interested in their replies; they were asked not to sign their names but to indicate their age and sex. All essays have been read and coded by this writer; the reliability of his coding, when subjective judgments were involved, was checked by having in some cases a Tyrolean and in other cases a German independently read samples of the compositions. Disagreements were few, since almost always it was necessary to note only the presence or absence of a topic.

The section of the study reported here involves only the conception of Heimat which seemed to underlie the compositions: what was each child writing about when he mentioned what he liked and disliked in his Heimat? Since both he and his teacher were located in his country, in his hometown, and near his home, he was presumably not controlled by external circumstances in selecting which of these three definitions he would assign to the word. Sixty-one compositions, 58 from South Tyrol, are not considered in this analysis because those children either forgot to indicate their age or inadvertently had not been instructed by their teachers to do so.

The results, expressed as percentages using the specified meanings as a function of age, are given in Table 1. The most general conclusion to be drawn is that with increasing age a higher percentage of the children tended to use the term Heimat to refer to larger geographical areas. No child in North Tyrol considered "home" to be his Heimat; the few in South Tyrol who did came from the younger age groups. In both regions the percentages defining Heimat as "town," either in a passing reference or exclusively, decreased as age increased. "Tyrol," in contrast, was designated as Heimat by more of the older children—but no such trend was found in North Tyrol for those implying (rather than stating explicitly or using the name) that this Austrian province was their Heimat. Not surprising, in view of South Tyrolean nationalism, is the fact that not a single essay in South Tyrol named Italy as the Heimat, although the legal nationality of the people is Italian. A bit more unexpected is the very small number in North Tyrol who thought of Austria, their native land, as the Heimat; this datum probably reflects not only provincialism but also the distinctive character of the Alpine area.

TABLE 1. *Tyrolean Heimat Study: Percentages Ascribing Various Meanings to "Heimat" as a Function of Age*[a]

| | | 8 | 9 | 10 | 11 | 12 | 13 | 14 | 15 | 8–11 | 12–15 |
|---|---|---|---|---|---|---|---|---|---|---|---|
| "Home" | S.T.[b] | 14 | 0 | 1 | 0 | 0 | 0 | 0 | — | 3 | 0 |
| | N.T. | — | 0 | 0 | 0 | 0 | 0 | 0 | 0 | 0 | 0 |
| "Town" | | | | | | | | | | | |
| any reference | S.T. | 60 | 73 | 54 | 46 | 33 | 18 | 33 | — | 56* | 28 |
| | N.T. | — | 46 | 40 | 37 | 24 | 24 | 17 | 17 | 40* | 21 |
| exclusive | S.T. | 41 | 49 | 36 | 30 | 13 | 9 | 22 | — | 37* | 13 |
| reference | N.T. | — | 26 | 25 | 26 | 14 | 10 | 4 | 7 | 25* | 9 |
| "Tyrol" | | | | | | | | | | | |
| implied only | S.T. | 2 | 21 | 33 | 30 | 56 | 67 | 48 | — | 25* | 59 |
| | N.T. | — | 44 | 44 | 41 | 27 | 31 | 42 | 48 | 43* | 34 |
| named at | S.T. | 10 | 2 | 18 | 15 | 18 | 16 | 26 | — | 13 | 19 |
| least once | N.T. | — | 15 | 18 | 24 | 55 | 42 | 43 | 38 | 19* | 46 |
| exclusive | S.T. | 2 | 0 | 11 | 9 | 13 | 16 | 26 | — | 7* | 16 |
| reference | N.T. | — | 5 | 5 | 13 | 35 | 27 | 26 | 28 | 8* | 29 |
| Country | S.T. | 0 | 0 | 0 | 0 | 0 | 0 | 0 | — | 0 | 0 |
| of citizenship[c] | N.T. | — | 0 | 1 | 2 | 2 | 7 | 5 | 4 | 1* | 5 |

---

\* Younger group differs significantly from older group ($p < .05$, chi square).
a. For South Tyrol, successive $n$'s for the 10 columns: 42, 47, 104, 78, 84, 57, 27, 0, 271, 168; age 8 includes one child of 7. For North Tyrol: 0, 96, 97, 128, 131, 135, 121, 29, 321, 416; age 9 includes six children of 8, age 15 three of 16.
b. S.T. = South Tyrol; N.T. = North Tyrol.
c. For South Tyrol, "Italy" named; for North Tyrol, "Austria."

What interpretation is to be given such a reasonably consistent trend? The tendency to include larger areas in the conception of Heimat with increasing age must reflect, as already indicated two chapters ago during a discussion of the land and its people, the changing experiences of the children. Some travel more as they grow older, or at least they have more contacts with those coming from more distant parts. Through the classroom itself they learn an ever-increasing number of facts about the outside world; two teachers in the South Tyrol stated that younger children are first taught about their immediate surroundings and then later, especially in geography, about the rest of their country.

If a common word like Heimat can evoke different meanings among Tyrolean children, then it seems necessary to return to the following question: at a given moment and in a particular society which attributes of the land and its people are likely to be noted? The question can receive no general reply: each culture pattern, each nation is more or less singular and therefore somewhat uniquely emphasizes certain attributes but not others. The reply can be more satisfyingly specific only by acquiring an intimate knowledge of the society. Superficially it can be stated, for example, that every modern nation has a flag which people notice and can associate with the name of the nation, but the precise emotions and convictions evoked by this symbol, varying as they do by nation and person, have to be empirically ascertained in each situation deemed worthy of a mighty investigation.

This section can be concluded by providing an equally inclusive answer to another pressing question: How often or by how many people must an attribute be perceived before it is considered a component of patriotism? Some attributes are obviously perceived by virtually all citizens. In a homogeneous society, every national who is not a hopeless moron uses the same name to refer to his country or tribe, or at least he recognizes the name. Other attributes, however, though apprehended only by segments of the population, can still belong to the national heritage. In modern societies, many traditional ways are confined to rural areas. Most sophisticated city dwellers smile with some condescension at a peasant wedding—their own ceremony certainly has been up-to-date—but the condescension may also be tinged with pride or with regret: 'It would be nice if we all could be so simple.' Sometimes it is asserted that those retaining the ancient custom are the "real" patriots and that those following modern ways are somewhat treasonous. Deliberate efforts have occasionally been made in the West to keep alive or to revive folk art and folk customs so that everyone may enjoy them without direct participation. In brief, an attribute associated with patriotism can be essential as shoes or as superfluous as a museum piece.

### Ethnopatriotism

A semi-ugly neologism has been selected to head this section in order deliberately to call attention to a recurrent methodological problem, that of discovering how people actually view their land, people, and culture. Ordinarily, as has been emphasized throughout this chapter, the outside observer, especially the anthropologist, reports the facts about all three of these stimulus patterns—at least the facts as he sees them through his categories, equipment, or prejudices. How the people view themselves, their environment, and culture is seldom indicated. That information on this point tends to be inadequate is shown in the Human Relations Area Files, a convenient and efficient system for organizing the most important studies of a society under a set of standardized, very inclusive rubics (Murdock et al., 1961, pp. xiii-xxv). Rarely is it possible to find therein any material for a society under ethnoscience, ethnobotany, ethnopsychology, etc., the very categories relevant to a psychological analysis of patriotism and nationalism.

How can ethnopatriotism be investigated? With patience, it would seem to this writer, nothing more is needed than the usual anthropological techniques: live among people, learn their language, win their confidence, and then note what they talk about, what they pay attention to—in short, the attributes of their land and their fellows which they single out to perceive, to judge, and to evaluate. One very germane study was conducted in the middle and late fifties of this century among the Wasco Indians on the Warm Spring Reservation in Oregon. Direct questioning produced very little information in spheres akin to our physical science; instead the attributes noted by people "in areas corresponding to our astronomy, geology, and mineralogy" could be classified as applied knowledge or "engineering." In contrast, informants possessed considerable information concerning fish and other animals and plants (French, 1956). The existence of one kind of information and the absence of another certainly affords an important clue to what these Indians perceive or do not perceive. A more specific study of their vocabulary is also relevant. Thus they have "almost no terms which refer to broad classes or categories of plants"; for example, they have no general word for "berry," although they do have names for particular berries. Presumably the absence of an abstract word reflects the absence of an abstract category and of a general way of perceiving the common attri-

butes of all berries. This rather common assumption of psycholinguistics, however, is a very Risky Stimulus Inference (Doob,
1960b).

Ethnopatriotism may be ascertained indirectly by examining
some cultural product or form of behavior and then utilizing it as
an index of people's predispositions and perceptions. Again the
dangers from a Risky Stimulus Inference loom. Proverbs may
provide a convenient, perhaps an accurate, clue to the aspects of
the land and the people likely to be noted within a society.
They must reflect people's activities and judgments in the past,
for otherwise they would not be as stereotyped, as concise, and as
frequently employed as they usually are. Then, since they are
popular and hence functional, they direct attention either literally
or metaphorically to the phenomena that are their content.

To illustrate this contention, a rather complete collection of the
proverbs current in the society must be available. Such a collection exists for the Jabo of Eastern Liberia (Herzog, 1936). Each
of the 406 proverbs appears, from the unbiased viewpoint of this
writer, to indicate how some aspect of the land and its people is
perceived and judged. A pair illustrating each of the attributes
mentioned in this chapter can be provided with dispatch:

*Composition and Physique*
  Pretty is the pebble, water doesn't carry it away.
  If you marry a beautiful woman, you marry trouble.

*Processes and Activities*
  The moon traveled on and on by night, until the day
    caught up with her.
  If you do not respect the child, he will not respect you.

*Traits*
  The pumpkin has no unripe parts.
  By his deeds we know a man.

*Development and Potentialities*
  What the sea has swallowed, it does not vomit out again.
  Children are the wisdom of the nation.

*Symbolizing*
  He is a centipede, he separates brothers.
  A grown-up who follows children is a fool.

Obviously such proverbs serve more important functions than that of giving the Jabo information concerning attributes of the land and of themselves: they explain behavior, they lay down rules of conduct. Simultaneously, and probably often only in passing, however, they must reinforce characteristic ways of perceiving and judging. The latter instruction may very well be effective because it is given merely incidentally and so effortlessly.

A Risky Stimulus Inference often is not only legitimate, but also compelling. Although accounts of an important ceremony in a society, for example, may describe events and not people's reactions to them, certain simple assumptions concerning those reactions appear reasonable. Thus among the people of French Somaliland, "the circumcision of boys is performed at about the age of puberty. The wound is healed with red pepper crushed in milk or by the smoke of a wood fire." Similarly, "the excision of girls may take place a few days after birth or at about the age of two or three or about the age of seven. . . . After the clitoris has been cut off, the two sides of the organ are made raw and joined with actual hooks made of thorns" (Leroi-Gourhan, 1953, p. 432). Certainly all Somali males and those females who reached six or seven before the rite was performed are not likely to forget the experience. For better or worse, the relatively unrisky (though ethnocentric) inference can be, home and country for them must somehow be associated with a rather ghastly ordeal.

Instead of making inferences, it seems legitimate to ask, why not approach people directly and ask them which attributes of their nation they generally perceive? An approximation of this technique has been used by the present writer in the Tyrol. In the spring of 1961 he presented a paper-and-pencil test to male and female students in a commercial secondary school in South Tyrol and a corresponding one in North Tyrol, and also to young men in Catholic seminaries in both regions. The first and by far the longer section of the questionnaire requested the subjects to fill in blanks of a document pertaining to their country; the results therefrom are presented at the conclusion of Chapter 8. The second part, the one being reported here, was a simple sentence-completion test, the instructions to which read as follows:

Complete each sentence with two or three words which from your viewpoint best meet the situation. "Among us" means "in my Heimat."

The meaning of the word *Heimat* has been discussed earlier in this chapter. There followed 25 incomplete sentences, the first three of which can serve as models for the rest:

1. Most *houses* among us are _____.
2. Most *families* among us are _____.
3. Most *farms* among us are _____.

This technique of eliciting the attributes of various stimulus patterns almost never produced a clear-cut modal response. Consider, for example, the replies on a dozen randomly selected papers from South Tyrol to the first item, "Most *houses* among us are _____":

1. gross und geräumig (large and roomy)
2. Neubauten (new buildings)
3. Holzhäuser (wooden houses)
4. zweistöckig und ohne Luxus (two-storied and without luxury)
5. neu; erneuert; Höfe (new; renovated; farms)
6. stark gebaut, mit Holz und Stein (strongly built, with wood and stone)
7. zweistöckig, und mit Holzgiebel (two-storied, and with wooden gables)
8. im Gebirge sehr niedrig, in der Ebene höher (in the mountains very low, on the plain higher)
9. der Landschaft angepasst (adapted to the landscape)
10. aus Steine, Holz, jetzt auch aus Ziegel gebaut (built from stone, wood, now also from brick)
11. der Heimat angepasst (adapted to the Heimat)
12. schmuckvoll, sauber (ornamental, clean)

These students must have been reporting different attributes of Tyrolean houses; on the level of their actual words each tended to give a more or less unique response. Here indeed is a phenomenon to be anticipated for most of the stimulus patterns composing the land, its people, and their culture.

Obviously, however, there was some agreement among the twelve respondents: four of them mentioned wood, three the height of the buildings, etc. On a higher level of abstraction all of them, with the possible exception of the two who referred to the way in which buildings are adapted to the landscape and the Heimat, reported an attribute involving the physical appearance of houses. Forcing the specific, discrete responses into such general categories, consequently, suggests some degree of unanimity in the responses. By means of this artificial but legitimate procedure, three groupings are shown in the columns of Table 2:

> *Development:* any reference to tradition, age in a flattering sense, history, ancestors, handing down from one generation to the next.
> *Symbols:* any reference to Heimat, German, Tyrol, peasant, Catholic, folk.
> *Praise:* any form of praise, including the use of words like beautiful, good, hospitable, friendly, happy, respectable, clean, healthy.

The reliability of these categories, determined by noting the agreements and disagreements in classification achieved by this writer and a patient assistant, was very high. The stimulus words themselves are grouped under three categories to conform to the exposition in this book, and the order in which they appeared in the questionnaire is shown by the number preceding each.

The statistically significant differences between the two samples which are indicated in Table 2 by asterisks may perhaps be attributed—after the fact, to be sure—to the stronger or more easily expressible patriotism of the South Tyrolean sample. In all four instances in columns 1 and 2 and also in all but one of the ten instances in columns 3 and 4 where these differences cannot be attributed to chance, a higher percentage of the South Tyroleans reponded to the words within a frame of reference involving, respectively, "development" and "symbols." A developmental response suggests an interest in tradition and the past, a symbolic

TABLE 2. *Sentence Completion: Percentages[a] Responding in Three General Categories*

| | Development | | Symbols | | Praise | |
|---|---|---|---|---|---|---|
| | South Tyrol | North Tyrol | South Tyrol | North Tyrol | South Tyrol | North Tyrol |
| **LAND** | | | | | | |
| 1. houses | 12 | 6 | 24* | 14 | 37 | 36 |
| 3. farms | 37* | 21 | 11 | 6 | 9 | 16 |
| 5. mountains | 3 | 2 | 1 | 0 | 17 | 11 |
| 14. villages | 14* | 2 | 9 | 4 | 28 | 30 |
| 17. flowers | 0 | 0 | 17 | 25 | 12 | 11 |
| 20. rivers | 0 | 0 | 0 | 0 | 8 | 3 |
| 21. animals | 0 | 0 | 1 | 0 | 3 | 4 |
| 23. streets | 0 | 0 | 0 | 3 | 27 | 31 |
| **PEOPLE** | | | | | | |
| 2. families | 0 | 0 | 42* | 9 | 9* | 23 |
| 4. children | 0 | 0 | 18* | 5 | 57 | 43 |
| 10. police | 0 | 0 | 0 | 2 | 3* | 57 |
| 11. tourists | 0 | 0 | 87* | 54 | 2 | 5 |
| 13. women | 0 | 0 | 12* | 0 | 41 | 41 |
| 19. peasants | 2 | 0 | 24* | 7 | 30 | 34 |
| 22. artists | 0 | 0 | 9 | 2 | 11* | 27 |
| **SYMBOLS AND CULTURE** | | | | | | |
| 6. flags | 8 | 8 | 42* | 64 | 7 | 5 |
| 7. tombstones | 1 | 0 | 9 | 2 | 14 | 13 |
| 8. costumes | 21 | 34 | 9 | 2 | 38 | 48 |
| 9. churches | 32* | 17 | 4 | 1 | 18 | 19 |
| 12. theaters | 2 | 3 | 48* | 21 | 10 | 19 |
| 15. bands | 7 | 8 | 12 | 4 | 33 | 28 |
| 16. festivals | 6 | 5 | 29 | 24 | 29 | 25 |
| 18. sports | 0 | 0 | 5 | 1 | 9 | 6 |
| 24. organizations | 0 | 1 | 41* | 25 | 10 | 11 |
| 25. newspapers | 21* | 1 | 18* | 2 | 4* | 13 |

---

\* Differs significantly from figure to right ($p < .05$, chi square).

a. Denominator for calculating a percentage includes those not replying to an item but replying to subsequent items; it excludes those not replying to an item and all subsequent items since a few papers were collected before the students had finished; hence the *n*'s for both groups gradually decrease toward the end of the series. The *n* for South Tyrol begins at 114 and decreases to 103; the corresponding figures for North Tyrol are 99 and 94.

one a tendency to identify the concept with the nation. In addition, not a higher but a lower proportion of these South Tyroleans reacted favorably to the four words producing reliable differences with respect to "praise"; it is possible that they were reflecting the frustration induced by what they considered to be the threat of Italian culture.

From the standpoint of ethnopatriotism, furthermore, Table 2 indicates that generally only a negligible number of these particular subjects replied in terms of "development." Evidently here was a set of attributes not likely to be noted. Most conspicuous of all is the relatively small amount of agreement that is observable even with such highly abstract categories. Indeed the fact of individuality shines forth no matter how the data are manipulated either in Table 2 or in countless other ways (the details of which the reader is spared because they show nothing more than just that).

The variability suggests that the students either perceived different attributes by and large or else, if their reactions to the referents themselves were in fact more uniform, that the words of the questionnaire were responded to out of context. Probably all of them at some time in their lives noted the various attributes which as a group they reported, but there were variations in the readiness to mention particular attributes as a response on the paper-and-pencil test. At any rate, the direct approach to ethnopatriotism utilized in this pilot study at least provides provocative hints concerning the kinds of reactions people ordinarily internalize and seldom overtly express.

This chapter began by recalling the proposition that perception depends upon the stimulus pattern and the predisposition of the perceiver. For patriotism to come into existence and persist there must be more than the continual perception of attributes: people in turn must react to the attributes their predispositions make them fated to perceive. The analysis, therefore, proceeds to the factor of distinctiveness.

# 5. Distinctiveness

At a given moment in time, the patriots whose reactions are being recorded here in slow motion can be said to perceive the land, the people, and the culture and to consider them more or less distinctive. Distinctiveness, therefore, is usually but not always evaluated quite positively. Not unexpectedly the concept is being employed in a psychological sense: what nationals prize as distinctive, others may consider most usual. Some attribute, it is believed, serves to distinguish a domestic stimulus pattern from other similar foreign patterns. In effect, 'our land, our people, our customs are different from theirs, and the differences are objective, observable, and desirable.' It is not necessary to have traveled or to have experienced other lands or people to be of the opinion that what is constantly observed at home is, somehow, unique, although such travel and experience facilitate the conviction. Indirectly people are able to learn that they are perceiving distinctive stimuli when those whom they respect tell them that the stimuli are distinctive.

No doubt the judgment of distinctiveness begins originally with the perception of differences which all living organisms must make. Thereafter the individual may come to believe that what he is perceiving exists in precisely the same form either nowhere else or much less frequently; his daily perceptions may grow commonplace for him but, in fact or in his opinion, others do not have this opportunity. 'What we see and hear all the time differs from what we would see and hear if we lived elsewhere; the usual in our country is most rare in the world.'

Any of the numerous perceived attributes of the land and its people can be singled out and adjudged distinctive. People point to the landscape and say that 'nowhere' is the vista so beautiful, varied, or cozy, without considering whether they have the empirical evidence necessary to validate the sweeping claim. They can believe that their drinking water is the clearest, the coldest, or the purest anywhere. Over the years they can devise a national dress whose materials, colors, and styles function as a medium of communication for those who know or learn their meaning and who consequently can identify the wearers as clearly and as easily as though they had been provided with a written sign or a spoken sentence. Each country in the modern world has, or thinks it has, its own peculiar literature, music, painting, handicraft, and perhaps also a form of dancing; again the feeling is that such distinctiveness can be immediately or at least eventually noted even by those who are neither nationals nor connoisseurs of these cultural products.

Scientifically distinctive phenomena may be overlooked psychologically, and phenomena considered psychologically distinctive may not be scientifically distinctive. A type of rock or disease in a country may actually be so rare that it is of great interest to the geologist or the microbiologist, but it can be virtually ignored or dismissed as unexceptional by ordinary men and women. Or, conversely, a geographer can prove objectively that landscapes like the one being praised can be observed in many regions of the world, but he is thinking in terms of the abstract categories of his craft. The nationals who view it, however, note that a particular ridge has a unique shape and is covered with very special vegetation. If the geographer does not concede the uniqueness of the shape and the special character of the vegetation, he may be forced to admit that the combination of the two is less common. Similarly the attributes of people provide limitless opportunities to stake claims for distinctiveness. 'Our women may not be particularly beautiful or intelligent, this we do admit; but nowhere else on earth can you find wives who coil their hair in such an alluring fashion or who cook such delicious dumplings.'

Claims concerning distinctiveness can seldom be contradicted or refuted because scientific criteria are difficult to formulate and then to satisfy. Natural phenomena may be measured with dispatch—the width of a river at a particular point or the height of the mountain is expressed in feet or meters—but such separate measures are not always psychologically adequate. For people's subjective feelings concerning distinctiveness usually include qualities which are not either immediately or even untimately measurable—'That wide river is mysterious'; 'That tall mountain is stark but beautiful.' Then distinctiveness as a psychological judgment is generally derived from the patterned effect of many characteristics, and patterns can be appraised less readily—'That river is wide, it is mysterious, sometimes it wanders in a straight line and sometimes it curves; there is no river like it in the world.'

In modern times the fruits of the frequently employed scholarly or scientific approach to the land and its people are communicated outside the circle of the actual investigators. Thus laymen may not have considered the old furniture of their region to be distinctive until antique dealers or historians provide evidence for the assertion. Then, having been made aware of the attributes, they become proud of the furniture and of the region and maybe also of the nation from which it comes.

The same problem of distinctiveness arises in connection with values, although here the so-called experts, the philosophers and the students of society, themselves offer contradictory views. The values men see in land, people, and culture certainly vary; but then it is also said, with sparkling originality, that there is 'nothing new under the sun.' Which is true? The answer, equally sparkling, equally original, must be that both views are correct. Although values fluctuate from society to society and from time to time, they must include certain referents because of the presence everywhere of "common problems for which all peoples at all times must find some solution." In any society, men come to grips with "the character of innate human nature"; with "the relation of man to nature (and supernature)"; with the question of whether men's temporal orientation should be toward the past, the present, or the future; with the issue of what they believe they can accomplish through their own activities; and with their relations to one another (Kluckhohn and Strodtbeck, 1961, pp. 10–11). If these be the universal problems of mankind, then it must be immediately added that each nation solves them in a particular way and, just as important, considers the solutions to be more or less distinctive. There may be, in short, uniformity on a highly abstract level, but distinctiveness in each society and—more important for this analysis—in most people's opinion is a subjective but palpable fact.

## National Character

The subject of national character, which without doubt must be included in a discussion of patriotism and nationalism, slips into its present place as gracefully as any other. For again the difference between an objective or scientific appraisal and people's convictions appears: whether or not a country has distinctive traits or a distinctive national character, its nationals almost certainly believe that it does.

The discussion must be pitched on only one of the three levels of analysis mentioned in the opening chapter of this book. Attention is turned neither to modal customs and culture traits nor to the modal circumstances under which patriotism or nationalism is expressed but to modal personality traits or behavior within a nation. Not all people in a society presumably reveal these traits and that behavior, but most of them do; and every person sharing the national character does not of course exhibit it at all times, but he does so sufficiently frequently to be so characterized. The emphasis, in brief, is upon similarities and not differences within a society. The possibility is not excluded, furthermore, that in a complicated society there may be several kinds of modal tendencies, each identified with the different groups who compose the society.

By and large such tendencies are discoverable by focusing upon the products of people or upon the people themselves. The products, which include all forms of art and literature as well as motion pictures and clothing, have been created for some reason in their own right; then, after coming into existence, they can be examined for possible clues to the society or the people for whom they have in the first place been created. The analytic procedure, however, is fraught with difficulties. First, there are usually innumerable products which can be selected for analysis, and so a sampling problem arises. No or relatively little consistency, for example, has been found in the themes contained in folktales of a given nonliterate society; and this discouraging but intelligible conclusion emerges from an examination of over 100 such groups (Child et al., 1958). Then in order to ascertain objectively and reliably the content of cultural products, specific analytic categories are explicitly defined and applied to a medium. The principal difficulty arises when the results of the analysis are used to make inferences about the creator. Just what do you know about a people when you discover that their temples are large and spacious or that their popular films contain slapstick? The very raising of the questions provides a temptation to reply—and the intuitive person is only too ready to do just that, but the objectively or scientifically inclined investigator must hesitate and wonder. The popularity of slapstick may indicate that people are demanding and obtaining the kind of gratification they obtain in real life, for art surely reflects life, doesn't it? Or they may be satisfying themselves vicariously since in real life such joy is beyond their reach or taboo and since art is supposed to provide such substitute joys, is it not? Likewise slapstick may serve to strengthen *or* to weaken whatever defenses people have against the expression of the impulses thus gratified.

A similar but even more difficult basis for inference is the society's "institutions, its collective achievements, and its public policy" (Ginsberg, 1942, p. 188). Here the data are almost infinitely numerous; hence, for example, an attempt to suggest the kinds of traits a people must have possessed when their leaders felt encouraged to formulate one colonial policy and not another seems perilous to the point of being foolhardy. Analysts employing the equivalent of this "indirect" approach by and large do not agree even on how to characterize Europeans of different nations, such as France or England, whose records and activities in the present and the past are part of the public and scholarly record. This disagreement is evidence that the approach itself is hopelessly subjective, impossibly difficult, or maybe just plain futile.

The direct alternative is to turn to a nation's people and to examine or observe them. The problem of sampling, dormant or implicit in connection with art or any other cultural product, intrudes again and most blatantly: have enough representative people been examined or observed? If a satisfactory sample has been obtained, then some kind of precise technique can be employed:

people are interviewed, they are given a questionnaire to fill out, they are asked to take a test whose purpose they may know (one that measures knowledge) or may not know (a projective instrument such as the Rorschach ink-blot test). Again, as when products are analyzed with a set of categories, quantitative scores are obtainable. The task of interpreting those scores in terms of traits or character, however, has not been well charted, especially when a test is originally devised for one society and then used in another. If people in the West who report the colors they see in ink-blots have been shown on the basis of some independent criterion to be emotionally disposed in a particular way, can one say that people in an African society who do not report the colors are consequently not so disposed? One cannot (Doob, 1960a, pp. 60–66).

Instead of working systematically with a sample of a nation, the investigator can employ the method of the anthropologist and the patient traveler: he lives among the people, he observes and talks with them in their own language for a long period of time, and slowly he absorbs their customs and values until he begins to appreciate the type of traits and characters they modally possess. A wife and also children may be of great assistance in penetrating a community since they automatically assume roles denied to the male researcher, and thus supplement the information he can gather. With such a method the aided or unaided investigator is the instrument. Though his appraisal is subtle and interesting, however, there is no real way of knowing whether his final judgment is valid. In a sense, even when he illustrates a particular trait by quoting the raw data of his observations from a notebook, he is engaging in as much interpretation as the investigator who judges emotions from responses to color on ink blots. He may be right; yet he has not submitted hard, convincing proof.

The student of national character, moreover, is confronted with still another problem: within a single nation there is the strong possibility that more or less distinctive traits are associated not only with different geographical regions but also with the different occupational, educational, and social-class groups of each region. The task of assessing national character carries with it, consequently, the responsibility of similarly and simultaneously measuring subnational characters. The difficulties in carrying on investigations of the latter both are and are not diminished by their smaller scale or range: the less extensive the group, the closer can be the scrutiny of the distinctive individual, but the greater the courage that is required to risk a generalization from the particular living details.

These quick references to the state of the art of delineating national character should first leave a dismal impression or at least the feeling that glib summaries of the modal personality tendencies of a nation must be viewed with deep suspicion. But the problem itself should not be abandoned. People's intuitions are likely to be broadly correct: though we cannot be precise or convincing, our brute experience suggests that there probably is a difference in personality between the modal Frenchman and the modal German or between the modal Eskimo in Alaska and the modal Eskimo in Greenland.

So much for the scientific issues. In real life, however, such perplexing problems concerning national character disappear. Superstition, casual impressions, stereotypes, replace factual measurements: ordinary men and women are usually not only willing to characterize themselves and others, as indicated in the last chapter, but they are also convinced that their compatriots have distinctive traits and hence that they all share a national character. The study of representative samples in various Western European countries, Australia, urban Mexico, and the United States during 1948, also cited in the last chapter, is illustrative. One question was worded as follows: "Do you think that our [name of nationality supplied] characteristics are mainly born in us, or are they due to the way we are brought up?" The question is clearly loaded, for it assumes that there are distinctive national "characteristics." A total of only 3 per cent of the Australian sample said they did not know the answer, thus perhaps implicitly rejecting the assumption of national character contained in the query; the remaining 97 per cent explicitly accepted that assumption by ascribing or not ascribing it to innate factors. The corresponding "don't-know" figure in Britain was 6 per cent, in France 14, in West Germany 12, in Italy 10, in urban Mexico 8, in the Netherlands 13, in Norway 20, and in the United States 6. In all these countries, except West Germany and Italy, furthermore, less or

far less than half of each sample believed that national characteristics are "born in us" (Buchanan and Cantril, 1953, pp. 62, 145).

Then during the same survey, the respondents were asked, immediately after they had indicated the social class to which they
considered themselves to belong, whether they felt they had "anything in common with" that same class of people abroad and also
with their own compatriots who were not members of the same
class as they. The analysis of the results: "In every country except the Netherlands, a higher percentage say they have something
in common with their compatriots than say they have something in common with their class members abroad" (ibid., p. 18).
With an exception, consequently, greater numbers considered
nationals of their own country, regardless of differences in social
class, to be more similar to themselves than people of the corresponding class abroad. Similarity obviously implies distinctiveness.
For the future, however, it must be pointed out that in this particular study the percentages of informants with contrary feelings
varied from country to country; and there is a remote possibility
that some of the people who felt more closely identified with foreigners of comparable status could have been leaning toward some
form of internationalism.

Sometimes hard facts make it difficult to claim distinctiveness
with respect to a character trait, but then partial facts can be interpreted as supporting evidence. In a study of "national differences in creativity," it has been shown that in various scientific,
humanistic, and cultural fields Germany has made more contributions since 1800 than any other nation (Lehman, 1947).
Germans by and large are certainly proud of these contributions
and, without knowing the facts precisely, claim creative distinctiveness. The preeminence of Germany, which is probably dimly
or fully recognized by educated people elsewhere, does not prevent nationals in other countries from emphasizing the lesser but
still distinctive contributions of their own countries. South Tyroleans often express pride in the fact that the inventor of the type-
writer—or one of the inventors—was born and died in their region.

In general, outsiders are always considered different from fel-
low-countrymen in some respects. 'Yes, we and they are Catholics, but we are much more pious than they are.' The ensuing

feeling of distinctiveness is likely to be converted into a virtue. Nationalists, for example, seek to retain their individuality by resisting innovations from the outside which, though desirable, are rejected just because of their origin. Paradoxically, however, they may be convinced that they are distinctively hospitable to ideas and practices from abroad; 'We are a cosmopolitan people; no narrow prejudices blind us or prevent us from participating in the best that the world has to offer.' Often, such apparent open-mindedness is accompanied by the feeling that the imports are incorporated into the existing culture only after being given some kind of a twist: 'We accepted it from them, but then we improved it and made it ours.' Differences in character which people ascribe to the separate regions inside their own country may be considered less distinctive or important than the traits allegedly distinguishing all peoples within the boundaries from those on the outside. 'We in the north are different from those in the south, of course; still northerners and southerners are basically alike and hence do not at all resemble foreigners.'

## Rewards

People emerge as adults with definite emotional attitudes concerning the home, the neighborhood, and the community in which they have been reared. Whether they later move away or remain in their birthplace, they necessarily are influenced by other people and events. They continue, nevertheless, to be affected by the values and criteria which they originally learned and employed and which, being theirs, must seem to be more or less unique. 'This is the way we once did it, this is the way it should be done, this is our way.'

There are other equally compelling reasons to treasure and hence to seek out distinctiveness. However dimly they are able to conceptualize the feeling, people value their own integrity: somehow they consider themselves to be different from everyone else, or at least from most others including members of their own ingroup. For they alone experience what seethes most privately within their consciousness. This value of self-identity they can sometimes extend to, or project upon, the objects and other people who are important to them. 'They are mine, hence they are like me, and so they are distinctive.' Being distinctive or possessing distinctive attributes means that persons so designated are distinguishable from their contemporaries and from outsiders; and being thus outstanding can bring greater prestige and higher status.

Usually, therefore, the perception of distinctiveness is accompanied by a judgment of superiority. 'Our way of doing that is not only different from theirs, it is better.' When the attribute in question must be considered inferior, nationalists can employ a number of devices to rescue their country's reputation. The inferiority is thought to promote other commendable virtues: 'Our scanty natural resources make us work all the harder in order to progress; it is for this reason that we have developed strong characters.' Another distinctive attribute with positive value may be placed alongside the one with negative connotations: 'We may be small, but we have been united for centuries.' The fact of distinctiveness rather than the attribute itself is believed to be attractive: 'Our town [county, country] is bedeviled by frequent fog, no doubt more frequently than any other place; we hate fog; our fog, though a very dubious claim to distinction, at least distinguishes us from outsiders.' A few people, finally, are able to perceive distinctiveness without much trace of ethnocentrism or envy: 'The world would be a dull place if all nations were the same.' Such a cosmopolitan view is likely to be expressed only by those who have achieved a sense of detachment and sophistication as a result of experiencing or being taught the joys stemming from diversity.

Nationalists not only believe that they and their country are distinctive, but they are also able to advance reasons for supporting their belief. Those reasons range from the simple to the profound, and they include both conscious and unconscious elements. 'This is our national soup, we love it, we have it every day, there is no soup quite like it in the world.' Why is the soup so good? 'It is prepared faithfully in accordance with the traditional recipe, it was used by our ancestors, it fortifies our bodies.' What significance should be attached to the fact that these people love their national soup so much and find it so distinctive? It may in fact contribute vital elements to their diet, of which they themselves are not aware. It may reflect the state of their economy: they are a poor people, and soup is a very economical dish. A psychoanalyst might discover or assert that such a form of nourishment represents infantile tendencies within the society: the people are really afraid of solid foods; they are so devoted to soup because "unconsciously" it brings them the feeling of security they once experienced at their mother's breast. Similarly, Germans say they like to see uniforms on government officials and other servants. This "passion" of theirs has been traced to certain needs they allegedly have. A uniform, it is asserted, not only unites one person with another but it also "covers" the wearer and isolates him from his neighbor who for him is considered "a disturbing figure and an object of hostility"; the latter need is also suggested by the rigid rules of behavior, the ceremonials, and the walled-in houses which can be found in Germany (Moellenhoff, 1947, pp. 40–43). In short, what people say concerning soup, uniforms, or any national custom may reflect objectively ascertainable facts or modal personality techniques within the society. Here is a very peculiar form of the Risky Stimulus Inference: people may be in error in interpreting their own behavior.

## Relativity and Universality

Previously the discussion has been concerned with the reasons for perceiving some attributes of the land and people and not others. A similar problem arises in connection with the factors determining which of the perceived attributes are judged to be distinctive. As in any judgment, objective and subjective processes interact. Objectively, the actual stimulus pattern available to people plays some role. A snowy countryside is not selected as the distinctive characteristic of a native land where snow is irregular or scanty. Subjectively, the factor of previous experience, as ever, must be taken into account.

The polar Eskimos may be called upon to serve as a real illustration of the complex interaction between the objective and subjective factors. When the European explorers reached them in 1818, "they had forgotten their origin and believed themselves the only people in the world" (Murdock, 1934, p. 218). From the standpoint of the anthropologist, they had developed rather distinctive ways of building snow huts, of shooting game, of fishing, and of transportation. Not having the opportunity to perceive an outgroup with differing traits, however, they probably could not have labeled their own traits as unique; at least that can be a Risky Stimulus Inference. A half century later they were visited by other Eskimos and apparently accepted from them innovations in the above respects; for example, they learned to use the bow and arrow as a hunting implement (Rasmussen, 1908, pp. 31–32). In this way they must have been made aware of their distinctiveness; simultaneously the acceptance of the changes strongly suggests that they judged the foreign traits to be more efficient to cope with a difficult environment. Previously, moreover, in spite of their small number—the total population was 271 in 1926—they did apparently perceive specific attributes of their own subgroups. Though nomadic, they classified themselves with respect to the sites of their permanent winter camps and the variations associated therewith, such as prevailing wind, available game, diet, clothing, and construction of houses (Rasmussen, 1921, pp. 20–23).

The presence of certain subjective factors in a society can thus be a function of the experiences nationals have had with some kind of outgroup. For unless a contrast or difference has been perceived or somehow communicated, it is difficult to imagine how they can consider their surroundings distinctive; in some respects conditions must be different from those elsewhere. The source of the insight can be tradition, a vague term whose concrete referent may be an historical contact in the past. Africans who served in the military forces of colonial powers outside their own territory during World War I and outside Africa during World War II learned that the world contains different people, different customs, and different landscapes; and they returned home with new orientations toward their own societies and themselves. The presence of tourists and travelers makes the inhabitants aware not only of foreign ways of behaving but of their own ways. 'I had not realized how loud we talk in public until I heard those foreigners; why, they seemed just to be whispering to one another.'

A complete inventory of the natural objects in a country could not suggest the particular ones likely to be singled out as distinctive: the subjective factors are so often critical. Whether or not people use as a national symbol the type of tree that grows most frequently and prominently in their land depends upon their associations with it: the way in which it is used, the customs in which it plays a role, and the general significance that is attached to it. Then, too, distinctive stimulus patterns can be created. Traditions are established to honor the Founding Fathers on some anniversary or other. Shrines are constructed. History is investigated so that the past can be extolled after it becomes known. Distinctive uniforms or costumes are designed and then made mandatory under specified conditions. In general, clothes relatively easily serve a protective function when materials are available; but thereafter, not in the conscious manner of the modern fashion expert who deliberately seeks to create novelty for his own financial gain but through some kind of trial and error extending over generations, distinctive attributes are added. Distinctiveness, in brief, is a relative matter.

In spite of the conclusion just reached, it seems necessary to ask whether it is not possible to survey coldly the welter of characteristics concerning the land, its people, and their culture that are capable of being labeled distinctive and then to select a limited number which are universally thus singled out wherever national unity exists. Clear-cut evidence is lacking, but a few attributes can be tentatively if incautiously suggested. First, people seize upon some properties of the land on which they live. As suggested earlier in this chapter, even nomads are probably aware of distinctive features of the area through which they move; when certain features disappear, they know they have reached a boundary, clearly or unclearly defined, and go no farther. The permanent inhabitants of a region become accustomed to the stimulus patterns engulfing them: they expect to see mountains or plains, to experience dry or wet weather generally or seasonally, to watch certain plants and not others grow to maturity and then wither. They may never be called upon to name the components of their customary constellation of environmental stimuli; but potentially the knowledge is within them and can be evoked when, for example, they are patiently questioned by an outsider or when they themselves suddenly travel abroad and then think of home. Perhaps the commonplace is part of that constellation only if it is also somewhat uncommon; thus frequent hail is more likely to be associated with a region than infrequent hail, but a never-changing phenomenon, such as heavy automobile traffic, may not be considered a distinctive attribute.

People are certain to apprehend or to try to apprehend something distinctive about their own compatriots. One attribute employed universally but not always successfully involves the body's appearance. The clearest perceivable attribute is skin pigmentation, which, however, cannot often serve the function of distinguishing the nationals of one country from another because the principal shades of skin coloring throughout the world are too few or because subtle variations in shading within each nation are too diverse. Thus this characteristic clearly distinguishes Africans from Europeans but not the inhabitants of two neighboring countries (such as Uganda and Kenya) or neighboring tribes within the same country (such as the Ganda and the Soga in Uganda). Other natural attributes of people—hair color, body size, physiognomy—are also difficult or impossible to employ as a result of the vast amount of racial intermixture everywhere. More frequently than not, as previously indicated, people believe, nevertheless, that they and their contemporaries constitute an identifiable type; or they deliberately add manipulatable attributes (scars, clothing) to the human body that achieve such a goal.

Less doubtful as universals are the cultural attributes that are singled out and labeled distinctive. People of a nation usually share a common language, which, consequently, they consider an especially important hallmark. Even when the same language is used in more than one country—English in England and America, German in Germany and Austria—a particular dialect can be claimed for the nation. In fact, the very same reasons, to be described in Chapter 12, that make a common language one of the essential conditions for patriotism and nationalism account for people's overwhelming desire to consider their own language distinctive.

At the same time as children learn their native language, they also acquire definite preferences for food and drink which they retain and treasure to some extent throughout their lives. After weaning, they gradually begin to eat and drink what their parents do, and they thus become accustomed to a distinctive diet and cuisine. Such preferences are so strong that most peoples, when confronted with choices, tend to select not the exotic or strange but the conventional or usual; young second-generation Italian males adopted innumerable American customs of the New England city where they lived, but all of them, even those rebelling against their parents' culture, tended to prefer and to adhere to Italian cuisine (Child, 1943, pp. 110–11, 197). Everywhere people say they have national dishes and national drinks that they consume either frequently or on special occasions. 'If you are a real American, you have coffee for breakfast every day of your life, not just coffee, but good American coffee which is distinctively different from any other cup of coffee anywhere, and so much better.'

Accompanying claims to distinctiveness is another tendency that must also be tentatively labeled universal: the desire to continue to be distinctive. Such a desire becomes somewhat difficult to satisfy when the customs or traits of outsiders invade the nation, which is certainly the situation again and again in modern countries. A number of alternatives then suggest themselves. The importations may be discounted: 'We are not outstanding in that respect, but we don't wish to be.' Or some qualitative distinction may be claimed: 'They have done more along those lines, but we were the pioneers, we produced the original invention.' It can also be maintained that a nation is not supreme in a given respect, only because it has devoted its energies to other tasks: 'We have a few great composers, but music does not seem to be our specialty; we lean more to literature and painting.'

One final paragraph from a scientific standpoint. In order to perceive and then claim distinctiveness, similarities must be deliberately or unwittingly disregarded. The casual traveler, for example, may be struck by the similarity in the physical appearance of people throughout the Mediterranean area; at a glance, he may not know whether a stranger is a Greek, an Italian, an Egyptian, or an Israeli. If he wishes, moreover, he may emphasize the similarities he observes among peoples considering themselves quite distinctive. And then, when a member of one of these national groups points out subtle or gross differences and if he is quite politically unbiased, he can make note of differences. But a traveler who can thus quickly alter his mode of perception in functioning like a scientist; he is not playing the role of a patriot hell-bent on noticing only the distinctiveness of compatriots. Nowadays international communication at least in the sciences tends to be relatively efficient, so that important contributors are likely to be recognized among most fellow-scientists; nationals, therefore, find it difficult to boast about distinctiveness in areas unsupported by the facts. The various Nobel prizes and the objectively ascertainable achievements ultimately validate or invalidate most claims. Possibly on some occasions the facts may not be known or, when known, may not prove critical, but they seldom can be completely overlooked.

More generally, though, as this chapter has sought to demonstrate, the people of every nation are convinced that their distinctiveness, no matter how small the area to which it pertains, is significant and virtually cosmic. 'Other nations are like us, but in some important ways we are happily and proudly different.' Here is a basis for mortal fame and for blessed immortality.

## 6. Evaluation

It is unnecessary to contend that all human reactions involve some kind of evaluation. Perhaps they do. Whether they do or not, however, value judgments unquestionably must be included among the components of patriotism. For the land, its people, and their culture are perceived as more or less distinctive, and they are praised. Outsiders are likely to be deprecated, if not condemned. In fact the strength of patriotism can be judged in terms of such values: people have strong or weak emotions when they consider the pattern or person they are judging to be very valuable or quite valueless.

Distinctiveness as such is a form of evaluation which is so important that it has been singled out for separate treatment in the preceding chapter. This is not to say that people consider all aspects of their nation extraordinary; but, it has been pointed out, when they believe that certain attributes of the land, their compatriots, and their culture are unique, they are usually expressing approval. The perception or the judgment of distinctiveness obviously involves some kind of comparison between what is being perceived and a standard. 'Our people are strong and healthy'— does this mean that their traits of strength and health are distinctive or that, by implication, they are stronger and healthier than some other group? Presumably whoever makes or subscribes to such a statement must be acquainted with some standards; he must know the nature of weakness and illness, but he may or may not consider the attributes distinctive or superior. And so, from a psychological standpoint, a conclusion emerges: the evaluations at the core of patriotism may or may not be accompanied by a conscious assertion concerning distinctiveness or a conscious comparison with another nation.

What are the values, then, that motivate people when they pass

judgment on the land, its people, and their culture? Obviously they
approve or disapprove of what they perceive for many reasons—
reasons in fact that are as varied as their feelings and emotions. Unfortunately, with a few notable exceptions (e.g. Lasswell and Kaplan, 1950), social scientists have not concerned themselves with
the problem of investigating these reasons empirically and classify-
ing them.

Help ought to be available from philosophers since they are
eager to assert that "what is actually the distinguishing mark of the
human species [is] the capacity not only to think and feel but to
*judge* and *evaluate*." But then they are quick to emphasize that
theirs is the special normative problem of validating the categories
behind ethical decisions and not the empirical one of determining
people's actual values or the ones they say they employ (Smith,
1958, pp. 8–14, italics his). When these empirical values are mentioned at some length, moreover, the data tend to be anecdotal
and incomplete (e.g. Cohen, 1954, pp. 15–18) or the list of values
is much too general to be followed as a guide to the description and
analysis of the concrete judgments associated with patriotism (e.g.
Baier, 1958, pp. 108–36). And so, sadly, gently, and semirespect-
fully the honorable discipline of philosophy must be cast aside.

The discussion in this chapter deliberately errs, it is hoped, in
the direction of completeness, without however suffering from the
delusion that the goal can be achieved. An arbitrary dichotomy
is introduced for the sake of convenience, and then under each
heading the evaluative criteria are given conventional labels for
purposes of quick identification and future reference. It is to be
understood, furthermore, that the values are not merely present or
absent when the attributes of land, people, and culture are judged,
rather that, when present, they vary in degree from extremely
positive to extremely negative. For purpose of exposition, however,
only the positive, strong variant of each value is usually indicated.

Hopefully to enliven and enlighten the discussion, each mode
of evaluation is introduced by two quotations from the children's
essays obtained for the Tyrolean Heimat Study, the broad outlines
of which have been given in Chapter 4. All the material here
comes from children in South, not North, Tyrol. The quotations
are not necessarily typical and they are given out of context; they

seek to illustrate the categories and not to prove a thesis. Each is followed by information indicating the sex, age, and residence of the child.

### Egocentric Valuations

'I like, I approve of this because of its effect upon me.' The values about to be considered have as a primary point of reference the person passing judgment. Often he indirectly mentions the significant groups to which he belongs: 'This pleases us.' Included here in large part are what have been called "welfare" values: "those whose possession to a certain degree is a necessary condition for the maintenance of the physical activity of the person" (Lasswell and Kaplan, 1950, p. 55).

1. *Hedonistic:*

> Old customs and traditions bring us a great deal of joy and love for our Heimat (boy, 12, rural).
>
> I would not like to live in a town because there harsh air must be endured which damages a person's health (boy, 14, semirural).

For reasons they may not be able to explain adequately, people react to some attribute of the land, its people, or their culture by feeling happy, content, proud, healthy, or gratified—or the reverse. They then evaluate the state of affairs which produces such internal feelings either positively or negatively. This most general type of evaluation—'I like it,' in effect, 'because I like it'—can be broad and vague, for it reflects the variety of emotions which people experience and the equally numerous ways in which they can express themselves. Love of countrymen, for example, can be concrete or abstract. Concretely the individual enjoys the company of his peers and therefore participates actively in national festivals. Or abstractly he is charmed more by the idea than by the reality: he avoids his countrymen, but thinks them the finest people on earth. In either case internal feelings increase his patriotism and can play an important role in nationalism.

Like some of the other modes of evaluation, this sense of physical or spiritual gratification can promote patriotism and nationalism at either end of its continuum. Unquestionably when people are satisfied with their country, they would have this state of affairs continue; and they are ready to make appropriate demands or take appropriate action in behalf of the status quo. But discontent can also goad them to action and increase their patriotism. Common defeats in the past, though not so cheering as common victories, may be just as binding: 'Our country has had its tragic moments, we cherish the memories of those who suffered and died then, we hereby resolve not to let history repeat itself.' It may be that a touch of bitterness renders the present not sweet but meaningful by revealing to people the connection between their welfare and their country.

The hedonistic criterion is usually employed at some point when differences between ingroupers and outgroupers are evaluated. Apparently people feel more comfortable or relaxed in front of those who are similar to themselves. 'If you belong to my family or my club or my nation, I can pretty well anticipate how you will judge the world, how you will react to my suggestion, in truth how you will behave because I generally have quite accurate anticipations about myself, and you are like me. But if you are a stranger and particularly if you are a member of some bizarre nation, I have to be alert most of the time; I really have no idea what you are going to do because you are so different from me.' A countryman, consequently, is evaluated with some contentment. Naturally the exotic, though it produces a strain, is also pleasant to some people; yet even they during a large part of each day probably seek the familiar, since no man can jump completely out of his background. In addition, the nonconformist, the bohemian, the expatriate, is relatively rare among those able to control their own existence.

2. *Aesthetic:*

What pleases me most is the church and the blossoming trees. The flowers and the bushes please me greatly because they are beautiful. The cross is beautiful because it has beautiful decorations. The cemetery is also beautiful (girl, 8, semirural).

The grey factories also do not please me. They also look very ugly (boy, 9, urban).

A more specific but still vague form of evaluation involves aesthetics: stimulus patterns are judged to be attractive or unattractive, beautiful or ugly in varying degrees. Of all values, this one is perhaps the most variable from culture to culture, from time to time within a society, and from person to person. In spite of such variability, however, at a given instant the society or the person reveals somewhat consistent, reliable judgments concerning those aspects of the land and its people that are singled out for aesthetic judgment. A certain type of physique or physiognomy is preferred by people, and the ideal is thought to persist in their own society and sometimes also, in varying degree, among outside groups.

Attractiveness and beauty are attributes to be appreciated in their own right, both students of aesthetics and ordinary human beings are likely to maintain. In many, perhaps in most instances, however, a stimulus pattern is aesthetically satisfying because it has served or might conceivably serve some other human need besides the sublime one of evoking subtle feelings. Thus arises no doubt the eternally fascinating though hackneyed problem of the connection between the beautiful and the useful. That relation involves a proposition and its converse which are by no means universal: some beautiful patterns are useful, some useful patterns are beautiful. An aesthetic evaluation, moreover, can usually be made with dispatch and without much deliberation: at a glance the woman or the flower bed is considered attractive or beautiful in appearance, and *de gustibus* there are likely to be neither disputes nor appeals.

3. *Moral-Religious:*

Otherwise what pleases me particularly above everything else is that we hold on to the correct religion (boy, 12, urban).

What does not please me in our Heimat is that there are wicked people who do not believe in God (girl, 8, semi-rural).

At some point, on some occasion, judgments are made with reference to the system of metaphysics prevailing in the society: the person feels that an attribute is good or bad in itself. Morally, a virtue such as honesty or righteousness is involved. For religion the values are oriented toward the sacred rather than the profane in terms of the rules for living which are sanctioned or tabooed. It is banal but necessary to stress the importance of moral-religious values; and so merely mentioning the problem of church and state or that of religion and nationalism suffices to substantiate the implied thesis.

4. *Utilitarian:*
> The forest pleases me particularly because it protects us from strong winds and because it provides us with shade. It is also a savings bank in time of need (girl, 11, semi-rural).

> But I do not like the storms and floods which cause so much damage (boy, 12, urban).

Here the mode of evaluation is quite practical: something about the land, its people, and their culture is appreciated or deprecated because it does or does not bring closer a goal whose value is acceptable without further inquiry. Utility is apparent in many different contexts. Tools are praised because they enable men to work with the expenditure of less physical or psychic energy. A shortcut is desirable for the same reason, provided that work and not play is involved. Fertile land is praised: it can be cultivated relatively effortlessly and it produces first-rate crops. The traits of people can be similarly judged: 'Our soil is poor, but we are conscientious and thorough enough to use every bit of it'; 'Their soil is excellent, but they are too lazy to take advantage of their good fortune.' The ability to perform efficiently may also be aesthetically appraised: there is something inherently attractive about elegant, delicate activity containing no waste motion. Finally, the utilitarian criterion can be applied to relations among people: deeds and devices are judged as means of strengthening or weakening such ties, and the ties themselves are considered valuable per se or helpful in the attainment of other ends such as power or prestige.

5. *Meaningful:*
> My Heimat is South Tyrol. I can be proud of a beautifully scenic Heimat. . . . My Heimat is so beautiful that I do not know what I should say, I do not know what does not please me about it (girl, 13, rural).

> These many-colored houses do not please me. But tech-
> nology makes such demands, and as a result no one can do
> anything to halt it (boy, 13, rural).

This mode of evaluating is very vague and least intimately connected with stimulus patterns in the external world: men are
deeply gratified when they have experiences which somehow provide perspective, explanations, understanding, in short, meaning
to their existence. Religion obviously offers or seeks to offer the
most cosmic meaning of all; it would explain human suffering or
death itself not as an unendurable, cruel misery or as an unavoidable fate but as an integral part of a divine scheme. Nationalism,
it has often been remarked, performs a similar function by promoting an earthly Weltanschauung which not only can command
men's allegiance and loyalty but can also provide them with an
explanation for many of the pleasant aspects of life as well as with
hope concerning the possible removal of many of its unpleasant
turns. In the nineteenth and twentieth centuries some men "who
might once have become priests in hope of salvation now became
superpatriots in pursuit of a national utopia" (Shafer, 1955, pp.
177–78). Freedom from colonial rule, peoples in the developing
countries have often been led to believe, will bring down the pie
from the sky and will quickly solve all national and personal problems.

In traditional or insular societies, existence finds most of its
meaning in daily routine; and so there the national goal usually is
simple preservation. In modern nations, especially in urban areas,
it is not easy to apprehend meaningful connections among the con-
flicting elements in the milieu; hence the goals being sought by a
nationalistic country as a whole can offer some consolation. While
separate events may not be considered beautiful, moral, or useful,
they can be viewed with approval in the context of the country's
destiny.

6. *Demanding:*
> I also like the winter in my Heimat. Even in summer I
> await it impatiently. I know how to take full advantage of
> it; in winter, I go tobogganing the entire day (boy, 9,
> urban).

> In my Heimat the many Italian workers do not please
> me. We are treated by the Italians as an inferior people
> (girl, 13, semirural).

Stimulus patterns are reacted to as signals that herald action for
the group to which a person belongs and that therefore promote
group action and unity. The bells ring and, as it were, demand
that the devout go to church; besides their aesthetically pleasing
sound, they are valued because they signify that the service is
about to begin. Some stimulus patterns associated with patriotism
or nationalism themselves exert demands that are close to zero.
'That landscape which I see now, which is so beautiful, which
means home to me, I need only admire; I do not have to do anything about it.' Other symbols, such as the passing of the nation's
flag during a parade or the command of a policeman, demand action which is then judged on its merits, that is, in terms of other
values: the flag is to be saluted, the policeman to be obeyed. In
fact, most stimulus patterns associated with government require
some sacrifice or abnegation with which people are or are not in
accord. Both the patriot and the less devoted citizen may agree
that laws and decrees should be followed, the former because he
would help his country, the latter because he would avoid landing
in jail.

### Ethnocentric Valuations

'I like, I approve of this because of its effect upon my relation to
other people.' The person who is passing judgment is considering
himself—all judgments are to some extent egocentric—but he is
thinking of that self primarily with reference to others inside or
outside his society. Such essentially social valuations are called
ethnocentric, though admittedly a trace of violence is being inflicted upon its usual meaning, in order to feature the personal
basis: 'I like, I approve of them because they share my values,' 'I
like this, they will like it too, and so we shall like each other more.'
To a certain extent homage is being paid here to the "deference"
values which constitute the other half of the dichotomy of the
authors previously cited: "those that consist in being taken into

consideration (in the acts of others and of the self)" (Lasswell and Kaplan, 1950, pp. 55–56).

7. *Conventional:*

And the ocean, that too I do not wish to see. I much prefer to remain in the mountains (girl, 13, rural).

Our Heimat is particularly defaced by the advertising posters on many barn doors and barns (girl, 12, semi-rural).

The peak of ethnocentricity is undoubtedly the branding of some activity or objects as desirable or undesirable simply because they do or do not conform to the conventional standards of the society. 'This just is not done, it is not respectable.' The gamut here is long, extending from personal habits of cleanliness and tidiness to such interpersonal relations as courtships and funerals. The value resembles but is different from the moral-religious one: the conventional standard is employed with dispatch and is not connected with any cosmic justification other than prevailing customs. The use of the value of respectability, however, does not signify that the individual is motivated only superficially, for the pain or the motives associated with trying to conform may be just as powerful as some of the more basic needs. In addition, conventionality is usually surrounded by a host of rationalizations and explanations. 'We do it this way because . . .' and then the sentence can be completed most variously: 'because we have always done it that way,' 'because any other way is ugly,' 'because this is the best way to do it.' The mass media of communication in modern societies and the formal education systems anywhere offer numerous grounds for following convention.

8. *Prestigeful:*

My Heimat is for me the most beautiful spot that exists on earth. It is very famous because of its good wine (boy, 13, rural).

Our Heimat is one of the most fertile regions. We can be very proud of the fact that we produced one of the most famous painters, Michael Pacher (girl, 12, semirural).

Receiving positive recognition from people inside or outside a society is judged to be valuable. Reputation and eminence spring from present or past performance. Often such an attribute becomes part of the society's tradition and persists over long periods of time. As will be repeatedly noted, modern nationalists seem particularly concerned with their reputations abroad: they seek fame and respect in one or more areas, and often a slur on their so-called national honor means only that they are convinced that the figure cut by the symbol of their country somehow has been tarnished. They would demonstrate that some of their citizens, long ago or now, have made substantial contributions to the world's culture in a valued field such as art, literature, science, discovery, or invention. In traditional societies, too, gratification can be obtained from the conviction that superiority over the foreigners has been attained, and so the strength of warriors or of wine can bring great joy.

9. *Interpersonal:*

My neighbors are Italians. They often play with me. We get along very well (boy, 12, urban).

Most of all the Dolomites please me. The Italians hate our land (boy, 13, semirural).

Relations between people, including those between the person passing judgment and some group, are evaluated. A criterion considered good in its own right, such as amicability, helpfulness, trustworthiness, or honesty, is implicitly or explicitly utilized. For it is felt that social relations of any kind are seldom if ever neutral: other people are judged in terms of the satisfactions they bring for all the reasons that attract and repel human beings. That satisfaction is not egocentric; reciprocity is a critical component of mutual esteem and affection.

10. *Powerful:*

All people in my town do not please me, many people are haughty. In my town there are both poor and rich people (girl, 8, rural).

What does not please me are the malicious people in the land. What does not please me is the fact that Italians oppress my Heimat land (boy, 11, semirural).

Ascendancy over others, actual or potential, is the bench mark of this value, and such ascendancy is either praised or condemned. Undoubtedly a very basic issue is involved, for the experience of being weak or strong in comparison with someone else is universal. The very words "children" and "adults" possess connotations relating to strength. Power may also be evaluated in its own right by focusing upon change; and in the West the values that appear usually have the common labels of reactionary, conservative, liberal, progressive, and radical. Again a basic tendency is evident: at an early stage it seems likely that children are torn between the conservative desire to continue to be weak and so to be protected by their parents and the more radical wish to have power in their own right by becoming independent.

The power being considered can consist of economic, social, or any other kind of domination; and the comparison can be confined to groups or individuals within or outside the nation. Within the society, for example, note may be taken of the fact that a class, sex, or age group occupies a dominant position—and there is always stratification of these types within any society. The point of reference on the outside may be to a foreign institution, to a foreign group, or in fact to the other nation as a whole: 'Our country is better than theirs.' The establishment of such differences can bring satisfaction or dissatisfaction. In countries like France and Germany titles tend to be used more conspicuously and frequently than in England and the United States; this method of clearly identifying status must bring pleasure to those whose high position is thus acknowledged and must somewhat please most people by reminding them of a hierarchy which they consider to be one of the distinctive and praiseworthy attributes of their society. Dissatisfaction after a comparison can lead to nationalistic demands: 'Their resources are more plentiful than ours, we must reach out and achieve at least equality with them.'

## The Organization of Values

The simple enumeration of the criteria employed by patriots and nationalists to evaluate their land, people, and culture suggests a number of generalizations concerning values. In the first place, usually more than one criterion operates when judgment is passed. Undoubtedly this tendency reflects the complexity of national stimulus patterns which evoke a variety of responses. Then, secondly, each of the values is culturally loaded: that which is considered happy, pretty, good, useful, intelligible, demanding, respectable, celebrated, honest, or strong fluctuates markedly from culture to culture and, within a given culture, from epoch to epoch.

In spite of the multiplicity and variability of the values, however, people's patriotic predispositions are generally neither disorganized nor chaotic. What emerges is a conviction best summarized by the unified tone of approval conveyed by the phrase "national pride." 'Our land is beautiful, our people are conscientious, our way of earning a living is difficult, we are closer to heaven than any other nation perhaps—but these are minutiae: the overwhelming, overpowering, the impressive fact is that our country as such is great and awe-inspiring.' Blemishes can be overlooked, in the light of such utterly convincing evidence of greatness and uniqueness.

In fact, the results of a very recently published study suggest that most people may be able to specify at least the superficial source of their pride even when suddenly called upon to do so by an open-ended question in the midst of a long interview. Carefully drawn national samples of approximately 1,000 people over the age of 18 in the United States and three European countries and a similar one in Mexico, confined to cities of 10,000 inhabitants or more, were confronted in 1959 or 1960 with a schedule containing 94 questions. Item 33 was: "Speaking generally, what are the things about this country that you are most proud of?" A total of only 4 per cent in the United States could think of nothing to mention; 10 per cent in the United Kingdom; 15 per cent in West Germany; 16 per cent in Mexico; and 27 per cent in Italy. The question also revealed the attributes of the land, the people, and the culture which, as judged by the spontaneous responses of those in the five samples, must have been perceived and viewed with approval. "Governmental, political institutions" was the modal reply in the United States (85 per cent), the United Kingdom (46 per cent), and Mexico (30 per cent); the "characteristics of people" in West Germany (36 per cent); and the "physical attributes" of the country in Italy (25 per cent). With such data in their possession, the investigators have formulated stimulating hypotheses concerning the feelings of the various nationals toward their countries. "The Americans and the British," they say, "with greatest frequency take pride in their political systems, social legislation, and international prestige"; in contrast, "Italians in the overwhelming majority take no pride in their political system, nor even in their economy or society" and therefore "to the extent that they have national pride at all, it is in their history, the physical beauty of their country, or in the fact of being Italian" (Almond and Verba, 1963, pp. 102–03). These findings, although they may not validly reflect everyday perception, judgment, and conduct, offer provoking clues to the major values currently, consciously, and verbally associated with each nationality.

The more or less organized values of patriotism are indeed exactly the same as those behind most or all of people's existence. For values come from the goals that are sought, and patriotism is involved in the attainment or nonattainment of the very goals that are considered significant. The organization of values, consequently, reflects the way of arranging the activities of life. If economic pursuits are more important to a person than political ones, the corresponding components of his patriotism will be more economic than political.

It is essential to be acquainted with the values of a society not only to anticipate, as indicated two chapters ago, how people assess personality traits but also to be able to deduce safely the components of their patriotism. In the same empirical, sympathetic study of the Hopi Indians that was mentioned during that previous discussion of social values, the author derived from his data (in a manner not specified) "a list of items valued by the Hopi," which he has arranged with "the apparently more important ones" coming first:

Good crops; rain; having sheep and horses; having money
Peaceable relations with other people; not being aggressed

against; not being an object of witchcraft; having a good
reputation; favorable attitudes of others in general; the ad-
miration of others (e.g., for causing rain, or working hard)

Sickness; the infirmities of old age; accidents; death; living a
long time; physical health

Your family and children; their welfare; the good behavior
and cleanliness of children; possible reunion with dead
loved ones

Being good; not being lazy; not being a witch

Not worrying about things

Abundance of food; the wife a good cook; being able to invite
your friends to eat

Having amusements; sexual enjoyments; having an easier life

Having an attractive wife; having good relations with her; her
not going about with other men; being attractive to the op-
posite sex

Having skills; running, weaving; one's children having skills
or good job

Having relatives; the size of one's clan

Ceremonies; attending ceremonies; taking part in them

Not going out in the dark; not having to have contact with the
dead; not being around snakes [Brandt, 1954, p. 46].

Unfortunately most societies are so complex and fortunately most
investigators are so sensibly timid that only rarely is a cataloguing
of a nation's goals so concisely set down. The patriotism of any society, then, will remain elusive until the task is assayed and such a
list at least approximated.

More modest investigations, however, can be relatively easily
conducted, one of which will be mentioned forthwith. Large
groups of German-speaking South and North Tyrolean and Italian
secondary-school students were given a very simple questionnaire
by their regular teachers; the actual numbers, respectively, were
108, 184, and 69. In addition, 36 Ladin children in a primary school
acted as subjects; a primary school had to be utilized because there
is no secondary school exclusively for Ladins in the South Tyrol.
All the students were presented with 60 pairs of words or phrases,
each separated by the word "or," and asked to "draw a line under

that word which better represents your point of view." The pairs, as can be seen in Table 3, were grouped under four different categories: pleasantness, importance, friendliness, and health. Because of a theoretical interest in certain linguistic phenomena that need not deter the present discussion (Doob, 1961, pp. 201–07), half of the South Tyroleans, half of a class of Italians in one of the schools in the South Tyrol, and half of the Ladins received this questionnaire in German, the other half in Italian. The study of Italian is compulsory in the German-language schools of the South Tyrol; hence the South Tyroleans knew that language reasonably well but by no means excellently. The Ladin children were acquainted with both languages, but they were more proficient in Italian. The Italians were studying German as an elective; their teacher re-

TABLE 3. *Paired Comparisons: Percentages[a] Favoring First Alternative*

|  | North Tyrol[b] | South Tyrol[c] | Italians[d] | Ladins[e] |
|---|---|---|---|---|
| MORE PLEASANT? |  |  |  |  |
| 1. age vs. youth | 5 | 6 | 8 | 0 |
| 2. village vs. city | 38[g] | 35* | 17* | 78 |
| 3. history vs. geography | 54* | 30* | 64* | 14 |
| 4. north vs. south | 25* | 43 | 44[i] | 58 |
| 5. carnival vs. Christmas | 42[f] | 37 | 31 | 6 |
| 6. Dante vs. Goethe | 24 | 13* | 69 | 62 |
| 7. Alpine roses vs. edelweiss | 27* | 46 | 33 | 19 |
| 8. statues vs. frescoes | 60 | 70 | 78 | 60 |
| 9. winter vs. summer | 30 | 35* | 14 | 9 |
| 10. Mozart vs. Verdi | 73 | 70* | 31 | 47 |
| 11. progress vs. old customs | 77* | 91 | 83* | 33 |
| 12. As a name: Johann vs. Giovanni | 66 | 78* | 33* | 74 |
| 13. As a building style: modern vs. traditional | 72[f] | 76 | 78 | 53 |
| 14. As a place to live: Spain vs. France | 51 | 41 | 49 | 38 |
| 15. music vs. painting | 67[f] | 77 | 79 | 83 |
| 16. green vs. red | 35 | 46 | 61* | 28 |
| 17. folk theater vs. movies | 32[g] | 32 | 28* | 78[i] |
| 18. tuxedo vs. peasant costume | 59[f] | 55 | 61 | 35 |
| 19. Rome vs. Berlin | 60 | 67 | 78 | 94 |

TABLE 3 (*continued*)

| | North Tyrol[b] | South Tyrol[c] | Italians[d] | Ladins[e] |
|---|---|---|---|---|
| 20. castles vs. palaces | 62 | 47* | 15 | 37 |
| 21. Bavaria vs. Switzerland | 45 | 46 | 31 | 18 |
| 22. folk vs. modern music | 30[g] | 20 | 15* | 71 |
| 23. professional vs. volunteer fire company | 49* | 28 | 22 | 15 |
| 24. white vs. black | 69 | 57 | 74* | 100 |
| 25. old vs. new part of town | 27[g] | 35 | 19* | 44 |
| 26. traditional work aprons vs. overalls | 29 | 42 | 33* | 68 |
| 27. skiing vs. marksmanship | 80[f] | 72 | 77 | 93 |
| 28. climbing down vs. up | 49 | 38 | 33 | 27 |
| 29. as tombstone: marble vs. metal | 70 | 72[h]* | 91 | 67 |

MORE IMPORTANT?

| | | | | |
|---|---|---|---|---|
| 30. success vs. happiness | 65 | 69[h]* | 14 | 15 |
| 31. art vs. science | 21 | 33 | 34 | 46 |
| 32. for news: newspaper vs. radio | 33 | 30 | 42 | 24[h] |
| 33. faith vs. love of country | 67 | 63 | 63* | 27 |
| 34. school vs. family | 12 | 10 | 19 | 14 |
| 35. joy vs. orderliness | 41 | 43 | 61* | 33 |
| 36. region vs. province | 63[f]* | 33* | 63* | 38 |
| 37. in clothing: elegance vs. durability | 41 | 39* | 60 | 36 |
| 38. for world history: Giuseppe Garibaldi vs. Adreas Hofer | 14* | 48* | 94* | 18 |
| 39. physician vs. lawyer | 87[f] | 93 | 86 | 88 |
| 40. future vs. past | 88[f] | 89 | 72 | 69 |

MORE FRIENDLY?

| | | | | |
|---|---|---|---|---|
| 41. "good day" vs. "Servus" [Italian: "ciao"] | 38[g] | 49[h]* | 14* | 61 |
| 42. neighbors vs. tourists | 70* | 49 | 46* | 76 |
| 43. folks vs. people | 52[g] | 54[h] | 36 | 42 |
| 44. correct German [Italian] vs. dialect | 30* | 54* | 81 | 69 |
| 45. strangers vs. foreigners | 47* | 21* | 47 | 42 |
| 46. scattered vs. not scattered farms | 61[f] | 49* | 72* | 32 |
| 47. English vs. Italians | 56[g] | 60* | 12* | 43 |
| 48. dachshunds vs. spaniels | 70 | 64* | 17* | 44 |

MORE HEALTHFUL?

| | | | | |
|---|---|---|---|---|
| 49. football vs. tennis | 49* | 19 | 14* | 78 |
| 50. beer vs. wine | 63 | 73 | 58 | 58 |

TABLE 3 (*continued*)

|  | North Tyrol[b] | South Tyrol[c] | Italians[d] | Ladins[e] |
|---|---|---|---|---|
| 51. milk vs. fruit | 52* | 21 | 26 | 17 |
| 52. ride vs. walk | 21 | 9* | 37 | 44 |
| 53. spaghetti vs. soup | 34 | 24* | 51 | 56 |
| 54. coffee vs. tea | 40 | 37 | 34 | 36 |
| 55. spring vs. autumn | 73 | 60 | 72 | 91 |
| 56. South Tyrol: at present or in 10 years | 48 | 48 | 64 | 50 |
| 57. Alpine pasture vs. valley | 84 | 90* | 49 | 66 |
| 58. central vs. stove heating | 48 | 42* | 77* | 49 |
| 59. farm vs. factory work | 91 | 98* | 81 | 92 |
| 60. joy vs. sobriety | 65 | 65[h] | 53 | 71 |

* Differs significantly from figure to immediate right; here and in all significance tests indicated in notes below, p < .05, chi square.

a. Of those choosing either alternative; hence the total *n*'s indicated in the next four notes are slightly smaller whenever some students, by choice or through carelessness, failed to make a choice on a given pair.

b. German version but only those in the same age range (14 to 20) as in column to right under "South Tyrol"; *n* = 131.

c. German version, entire school; *n* = 54.

d. Italian version, entire school, in same town as "South Tyrol" sample; *n* = 36. For the comparison indicated below in notes *h* and *i*, not this school but an Italian school in another town was used.

e. Combination of German and Italian versions; *n* = 36.

f. Younger students (10 to 13) significantly *lower* than the older (14 to 20).

g. Younger students significantly *higher* than the older.

h. Those receiving Italian version significantly *lower* than those receiving German version.

i. Those receiving Italian version significantly *higher* than those receiving German version.

ported that their knowledge of the language in general was not very advanced.

Major results appear in Table 3. There, except for the Ladins, similar groups can be compared. Since the ages of the South Tyroleans and the Italians ranged from 14 to 20 or 21, only those North Tyroleans are represented in Table 3 who fall within the same range. The Italian and both Tyrolean figures come from those offered the questionnaire in their native language. The Italian students lived in the same town as the South Tyroleans;

in fact, they were also housed, though segregated on different floors, in the same building; they knew little or no German and so were not used in the experiment involving the comparison between the German- and Italian-language versions. The Ladins were younger, with ages ranging between 10 and 13; the Ladin figures are based upon both linguistic versions in order to make the total size of the sample large enough to permit statistical comparisons.

Many of the 23 statistically significant differences between the South Tyroleans and Italians and of the 20 between Italians and Ladins that are shown on Table 3 can be attributed, at least on the surface, to patriotism and cultural influences. It seems perfectly obvious, for example, that, in comparison with the Italians, a higher proportion of the South Tyroleans would prefer Goethe to Dante (#6); would consider the Tyrolean hero, Andreas Hofer, to be more important in world history than Garibaldi (#38); would call the English more friendly than the Italians (#47); or would be convinced that soup is more healthful than spaghetti (#53). Similarly the Ladin children can be said to display a conservative tendency since even at their age they know their culture is threatened by both the German and Italian cultures. The hypothesis may be advanced, consequently, that more of them than the Italians must have been attracted to the first rather than the second word in each of the following pairs: village vs. city (#2), old customs vs. progress (#11), folk theater vs. movies (#17), folk music vs. modern music (#22), old vs. new part of town (#25), traditional work aprons vs. overalls (#26), love of country vs. faith (#33), neighbors vs. tourists (#42), stove vs. central heating (#58).

All differences in evaluations, however, cannot be so easily explained by casual references to patriotism. In the first place, some choices were unrelated to nationality or to any of the other factors ascertained in the study. The vast majority of the children in all four samples considered youth rather than age (#1) and skiing rather than marksmanship (#27) to be pleasant; the family rather than the school (#34), physicians rather than lawyers (#39), and the future rather than the past (#40) to be important; and spring rather than autumn (#55) and farm rather than factory work (#59) to be healthful. Then on Table 3 there are a dozen differences between the North and South Tyrolean samples which cannot be ascribed to chance and which in some instances may not be due to variations in the two cultures. Why should a higher proportion of the North Tyrolean sample find history more pleasant than geography (#3)? It would be difficult to argue that, for patriotic reasons, history is more important in the North than in the South; could the children have been subjected to different methods of teaching or to different topics within the two fields of knowledge in view of the fact that an Austrian syllabus is followed in North Tyrol and an Italian one in South Tyrol? Does the higher proportion of South Tyroleans considering Garibaldi more important than Hofer (#38) reflect Italian influence? Table 3 contains, however, a fact that increases confidence in the validity of a cultural thesis: there are almost twice as many significant differences between South Tyroleans and Italians as there are between the former and North Tyroleans.

Some of the significant differences between Italians and Ladins cannot be glibly subsumed under the explanation of Ladin conservatism and the Italian threat suggested two paragraphs ago. More of the Ladin children, for example, found the color red pleasanter than the color green (#16). Could this preference reflect greater sympathy for the Tyroleans than for the Italians, since the Tyrolean flag contains red and the Italian green? Perhaps, but then why did roughly the same proportion of the Italians and the Ladins consider spaghetti more healthful than soup (#53), whereas a significantly smaller number of South Tyroleans voted for that Italian dish?

The comparison of the South Tyrolean and Italian samples also provides instances in which the hypothesis of patriotism or culture seems inadequate. The patriotic Tyroleans might have been expected to prefer traditional rather than modern architectural style; in fact, however, about three-fourths of them in the North and the South as well as the same proportion of Italians considered a modern style more pleasing. It is not surprising that more South Tyroleans than Italians preferred the name Johann to Giovanni; and yet one-third of the latter also voted for the German name.

Then the superscripts attached to some of the percentages in Table 3 specify two factors other than nationality that were associated with evaluating the pairs of concepts. The children in North Tyrol have been divided into two groups: the younger, whose ages ranged from 10 to 13, and the older (represented in the first column of the Table), who were between 14 and 20. The letters indicate the questions on which significant differences appeared and the direction of the difference; thus for "village vs. city" (#2), the letter "g" suggests that the figure of 38 per cent is significantly lower than that for the younger group (which actually is 64 per cent) and hence more of the younger than the older found a village more pleasant than a city. A total of 16 such differences appear on Table 3; in over one-quarter of the cases, consequently, age played an important role. That role seems to be fairly consistent: more of the younger than the older children subscribed to what might be called the traditional viewpoint.

In the remaining three columns the superscripts symbolize not differences associated with age but those emerging when a comparison is made between results from the Italian-language version of the questionnaire and the German. Language, it can be seen on Table 3, sometimes though infrequently produced significant differences, which appear five times among the South Tyroleans, once among the Italians, and twice among the Ladins. When the South Tyroleans, for example, were asked to indicate whether they found a marble or metal tombstone more pleasant (#29), 72 per cent of those receiving the German version (*Als Grabstein: Marmor* oder *Metall*) but only 45 per cent of those receiving the Italian version (*Come monumento funebre: marmo o metallo*) chose the former rather than the latter. Among the Italians, 53 per cent preferred the north rather than the south (#4) when presented with the German version (*Nord* oder *Süd*), 74 per cent when seeing the Italian version (*Nord o sud*). For the Ladins, 61 per cent selected the alternative of folk theater rather than movies (#22) when confronted with German (*Volksbühne* oder *Kino*), 94 per cent when reacting to Italian (*Teatro popolare o cinema*). The explanation of such results is not easy to discover. In the illustration from the Ladins, all four of the words are quite different and hence may possess varying connotations; but in the examples from the South Tyroleans and the Italians, the pairs in each language are virtually identical. For this last case the possibility that each language evokes a somewhat different general mental set must be mentioned. At any rate, if in this study language mediated nationality, it exerted a subtle and not always consistent effect. And so once again the same conclusion emerges: evaluation probably results not from nationality alone but from many other factors that can be simultaneously efficacious.

# 7. Patriotic Convictions

The dissection of patriotism has now reached its culmination, and only a gentle flip is needed to enter the region of nationalism. It has been shown how the media of communication enable men and women to perceive various attributes of their land, their country-men, and their culture as well as foreign countries, foreigners, and foreign cultures. In all probability nationals find themselves distinctive and, with exceptions here and there, praiseworthy in terms of their own value system. At this point in the analysis, people can be considered patriotic: they are convinced that their own welfare and that of the significant groups to which they belong are dependent upon the preservation or expansion (or both) of the power and culture of their own society—the original definition of patriotism is thus repeated with little paraphrasing. Patriots are of the strong opinion that certain activities are necessary for the preservation or expansion of their society, but they do not necessarily make demands in support of that opinion, nor do they always possess the remaining psychological paraphernalia associated with nationalism.

## Preservation and Expansion

'We love our country dearly and are always ready to spring to her defense.' The emphasis here is upon actions in the present or the past which obviously are needed if the nation is to be preserved or expanded. New action is not called for when it is believed that what is occurring at the moment is indeed preserving important aspects of the culture. The empirical problem is to ascertain the particular features or institutions that are so valued. Do patriots wish, for example, to have the characteristic bad weather of their country remain unaltered? Would they retain a tradition of hard work and little leisure time? Is it important for them to keep their country "pure" and hence prevent contact with others?

People probably do not possess a catalogue of priorities ready to be unfurled but, when challenged by a searching or impertinent question from an outsider or by the possibility of change, they demonstrate through their reactions and activities the features of their society they consider important or unimportant. In the United States, the literature on race prejudice suggests the type of relations among ethnic groups which Americans believe should be preserved and, by implication, those which they also would alter or permit to be altered. Of all the scales measuring prejudice in the United States, for example, perhaps the most popular, certainly one of the oldest, involves the notion of social distance. Informants are asked whether they would admit various ethnic groups "to close kinship by marriage," "to my club as personal chums," "to my street as neighbors," "to employment in my occupation," "to citizenship in my country," and as "visitors only to my country"; in addition, they say, too, whether they would "exclude from my country" members of these same nationalities (Bogardus, 1928, p. 25). The opposition of the prejudiced or dominant group, it has been found and then really confirmed in the 1960s during the determined struggle of American Negroes to eliminate segregation, decreases as the social distance increases from the beginning to the end of the above list.

Any particular institution is probably valued differently from society to society. During the survey of samples in the United States, in three European countries, and in Mexico that was mentioned in the previous chapter, the respondents were asked whether they thought "the national government" had much effect on "your day-to-day life"; and those believing that government had at least some effect then specified whether they thought "the activities of the national government tend to improve conditions in this country." A slight reworking of the investigators' own data by the present writer indicates that 65 per cent of the sample in the United States believed the effect of government was to improve conditions; alternative replies included "sometimes improves conditions, sometimes does not," "better off without national government," and "national government makes no difference." The corresponding affirmative figure for the United Kingdom was 56 per cent; for West Germany, 43 per cent; for Italy, 36 per cent; and for Mexico, 17 per cent (Almond and Verba, pp. 80–82). The great contrast between the American and the Mexican samples does not of course mean that Americans are generally more patriotic than Mexicans, rather the evidence suggests only that greater numbers of Americans see a connection between their personal welfare and central political institutions. You may love what you call your country with or without simultaneously loving its government.

The people of a nation, furthermore, may note the presence of change without demanding action. For they may approve of deviations from the past or the present or, when their attitude is neutral or hostile, they can be convinced that action would be futile or dangerous. Strongly inclined nationalists, however, are not likely merely to describe changes without demanding or engaging in appropriate action.

The changes that are, ostensibly, merely described can be attributed by people either to internal or external sources. Internally, for example, peers may be thought to be less conservative or more progressive than formerly. Such a judgment can arise even in the most traditional or stable society because customs are never followed exactly by people who differ with respect to skill, intelligence, and temperament on the one hand and blunt experience on the other. In addition, people inevitably detect changes during their lifetime. The usual ways of behaving appear different as they grow older: what children think arbitrary and frivolous adults may believe sacred and profound. The personnel of a society, furthermore, is in fact always changing as people die and as what is arbitrarily considered to be a new generation gradually or abruptly assumes power.

The external sources that are held responsible for change may be natural or human. Natural causes are confined to phenomena over which people have or are thought to have no direct control, such as fluctuations in climate and weather or many activities of animals. Traditional modes of horticulture must be altered when plants are attacked by a new variety of insect or fungus. On the human level, foreigners sometimes appear to be affecting the nation's people or its institutions. Immigrants arrive or alien merchandise or ideas circulate. Many influential outsiders, therefore, function from far afield; thus Hollywood films are said to produce minor or major changes in the behavior of the people whose countries permit them to be imported and exhibited. Or strangers dispatch their representatives to effect the changes, in the manner of colonial officials who control an area through force, decrees, and example—or at least once did.

This discussion of preservation and expansion once again suggests the close link between patriotism and nationalism. It seems possible for people merely to note a connection between their own welfare and the preservation of their culture without making active demands that it be preserved. But when they are convinced that expansion is desirable or is in fact occurring, they are usually inclined to express appropriate demands. Patriotism without some nationalism is a bit unlikely.

### Social Origins

What causes people to become convinced that their welfare and that of the significant groups to which they belong depend upon the preservation and sometimes also upon the extension of their culture? The answer to this question can be split into two parts, as is always the case when any aspect of culture is dissected: (1) the presence of the conviction within the society and (2) its transmission to children of succeeding generations.

At some period in the past, if a country is intensely patriotic or nationalistic, people have been forced by an event or a series of events to see a connection between their own welfare and the land in which they live. In the development of the United States, for example, Turner's famous hypothesis suggests that

> the frontier promoted nationalism: the pioneer looked to the national government to adopt the measures he needed—to provide him with internal improvements, to administer the public domain, and still more to accord to the area in which he had settled territorial status and, later, statehood; moreover, the pioneer, on the frontier, mingled with other settlers from other states and even from other countries [Potter, 1954, p. 152].

If this analysis is correct, then the pioneers experienced difficulties which only the central government could solve for them; under such conditions, the connection between the nation and virtual survival must have been apparent. The second part of the theory assumes that the frontier provided an opportunity for men to perceive the attributes of various social groups and then to consider them all countrymen.

Two points are suggested by the hypothesis. These experiences of the pioneers were somewhat unique on a comparative basis. The factors causing men in the West to feel dependent upon government were not duplicated precisely in Europe in the nineteenth century as modern nations, such as Germany and Italy, came into existence. And they are certainly not being duplicated today in the newly independent African states. The details are different, but one abstraction remains: something, some event, some series of events, produces the conviction. The intense patriotism of South Tyroleans has nothing to do with a frontier, according to Turner's use of that concept, but these people believe their leaders are playing a vital role in preserving their culture from Italian influence.

Then, secondly, the Turner hypothesis presumes that, when once it had been strengthened, the conviction concerning the importance of the government in Washington must have become part of the American tradition. Nothing mysterious is meant here, nor is the easy proposition being advanced that the fruits of earlier experiences are automatically perpetuated "by culture." The elaborate media of communication within a society do transmit the patriotic conviction to future generations and reinforce it among adults, but the transmission and the reinforcement are possible only because patriotism performs psychological functions for the people here and now.

Patriotism, therefore, is learned in the past by one's ancestors for one set of reasons but, as a result of changing conditions, it usually brings gratification in the present for quite different reasons.

### Psychological Development

To understand the psychological functions served by well established patriotism, it is necessary first to turn again to the process

of socialization. Adequate data concerning the growth of patriotism in children do not exist. Whatever crumbs there are must be
used, consequently, whether from the literature on race prejudice
or from direct studies in patriotism; but for some of the crucial
problems the only guide can be speculation.

Studies of prejudice, especially in the United States, show that
hostile or unfriendly feelings and beliefs concerning outgroupers
are acquired in one of four ways: from a general fear of strangers
that the child gradually learns to restrict to one or more distinguishable outgroups; from a severe emotional experience with one
person that the child subsequently generalizes to all members of
that person's group who resemble him or who have similar attributes; from a series of petty, unpleasant experiences with members
of some distinguishable group which the child soon generalizes
to everyone in that group; or, most frequently, from observing
and listening to respected adults who verbally or actually reject
members of an outgroup or who disparage its name (Allport,
1954, pp. 297–325). The first three of these methods—discrimination, trauma, and petty incidents—all involve personal experience of the kind that generations in the past must originally have
had as the prejudice was established in the society and thus
became a part of its culture. But the fourth demands no experience
with the ethnic group as such, only with parents and others in the
milieu who are the transmitters. A preliminary assumption must be
that patriotism and nationalism are similarly learned.

Part of patriotism consists of responding in the approved way to
the name of the country. It is to be expected that the response to,
or the meaning of this symbol, like that of any other verbal sur-
rogate, is only slowly learned and defined correctly from the adult
viewpoint. According to an impressionistic study of about 30 Swiss
boys between the ages of 7 and 10, the child at first imagined that
his country was another geographical unit such as a town or a dis-
trict. Then he began to realize that towns and districts were part
of the country, but he did not consider them to be incorporated
within it: "Switzerland surrounds Geneva and Vaud. These are in
Switzerland but do not really 'form part of' Switzerland." Finally,
he could give the correct response. Up to the age of 9, for example,
three-quarters of this group denied the possibility of being both

Swiss and a Genevan or member of some other canton (Piaget, 1959, pp. 119–28). The finding here resembles that adduced by the Tyrolean Heimat Study (reported in Chapter 4): the definition of Heimat tends to broaden with increasing age. Important in the Swiss research is an additional datum suggesting that many of the children defined a country as "a piece of land that has a name."

The meaning of other national symbols probably is also gradually learned. Investigators in the United States once used a very simple technique to study the process: subjects were shown 20 or more flags of different nations and were asked to rank them on the basis of the "best-looking." Among college students these rankings correlated significantly with a measure of nationalism on a paper-and-pencil test. In a study of over a thousand school children in New York City, the American flag was rated among the top five by 74 per cent of the children in kindergarten; this percentage did not change appreciably with increasing age. Apparently knowledge about the flag had been acquired very early in life. With respect to the flags of other lands, however, significant changes with age did appear. First, progressively fewer children gave a high rating to the flag of Liberia which is very similar to that of the United States; undoubtedly, therefore, the confusion of the two flags slowly diminished. Then there was a sharp rise in the popularity of the flag of the United Nations and an increase in the number of children rejecting the Soviet flag. The latter increase could be only slight because the hammer and sickle had already been rejected by most kindergarten children (Lawson, 1963). These shifts obviously reflect learning, first of the significance of the United Nations and secondly of the prevailing attitude in the United States regarding Russia.

The literature on prejudice indicates that the learning curve for information concerning, and attitude toward, members of an outside group also ascends slowly. As early as kindergarten and first grade, it was once reported, children begin to express the prejudices of their elders; for example: ·

> Elaine, showing costume doll to the class: "This is a Spanish doll."
> Teacher: "How can you tell she's Spanish?"
> Tommy: " 'Cause she's fat" [Trager and Radke, 1947, p. 19].

In an area of New York City in which there was a mixture of various ethnic groups, a sample of 86 children was asked, among others, these questions: "What kinds of people live around your house?" "What are you?" "What is Daddy?" "What is Mommy?" The most frequent answer, ranging from one-third to one-half of all replies, referred to ethnic affiliation: Jewish, Italian, Spanish, colored, American, etc. Though the subsamples were small, it seems clear that almost no children around four years of age answered in ethnic terms, but that thereafter the percentage jumped sharply and rose steadily until the age of 10, the oldest age group of the sample. At an early age, the modal reply to "What are you?" was, for example, "My name is Carol"; later it became one such as "I'm Jewish." When a girl slightly over four was asked, "Are you an American?" she declared, "No, my father is American; I'm a girl." Another slightly younger child provided this definition of the word *American* "I was an American when I had my gun, but when they took my gun away, I wasn't an American any more" (Hartley et al., 1948). The following question, once asked by a six-year-old girl, dramatically illustrates and perhaps also epitomizes the entire learning process: "Mother, what is the name of the children I am supposed to hate?" (Allport, 1954, p. 307). Parents, teachers, and peers are, as ever, the intentional or unintentional instructors.

Learning to distinguish among various nations undoubtedly follows an analogous course. In Glasgow, Scotland, 144 primary school children between the ages of 6 and 11 were interviewed individually and informally concerning foreign countries. The number of nations and continents they could name increased slightly with age. The youngest tended to be attracted by "the unusual or picturesque, especially of distant places"—a child of 7 said he liked Africa because "they've got lions, tigers, elephants, and polar bears." By the age of 11, they were inclined to emphasize "people and their characteristics"; most Americans, as noted by a child of 11, "have a good sense of humour—you never see them with dour faces." According to the investigator, the progression from "rudimentary" to "geographical and historical concepts in the stricter sense" was not simple and straightforward. At each age middle-class children possessed more information concerning other nations than working-class children, and their sources of informa-

tion were somewhat different. A "wide range of variation" was
also evident within each age group. One of the oldest children explained, in a manner more characteristic of a younger child, that
"I like Germany better than Britain—they have smashing stamps.
. . . I don't like Rumania, it's the only country I have only a few
stamps for." In contrast, a very young child rather precociously
disliked Germany because "they fought against us" (Jahoda,
1962).

All the attributes that are modally perceived in the land, its
people, their culture, and the equivalents outside are, presumably, similarly learned. The adverb "presumably" has been in-
serted with great deliberation, for again evidence is lacking and
indeed difficult to collect. The complexity of the problem can be
illustrated rather luridly in Table 4, which is derived from the Tyrolean Heimat Study already mentioned in Chapters 4 and 6. Children in various schools in South and North Tyrol wrote essays in response to the broad question: "What do you like and what do you
not like about your Heimat?" Table 4 indicates the percentages
who mentioned, whether at length or just in passing, the indicated
themes. Of course a great many additional themes also appeared,
but the ones on Table 4 are sufficient to indicate the scope of the
essays. A pair of schools, both from semirural areas in North and
South Tyrol, have been selected for illustrative purposes. In the
last two columns of the table appear the figures for all the schools
investigated in the two regions: 8 in South Tyrol with a total of
497 essays, and 6 in North Tyrol with a total of 740.

The breakdown for the two schools in South Tyrol and for one
school in North Tyrol is in terms not of age but of school grade. For
the latter is probably a better index of the children's experience
with their country since teachers in the school systematically introduce them to historical, cultural, and geographical artifacts.
The dichotomy is between those in the third and fourth grades
("L" for lower on Table 4) and those in the fifth through seven
grades ("H" for higher).

The outstanding impression to be gained from Table 4 is that
education thus measured played a role in determining the content
of the essays but not a relatively dramatic one. In the case of Town
1, only two of the obtained differences with respect to educational

TABLE 4. Tyrolean Heimat Study: Percentages Mentioning Selected Themes as Function of Education, Locality, and Sex

| | South Tyrol | | | | | | North Tyrol | | | | | | Totals | |
| | Town 1 | | | Town 2 | | | Town 3 | | | Town 4 | | | | |
| | L | H | T | L | H | T | L | H | T | M | F | T | S.T. | N.T. |
| **LAND** | | | | | | | | | | | | | | |
| Landscape | 52 | 68 | 61* | 77* | 96 | 88 | 95 | 94 | 95* | 91 | 82 | 85 | 75* | 87 |
| Churches | 37* | 19 | 27 | 48 | 27 | 40* | 11 | 14 | 12* | 44 | 42 | 43 | 31* | 38 |
| Buildings | 81 | 72 | 76 | 87 | 86 | 86 | 93* | 69 | 84 | 91 | 83 | 85 | 82* | 89 |
| Land and buildings | 93 | 95 | 94 | 100 | 100 | 100 | 100 | 100 | 100 | 100 | 98 | 99 | 97 | 99 |
| **PEOPLE** | | | | | | | | | | | | | | |
| Historical figures | 4 | 12 | 8 | 3 | 10 | 7* | 34* | 3 | 22 | 7 | 15 | 13 | 9* | 23 |
| Leaders | 0 | 0 | 0 | 0 | 0 | 0 | 2 | 0 | 1 | 0 | 0 | 0 | 1 | 2 |
| Family and children | 2 | 8 | 5 | 10 | 10 | 10 | 5 | 11 | 7 | 12 | 18 | 16 | 8 | 12 |
| Ingroup | 25 | 28 | 26 | 18* | 46 | 36* | 55 | 50 | 53 | 61 | 62 | 61 | 39* | 65 |
| Italians | 10 | 23 | 17 | 6* | 32 | 22* | 61 | 0 | 37* | 5 | 3 | 4 | 15* | 10 |
| Outgroup | 16 | 26 | 21* | 26 | 44 | 38 | 62* | 34 | 49* | 5 | 8 | 7 | 29* | 36 |
| Human beings | 35 | 43 | 38 | 28* | 73 | 51* | 89* | 61 | 78 | 65 | 65 | 65 | 53* | 78 |
| **CULTURE** | | | | | | | | | | | | | | |
| Symbolic objects | 12 | 14 | 13 | 24 | 11 | 16 | 16 | 6 | 12* | 37 | 35 | 36 | 10* | 32 |
| Cultural objects | 37 | 29 | 33 | 41 | 46 | 44* | 33 | 19 | 27* | 68 | 66 | 66 | 34* | 60 |
| Cultural products, of activity | 22 | 15 | 18 | 6* | 27 | 20 | 22 | 42 | 31* | 45 | 45 | 45 | 24* | 49 |
| **MISCELLANEOUS** | | | | | | | | | | | | | | |
| Weather | 21* | 48 | 35 | 39 | 37 | 38 | 23 | 25 | 24* | 49 | 40 | 42 | 27 | 32 |
| No "dislike" | 25 | 26 | 26 | 28* | 11 | 17* | 7 | 5 | 6 | 7 | 17 | 14 | 27* | 12 |

* Differs significantly from the figure to the right (p < .05, chi square); for a figure under T of a Town, however, the comparison is with the one under T three columns to the right.

L  Lower school grades, 3 and 4
H  Higher school grades, 5, 6, and 7
M  Males    F  Females

T  Total
S.T.  South Tyrol
N.T.  North Tyrol

n's:
Town 1, L = 52, H = 61
Town 2, L = 39, H = 70
Town 3, L = 56, H = 36
Town 4, M = 43, F = 99
S.T. = 497, N.T. = 740

groups are statistically significant; for Town 2, six; and for Town 3, four. The trend for fewer of the children in the lower grades to refer to the various categories under "people" is contradicted in Town 3 of North Tyrol. By and large, however, an examination of the themes represented in Table 4 and of the numerous ones not represented there indicates that a larger proportion of the children in the higher grades referred, at least in passing, to more topics in their essays than did those in the lower grades.

Even the purity of this last, unastonishing observation, it must be added, is tarnished by other data. In the first place, some younger children, however few in number, touched upon every theme mentioned by the older children; all differences, including the significant ones, are relative, not absolute. Then, as in the Scottish study, exceptions to the general trend can be noted; for example, 31 per cent of all those in the lower grades and only 14 per cent of all those in the higher grades in South Tyrol referred to themselves in discussing their Heimat. Such exceptions might be rationalized were it not for the fact that often schools in some of the communities did not conform to a statistically significant trend for the region as a whole. In South Tyrol, for example, 58 per cent of the lower- and 87 per cent of the higher-grade children mentioned the landscape; the same kind of difference appeared in all four of the other communities where comparisons of grades are feasible; but an overall difference in the same direction (23 per cent and 41 per cent) regarding references to the hometown as such appeared in only four of the six schools. On Table 4 it is possible to observe two significant differences between the two schools in South Tyrol and eight between the two in North Tyrol. In some instances, finally, these latter differences embody different results within the two educational groups for all the schools in both regions. In South Tyrol, for example, roughly the same proportion of the samples in both educational groups noted churches, but in North Tyrol significantly more of those from the higher than from the lower grades did so. In passing, it is to be observed that the breakdown in terms of sex on Table 4 reveals no significant differences.

Education as an index of age, in short, has been shown to be associated with ways of reporting impressions concerning home town or country but is certainly not an unequivocal index. There were other differences which must have been influential such as variations in local customs, in landscape and other natural features, and in instructions received from the teachers. In addition, the validity of the essay as a technique for gathering information concerning perception and memory is open to question: the children may have been reporting only the common verbal clichés they were accustomed to hear in connection with the word Heimat; and certainly some of them must have been trying to write down those ideas they knew would please their teachers. It is also well to recall here a finding in the previous chapter in connection with the choice of paired associates by Tyrolean children: adherence to traditional concepts seemed less prevalent among the older than among the younger children. Perhaps, after some initial learning of parental values, they rebelled against their parents or they were influenced by new ideas and practices in their milieu.

The discussion, so far confined to the content of patriotism, now turns to the development of patriotic judgments. The differing values placed upon personality traits attributed or not attributed to other nations must also—at least in theory—be traceable to childhood experiences. Children between the ages of 5 and 15 were once observed at play in various European countries and the United States. In a manner not clearly indicated, national differences were adduced; American children above kindergarten age, for example, were said to reveal a "conflict between competitive aggressiveness and cooperative sociability" and Austrian children were believed to be "much more aggressive and schematic than any other group" (Bühler, 1952, p. 49). If the children themselves already possessed such distinctive traits, then they probably also showed a preference for others with similar traits; and so the process of identification with patriots must have begun. In addition, a pilot study of the stereotypes of children 6, 10, and 14 years old in four nations suggests that perceived similarity between one's own and foreign countries is associated with friendly attitude toward those outsiders (Lambert and Klineberg, 1959).

It seems reasonable to assume that infants at a very early age learn to perceive distinctive attributes in an object or person. For experience can be profitably utilized in the future only when there has been generalization and discrimination in the past. The mother quickly comes to mean comfort and security for the child since her presence and actions evoke such feelings within him. Other people onto whom he wishes also to generalize his attachment do not provide the same joys. He discriminates between his mother (including usually members of his immediate family) and other people in his milieu. Safety and welfare, consequently, depend upon extending and simultaneously limiting the stimulus patterns from which rewards can be anticipated; criteria for distinguishing between the helpful and the harmful (or the indifferent) must be apprehended and stored. Distinctiveness is a judgment that is both basic and precious. Thus there is generalization from perceiving distinctiveness in the early environment to valuing distinctiveness as such; and also, as previously contended, that environment is considered at least somewhat distinctive forever after.

The main point in the evidence now examined seems to be that the learning of all aspects of patriotism is a slow, gradual process and, like prejudice, may be derived from secondhand or socially determined experiences. Feelings concerning foreigners in most instances are forms of prejudice and also are likely to stem not from personal contacts but from the prevailing views within the society. From the children's standpoint, however, a television program or a film, as well as the occurrence of an event, whether reported to them by the press, the radio, or their own parents, may be an experience almost as "real" as such contacts. Firsthand experience becomes critical under unusual conditions, for example, when children travel abroad or when their country is occupied or otherwise controlled by outsiders.

In any case, some persons in the milieu significantly affect the learning process because children are strongly and emotionally identified with them. Although originally the identification has not been patriotically motivated, it eventually facilitates the learning of patriotism. You love your mother for reasons best known to you, you love your teacher because he or she is so kind and gentle; and then you grow to love your country because they whom you love urge you most subtly to do so. The following sentence, though derived through necessity in large part only from American studies, represents the best available generalization: "In the same way that the child becomes identified with his parents and his social class he also learns to identify with the other subcultural groups (ethnic, religious, racial) to which they belong" (Mussen et al., 1963, p. 409). To be prejudiced and to be patriotic is to participate in one's society.

## A Patriotic Personality?

So far similarities and dissimilarities concerning the learning of prejudice and patriotism have been suggested. Now a realm must be approached in which there is no evidence whatsoever, to the best of this writer's knowledge, for patriotism as such. Studies in the United States (e.g. Frenkel-Brunswik, 1948) suggest that prejudiced children, even before the age of 11, have personality traits differing from those of their nonprejudiced counterparts. In comparison with people at the other end of the continuum, the strongly prejudiced tend to be rigid, intolerant, authoritarian, moralistic, aggressive, lacking in insight, generally aggressive (Allport, 1954, pp. 73–74, 395–409). Name a nasty trait, in fact, and research motivated to expose prejudice has probably demonstrated that great numbers of prejudiced persons possess it. In short, being or becoming prejudiced in our society means not simply reflecting the prevailing view of the environment but also satisfying deep-seated needs connected in many instances with parental treatment and behavior. Now the question at hand is whether a similar state of affairs characterizes patriotism. Do superpatriots have personalities markedly different from the mildly patriotic or the internationalists?

On the one hand, there are weighty reasons for suspecting the existence of a similar relation between personality and patriotism. Strong dispositions, such as those which characterize patriotism, seldom function without being connected to central personality traits: powerful needs spill over. Then support is obtained from some available empirical evidence. In a highly publicized California study, one component of an ethnocentrism scale measured "patriotism." Scores thus obtained were found to correlate significantly with attitude toward Negroes, Jews, and other minority groups; and there was also a high correlation between the main ethnocentrism scale and authoritarianism which in turn was related to personality traits (Adorno et al., 1950, pp. 113, 122, 179, 263). Prejudice regarding foreigners, furthermore, is one of the components of patriotism as that term is being employed in the present analysis.

Straws galore are flying about which suggest, on the other hand, that patriotism may not be related to personality or may not be so intimately related. The evidence connecting prejudice and personality comes largely from the United States; there is no theoretical or superstitious reason to expect similar results elsewhere. Patriotism is evident under so many different societal and historical conditions that universals appear rather unlikely. For cultural reasons people living in a strongly nationalistic area most certainly become on the whole highly nationalistic too; their nationalism, consequently, reflects their environment to a greater degree than it does their personalities. In fact, some data lead to such a conclusion even in the case of prejudice. On the basis of an unusually first-rate investigation of college students in South Africa and of white adults in four Northern and Southern communities in the United States and from a consideration of the relevant scientific literature, for example, one investigator concludes that, in areas having strong traditions of racial intolerance, "sociocultural factors are unusually crucial and account for the heightened racial hostility." Under such conditions, "personality factors" seem less important (Pettigrew, 1958). A significant relation between patriotism and personality may similarly come into existence only when strong patriotism is not the norm in a country and when, consequently, the outstandingly patriotic are thereby expressing their own personal problems or difficulties. In addition, whatever relation does in fact exist between the two is probably different from that between prejudice and personality. For there is no reason to suppose that the personality traits associated with love of country are the same as those connected with hostility toward foreign countries or foreigners.

The same literature on race prejudice does provide another clue to a problem involving personality, viz. the effect of patriotism and nationalism in one society upon the people who live in another society. In the United States, the victims of prejudice are reported to reveal traits ranging from simple "ego defenses" to genuine symptoms of "neuroticism" (Allport, 1954, pp. 142–62). The people developing such defenses or neuroses are aware of the minority or underprivileged position they occupy. Outsiders against whom patriotic or nationalistic predispositions may be directed, however, may or may not realize that they are the target for hostility; only when they do, of course, are they likely to be affected. In the modern world it seems probable that nationalism in one country breeds nationalism in another: the better organized the patriotic predispositions in one nation, the more frequently they are likely to be expressed; and the more frequently they are expressed, the greater the probability that foreigners who are the targets will react defensively, aggressively, and hence similarly. Another Spiral Phenomenon.

This discussion of patriotism and personality cannot be brought to a halt without introducing a question which will then be ruthlessly pursued throughout the rest of this book: Why does, why can, the patriotism of some men become so influential under certain circumstances? Why are men willing to risk their lives or to sacrifice themselves for their country? When the learning of patriotism can be discussed in the same terms applicable to any other learning process, such as skiing or the rules of a social club, it may seem as though the culmination of the trials-and-errors ought to be something not especially extraordinary; you don't ordinarily consider skiing or club etiquette a matter of life or death, do you?

The fruits from learning patriotism, it must be quickly said, are not allowed to perish. As the chapter on the media of communication has already suggested, each society has an extensive system of media which forever bombard people with patriotic communications. These communications reiterate what adults already know, but in the changing contexts of their existence, so that love of country becomes linked in some way to many events. Ultimately, therefore, all citizens and especially the patriotic ones continually see a connection between their important values, their way of living, and their surroundings. The surroundings are their country, and they have come to possess an impressive arsenal of words, symbols, and objects which frequently remind them of that link.

A man will fight if his life is threatened. Undoubtedly, he will behave similarly to protect his family under comparable circumstances. Obviously, he is identfied with himself and also with his family. That identification is extended to other groups and, as has now been indicated, to the nation itself. The identification with the nation, however, is not as easy to maintain as identification with the family to which one is devoted; and for this reason, presumably, the call to make sacrifices in behalf of the country is not always answered with the same degree of enthusiasm and promptness.

Over and over again reference is being made in this analysis to people's consciousness concerning the connection between their own welfare and their country. Here the suggestion is timidly advanced that such conscious ethnopatriotism may be produced or facilitated by the kind of nationalism characteristic of the modern world. In more traditional societies, even though their welfare is just as intimately linked with their tribe, people have good reasons not to dwell on the fact or even to become aware of it. A Burmese politician, troubled by the problem of "choosing a national identity," has made the following statement:

> I had never given any thought to what it meant to be a Burmese. I must have filled in countless forms in which I called myself a "Burmese Buddhist," but it didn't have much meaning. I grew up in Rangoon and there were always Indians, and Karens, and Arakanese, and all kinds of people around; so it didn't seem strange that people were different from each other.
>
> In my second year at the university, I met this young Englishman who was very keen on learning all about Burma. He had read more about Burmese history than I had, and he knew more than I did about the old days of the Burmese kings. I remember telling some of my friends at the university some of the things he had taught me about Burmese history, and they all said that it was foolish to think about such things, for we should be looking to the future and to a modern Burma which would be much better. My English friend was most interested in learning about Burmese customs. He was always asking me questions about why the Burmese do all the things

they do. Sometimes I didn't know, sometimes I just couldn't explain it to him.

Then one day, I still remember very clearly, he got quite angry with me when I could not answer his questions and could only laugh at the customs he wanted to know more about. He said, "Don't you know anything about your own beliefs; what kind of a Burmese are you?" The question really bothered me. You can't imagine how awful it was [Pye, 1962, pp. 258–59].

The speaker obviously was not experiencing a change in his own dependence upon Burmese culture and upon Burma; rather through the kind of reflection which his English friend fostered, he was being made aware of that dependence; and so he felt compelled to justify what he then knew to be true.

Another way of accounting for the fire and strength of patriotism is to note the differences between nationality and membership in almost any other group. These other groups, with the possible exception of the church under some circumstances (Znaniecki, 1952, p. 127), command only part of the person's activities; in contrast, the nation can be involved in almost everything he does, or at least can be made to appear so. Government or the threat of governmental action is always present; the state has "a monopoly of organized force" (Royal Institute, 1939, p. 329). Then the society demands and usually obtains complete sovereignty, and displays its power by punishing those who do not obey. The very inclusiveness of the nation, moreover, is impressive: everyone belongs, and ordinarily it is difficult to shift allegiance from one country to another. You can resign from a club and join a new one, but you need permission to leave a modern country and then you have problems becoming a citizen elsewhere. As will also be indicated in a subsequent chapter, the critical institutions of a society are likely to have, or to seek, some intimate link with the nation. Finally, the components of patriotism almost always and repeatedly are appraised in two ways which bring them close to the core of a person's very existence: they are thought to be more or less distinctive, and they are linked to central values of conduct and judgment.

## 8. Demands and Actions

When patriotic convictions are so firm and enduring that they give rise to demands, by definition, or at least by the definition of this book, nationalism comes into existence. The query as to whether some nationalism inevitably accompanies patriotism, having been previously discussed, must now be considered moot. Instead attention is turned to situations where nationalistic demands and actions are perfectly apparent.

### Demands

During the present era, it has been observed frequently and often sorrowfully, the rate of change everywhere—or almost everywhere—has been accelerating. The now broadened cultural base facilitates the emergence of more and more inventions. International communication and transportation literally diffuse innovations with dispatch. Industry in some form is universally attractive because it brings people the goods and services they think they want.

Nationals who are strongly attached to their traditional culture are likely to resist such changes; and others, seeking for themselves the kind of nation the great powers have, welcome modernization and change. The wave of the future, whether it be resisted or welcomed, causes most people not simply to describe the changes on their horizon and in their midst; rather it sets them in motion, creates demands within them, and impels them to action. Nationals become nationalists when they are so discontent with their present mode of life or with the observed changes in their milieu that they deliberately, unblushingly seek the action they believe will change or preserve what they have—or what they think they once had.

Patriotism is universal because the preservation of the cultural heritage, broadly or narrowly defined, is always sought by all people at some time: that heritage is a critical ingredient of the life which they have learned to live as infants and children and which consequently they more or less cherish forever after. Ordinarily there are customs and regulations ensuring preservation to some degree. Each society has evolved ways of perpetuating itself not only by the reproduction and socialization of children but also through current practices that reinforce the modes from the past. Whenever the normal methods are, or appear to be, insufficient to preserve the way of life, direct action is called for. That action may be, first of all, defensive. Literally or figuratively, the moat is deepened, the fortification rebuilt to keep the enemy out. Or the institutions themselves are strengthened and people become more patriotic: the rigor of a rite de passage is increased, the greatness of the past is further emphasized in history textbooks.

The power and culture of a society may also be preserved through offensive measures directed against outsiders who are viewed as threats. The goal of political independence may ostensibly involve no change in culture other than the expulsion of intruding foreigners. Or, in the trite but compellingly important phrasing of our time, the best defense may be considered to be an offense directed against enemies before they strike. Whether the threat is real or unreal is an important question, but in an analysis of nationalism the more relevant facts are the claim that there is a threat and the consequent demands.

People who would defend or preserve their culture through some offensive action demand both a shift in a present institution or custom and also a more radical change. Such incitement may be concerned with internal changes in the society itself. The rite may be altered, or a relatively new one introduced; or a different textbook for history may be distributed. Deliberately planned changes win approval when beneficial results seem likely. The outcome, however, cannot always be precisely anticipated. Thus the one modern innovation sought and obtained most frequently by people in relatively isolated communities of the West is electricity. For wires can be more easily erected than roads or railways and more cheaply than airports especially when power is to be brought to an island, a desert, or a mountain top. But then Pandora's box is likely to spring open: in addition to the motors, lights, refrigerators, radios, telephones, which people crave in order to make life easier and more pleasant, other devices and customs of a mechanized, urbanized culture quickly appear. Similarly the industries sought by rural societies or communities to improve their economy and sometimes also to provide employment for surplus labor which might otherwise move away has, eventually, unforeseen influences upon the very traditional ways which people believed they could retain unaltered. For these and other reasons, a strong trend toward uniformity is everywhere discernible.

The changes sought or not sought by people may pertain not only to their own land, compatriots, and culture but also to foreigners who, they may be convinced, do or do not promote or affect the national welfare. When it is believed that outsiders are a threat, then demands for actions are likely to arise. Such demands and actions themselves fall along a continuum whose endpoints are nonovert and overt behavior. At one extreme there is fantasy: 'These are the very people,' it is whispered, 'who should be exterminated; it is they over whom I triumph in my dreams.' At the other end, actual extermination is sought. Between the words and the incitement to deeds are calls for verbal attacks, snubbing, discrimination, segregation, etc. These rejections are in effect identical with the ones practiced in connection with prejudice (Allport, 1954, pp. 48–81).

The demand for expansion, an important ingredient of most modern nationalism, naturally also involves an outgroup. For if the welfare of the society is thought to be dependent upon action leading to greater power or more land, then someone on the outside must relinquish the power or land. To justify expansion, defensive pleas may be uttered, but they need not be. Some nationalists in the modern world, for example, firmly believe that the boundaries of their land must be extended to include additional people who, being considered countrymen of theirs, should be allowed to enjoy or benefit from cultural conquest or should join the society in order to help it remain intact or survive or progress. Opponents seldom label the expansion so demanded or obtained in a neutral or objective fashion; instead they fling an epithet at the proposal: imperialism, exploitation, colonialism, neocolonialism, world revolution, conquest. To avoid the stigma attached to such words, the expansionist plans of modern nationalists are not paraded in their naked simplicity in front of either insiders or outsiders. They are described and then justified in terms of values to be considered subsequently at some length in Chapters 10 and 11.

National demands, like all human demands, may express quite truthfully or conceal most subtly the underlying motives of the communicators or their audience. The goal of a crusade to seize foreign territory may indeed be the one inscribed on the banners of the warriors, but often more than the glory of God is also at stake, such as raw materials, adventure, or power over others. These latter goals can be totally unconscious or absent in the pious and be conscious but suppressed in the crafty. In any case, the demands at the surface serve some rallying function for everyone.

Demands can be experienced and expressed with different degrees of enthusiasm and vehemence. A distinction that has been drawn (Lasswell and Kaplan, 1950, p. 17) between "preference" statements ("Full employment seems desirable") and "volitional" statements ("There *must* be full employment") suggests the range involved. A significant, but not always completely valid measure of the content and strength of a demand is the action to which it leads.

### Actions

The convictions and the demands of people always refer or give rise to actions which cannot be rigorously catalogued because they literally involve all forms of human activity. Preservation, for example, may be advocated quite variously: 'Let us remain relatively isolated, do not build modern highways to our towns and villages'; 'To prevent their poison from reaching our people, we must ban their newspapers and jam their radio programs'; 'The textbooks must be altered, they do not sufficiently glorify the deeds of the heroes who are our ancestors'; 'We must explode this nuclear device, otherwise we shall lack crucial information enabling us to defend our country in case of attack.' Expansion can mean numerous actions, such as: 'Let us seize the land'; 'We must send volunteers to work in that country so that they will grow to love us'; 'Our exhibit at the world's fair must be second to none'; 'We must reach the moon first'; 'We must capture them alive, we need more slaves.' While these demands serve the same or similar functions, they have quite different consequences in terms of political power or international relations. There is thus a significant practical distinction between the conviction that 'we must be free from domination by this foreign power' and one suggesting that 'we must bring home from abroad our brothers who speak the same language and have the same traditions as we.' Likewise there is a sharp line between the feeling that 'we must reform for the sake of progress' and the conviction that 'we must change our national policy so that our kind of civilization can impress more people in the world.'

Attention may be directed to three important points concerning the actions of people motivated by patriotism and nationalism. In the first place, a universal goal of these actions appears to be to obtain those conditions which in the opinion of the people and their leaders will promote the welfare of their nation and produce "national consciousness" and unity (Hertz, 1944, p. 21). The conditions are met when people are convinced that:

> 1. Their society controls its own destiny. By society is meant in effect the state which in turn is controlled by leaders or, to a certain degree, by the people themselves. The phrasing in modern terms includes words such as "freedom," "liberty," "self-determination," "sovereignty," "autonomy," "independence," "emancipation," "liberation," etc. One of the rights assumed by a modern nation under this aegis is that of protecting or, in some instances, furthering its own interests by resorting to war (Wright, 1942, p. 347).
>
> 2. All people believed to belong to a society are in fact members of it and thus are subject to its regulations and contribute to its welfare. "Unity," "irredenta," "our brothers overseas," "solidarity," "union," "integrity," etc. are some of the concepts invoked in this connection.
>
> 3. Society provides a satisfactory existence for its people or at least for the important or ruling strata. That existence, moreover, is likely to be considered satisfying only when it

enables people simultaneously to believe that their way of life is, in some vital respects, distinctive: they have individuality and a national character.

4. Their society has prestige in the opinion of outgroupers whose opinion is valued. Here the vocabulary is so diverse that no abbreviated lexicon seems practical.

Then, in the second place, the actions of nations can be conceptualized in terms also applicable to the actions of people. As indicated previously, when people are frustrated, they have at their disposal a wide range of alternatives which begin with direct aggression against the source of annoyance and end with withdrawal and suicide; and they can also be constructive and creative by turning their energies elsewhere. Similarly national demands can spill over into fierce belligerence or meek submission. The National Socialists in Germany represent one extreme. While climbing into power, Hitler and his associates advocated a kind of nationalism which included resistance to those they chose to call their nation's enemies; and after 1933 they clearly carried out the demands. People, no matter how patriotic they are, can find that resistance is hopeless, and then they seek some type of substitute. An extreme illustration is provided by the Comanche Indians who, after they had discovered that the reservation to which they were assigned provided too few of the old satisfactions and after they had come to realize that overt resistance against whites was futile, retreated from the realities engulfing them. They combined elements from their traditional religion with the drug peyote, and at their meetings once again experienced the joys of companionship and power (Wallace and Hoebel, 1952, pp. 328–37). Emigrants who voluntarily leave their native country may be patriotic, but for reasons associated with other drives—standard of living, mobility, etc.—they choose not to withdraw into fantasy but to adopt a different way of life; still in their new home they usually cling, as well as they can, to some of their old ways.

Finally, a very significant, though negative index of the strength of patriotic convictions is the ability of people to withstand temptations to commit what is officially called treason. To be disloyal to one's country is of course a crime, the penalties for which are likely

to be known by most citizens. If they become traitors, nevertheless, then certainly they are connecting their welfare with some
other goal. Obviously they may be motivated quite simply by the
money they receive as spies; so-called quislings seek power or social recognition; and the frustrated or the idealistic reject national
loyalty for one they consider more compelling or righteous, such
as the alleged betterment of mankind. The last group is most difficult to comprehend, and yet it is important to do so since from
them have come many of the important traitors of our time. One
journalist thus describes members of "the lost generation" after
World War I:

> They had been caught up, as unsuspecting boys, in the fire
> and torment of the trenches, and returned determined to re-
> volt against everything, especially against the artificial bar-
> riers which they viewed as one of the prime causes of the
> great disaster. At first, many thought that they had found the
> answer in communal life, in wandering, in the flickering
> twilight of the campfire. Their searing and terrible war ex-
> perience, which they had in common, would conquer all
> boundaries between nations and individuals and bring about
> a truly international movement for peace [Boveri, 1963, p.
> 26].

Men and women with such feelings and predispositions could be
converted to movements of protest (such as communist and fascist
groups) that sought to transcend national boundaries and, in fulfilling their new loyalties, could be made to betray their old ones;
or, as was true of most of them, they eventually returned to the
fold when their country of origin was threatened, for example, in
World War II.

### A Patriotic, Nationalistic Credo

Before proceeding to a discussion of the justifications that are
advanced to support nationalistic claims, it seems desirable to present in some sort of unified fashion the credo of at least one nation. After living in the South Tyrol for over half a year, this
writer felt he could intuit the modal beliefs of the German-speak-

ing inhabitants; he had carried on long conversations with people from all social strata, he had converged deliberately upon informants who were vocal and well informed about their contemporaries, and he had read very carefully the newspaper, the journals, and other printed matter that reflected the Tyrolean point of view. Next, in a manner described in greater detail elsewhere (Doob, 1962), he verified these hunches by asking two dozen key people whether in their opinion "most South Tyroleans" agreed with a series of 75 beliefs which he presented to them, one by one, typed on small cardboard cards. Some corrections were made; and the wording of the beliefs was then changed slightly so that all of them could be woven together into a single, somewhat unified document. Related statements were grouped into sections with appropriate headings. Each sentence, however, was incomplete: the key word or words pertaining to the belief therein expressed were missing and replaced with an underscored blank. Thus the first heading was "Land," and the first three incomplete sentences read as follows, in German:

> Our landscape is ———. Life in the mountains is ———.
> Everywhere people ——— every square meter of fertile land.

Subjects were instructed by their teachers to fill in the blanks with "the word or words which are closest to your point of view or to the fact." Papers were obtained from 124 boys and girls in a commercial secondary school in South Tyrol and from 101 in a similar school in North Tyrol, and also from 26 young men in a Catholic seminary in South Tyrol and from 22 in a similar institution in North Tyrol. (Results from another part of this same study have already been described in Chapter 4.) The entire document is reproduced below but with the blanks completed by means of italicized words or phrases representing the modal response of the students. Naturally a deliberate effort had to be made to locate that modal response in each instance. Two steps were involved: first, all the responses were coded into twelve categories, twelve because that is a convenient number for IBM analysis; and then, after the number in each category had been counted, an effort was made to combine fairly similar categories. The procedure can be illustrated by means of the first sentence, "Our landscape is _____." The coding is given in German because these are the words that literally appeared in each category. The figures are the numbers so replying; the columns are based upon breakdowns which will be disclosed in just a moment.

|  | S | N | M | F |
|---|---|---|---|---|
| no reply | 0 | 0 | 0 | 0 |
| *schön, wunderschön, sehr schön | 64 | 43 | 23 | 30 |
| prächtig, anziehen, bezaubernd, wundervoll, grossartig | 5 | 4 | 0 | 2 |
| *anreizen, reizen, reizvoll | 1 | 2 | 1 | 0 |
| einzigartig, eigenartig | 1 | 1 | 0 | 0 |
| herrlich | 13 | 3 | 4 | 7 |
| *lieblich, bunt, sehenswert, malerisch, romantisch | 5 | 3 | 3 | 1 |
| abwechslungsreich, vielgestaltig | 7 | 13 | 0 | 3 |
| einmalig, klein | 5 | 3 | 1 | 2 |
| gut gebaut, fruchtbar, besucht | 8 | 0 | 6 | 1 |
| gebirgig, or anything with Berge | 15 | 26 | 10 | 4 |
| miscellaneous | 1 | 3 | 0 | 0 |

In the Credo itself which follows, the three categories preceded by an asterisk have been somewhat arbitrarily combined and translated simply as "beautiful, very pretty."

The document given the students was headed "Heimat," whose meaning, as the reader (whether acquainted or not acquainted with German) must now be bored to hear as a result of the frequent reminders in this book, is home, hometown, or country. In the text below, only that word has not been translated. Each modal response is numbered (the blanks on the original questionnaire were not numbered) so that easy reference can be made to the five columns appearing to the right of the credo. Words in brackets suggest the form of statistical breakdown or, when also italicized, the abstract category employed in the content analysis. The five columns have the following meaning:

#:  the *identifying number* in the text
S:  the percentage of all the students in *South Tyrol* actually giving the indicated modal response
N:  same as previous column but *North Tyrol*
M:  the percentage of all the *males* in the commercial high school of South Tyrol actually giving the indicated modal response
F:  same as previous column but *females*

As ever, an asterisk indicates that the differences between the percentage so marked and the one to the immediate right is statistically significant ($p < .05$, chi square).

| *The Land* | # | S | N | M | F |
|---|---|---|---|---|---|
| Our landscape is (1) *beautiful, very* | 1. | 66* | 48 | 58 | 62 |
| *pretty.* Life in the mountains is (2) | 2. | 48 | 52 | 44 | 46 |
| *difficult, rugged.* Everywhere people | | | | | |
| (3) *use, cultivate* every square meter | 3. | 91 | 83 | 91 | 91 |
| of fertile land. Our towns and villages, | | | | | |
| when untouched by strangers and the | | | | | |
| modern world, and also our churches | | | | | |
| and castles are (4) *beautiful, artistic.* | 4. | 29 | 34 | 27 | 38 |
| The quality of our products, | | | | | |
| especially fruit, wine, lumber, and | | | | | |
| grain is (5) *outstanding, very good.* | 5. | 56 | 56 | 71 | 54 |

### History

| | # | S | N | M | F |
|---|---|---|---|---|---|
| Our country has an (6) *old, long* | 6. | 40* | 31 | 48 | 50 |
| *history.* Between the North and | | | | | |
| the South we have always been (7) | 7. | 47 | 46 | 46 | 40 |
| *a bridge, a connecting link.* Our | | | | | |
| country has been settled and influenced | | | | | |
| most by (8) *Bavarians, Germans.* Our | 8. | 50* | 68 | 56 | 48 |
| democracy is (9) *not genuine,* | 9. | 37* | 26 | 48 | 28 |
| *unpopular, etc.* We have been able to | | | | | |
| produce famous people in (10) *all,* | 10. | 40* | 62 | 33 | 38 |
| *most* spheres of culture. We can indeed | | | | | |
| be (11) *proud, very proud* of our | 11. | 81 | 87 | 85 | 76 |
| ancestors. The greatest hero of our | | | | | |
| Heroic Era was (12) Andreas | 12. | 88 | 85 | 92 | 84 |

|  | # | S | N | M | F |
|---|---|---|---|---|---|
| Hofer. The two worst periods for our country have been (13) *the Fight for Freedom in 1809* and (14) | 13. | 53 | 40 | 56 | 46 |
|  | 14. | 53 | 62 | 54 | 70 |
| *World War II.* The first period was bad because of (15) [of those so saying] *repression, foreign domination,* and the second | 15. | 45 | 41 | 46 | 41 |
| because of (16) [of those so saying] *human lives lost, air war, general misery.* For all people the | 16. | 47 | 49 | 71 | 59 |
| knowledge of our history is (17) *important, informative.* | 17. | 50* | 72 | 42 | 56 |

### People

| | # | S | N | M | F |
|---|---|---|---|---|---|
| As a people we are called (18) *South Tyroleans, Tyroleans,* and we | 18. | 90* | 66 | 94 | 86 |
| conduct our lives the way (19) *the German people do.* We are a | 19. | 31* | 10 | 33 | 20 |
| (20) *unified, healthy, ambitious, etc.* people. Our love of country is | 20. | 26 | 30 | 23 | 32 |
| (21) *great, deep;* and so whenever | 21. | 69 | 62 | 67 | 72 |
| we are away we experience (22) | 22. | 61 | 64 | 67 | 56 |
| *homesickness, grief.* For us "Heimat" means (23) *land, fatherland.* In | 23. | 19 | 17 | 17 | 6 |
| our country every place, every valley, every range of mountains, and every region has distinguishable characteristics such as (24) | 24. | 45* | 65 | 23 | 48 |
| *customs, language.* The status of a person (his social position or profession) should be respected (25) *always, by all.* Our peasants | 25. | 81 | 82 | 84 | 80 |
| love, most of all, their (26) *Heimat* | 26. | 26 | 20 | 25 | 22 |
| and their (27) *farms, property.* | 27. | 47* | 24 | 25 | 22 |
| The rule of primogeniture is for us (28) *necessary, important.* The | 28. | 65* | 7 | 81 | 54 |
| higher one goes in the mountains, the (29) *more silent, shier* the | 29. | 16* | 32 | 23 | 10 |
| inhabitants become. Inhabitants of towns, particularly businessmen and officials, are not so (30) [*praise-* | 30. | 48 | 62 | 42 | 48 |

| | # | S | N | M | F |
|---|---|---|---|---|---|
| *worthy*] and (31) [*unpraiseworthy*] as those living in villages and the peasants. The principal attributes | 31. | 23 | 25 | 27 | 24 |
| of our character are (32) *love of* | 32. | 40* | 30 | 35 | 36 |
| *Heimat*, (33) *friendliness, hospitality*, | 33. | 14 | 14 | 17 | 12 |
| and (34) *fidelity*. Among us differences between rich and poor | 34. | 32 | 28 | 29 | 26 |
| people are (35) *not great, not* | 35. | 62* | 79 | 54 | 66 |
| *significant*. Generally we think about the past (36) *more, more willingly* | 36. | 56 | 67 | 46 | 62 |
| than we do about the future. From the pronunciation of an unknown countryman, it is possible to | | | | | |
| recognize his (37) *origin, residence*. | 37. | 57 | 78 | 37 | 60 |
| From an economic standpoint our people are (38) *prospering, in good* | 38. | 77* | 48 | 81 | 78 |
| *condition*. | | | | | |

### Culture

| | # | S | N | M | F |
|---|---|---|---|---|---|
| The culture of our land and also its principal characteristics can be designated as (39) [*any* | 39. | 27 | 28 | 31 | 18 |
| *anthropological conceptualization of "culture"*]. In recent times the following folkways and customs have gradually become different: | | | | | |
| (40) *clothing*, | 40. | 25 | 18 | 31 | 22 |
| (41) *festivals*. Changes in the above | 41. | 19 | 9 | 27 | 14 |
| folkways and customs have had (42) *little, no* influence on the | 42. | 95 | 91 | 93 | 92 |
| strength of our love of Heimat. Folkways and customs that can be immediately recognized as | | | | | |
| genuinely Tyrolean are (43) | 43. | 37* | 16 | 48 | 32 |
| *traditional costumes* and (44) | 44. | 15 | 21 | 21 | 14 |
| *religious processions*. Gradually the modern world has had (45) *strong,* | 45. | 53 | 58 | 48 | 58 |
| *considerable* influence on folkways and customs in mountain areas. The room in every farmhouse which plays an important role in preserving | | | | | |

| Text | # | S | N | M | F |
|---|---|---|---|---|---|
| the family and the culture of the land is (46) *the living room*. Our festivals | 46. | 44 | 47 | 13 | 70 |
| are particularly beautiful and agreeable because (47) [*worldly or hedonistic character*]. Customarily | 47. | 34* | 14 | 35 | 38 |
| people think (48) *little, not at all* about our comprehensive culture. | 48. | 23* | 34 | 35 | 12 |
| Very important for the preservation of our culture are (49) *our customs,* | 49. | 22* | 13 | 27 | 14 |
| *festivals*. We must always (50) | 50. | 59 | 59 | 69 | 46 |
| *protect, cultivate* our culture. We have our own folk characteristics, for example, (51) [*reference to a* | 51. | 23 | 18 | 27 | 8 |
| *region*]. | | | | | |

## Problems

| Text | # | S | N | M | F |
|---|---|---|---|---|---|
| In comparison with the time before the First World War, there are now (52) *bigger, more difficult* problems. | 52. | 57 | 51 | 50 | 52 |
| Today the principal problems in our country are (53) [*related to Italy*]. | 53. | 86* | 72 | 90 | 74 |
| The living standard of peasants in the mountains is in general (54) *low,* | 54. | 63 | 69 | 65 | 66 |
| *not satisfactory*. We need for ourselves (55) *more, useful* | 55. | 37* | 69 | 23 | 46 |
| *factories*. The origin of many of our problems is (56) [South Tyrol | 56. | 56* | 12 | 63 | 40 |
| only] *Italy*, [North Tyrol only] *South Tyrol*. Our schools, which always remain important, must be (57) | 57. | 63 | 72 | 83 | 52 |
| *preserved, improved*. In the world our problems are (58) *well, better* | 58. | 48* | 25 | 50 | 56 |
| known. | | | | | |

## The Italians

| Text | # | S | N | M | F |
|---|---|---|---|---|---|
| The Italians who have been in South Tyrol for 40 years in general have had (59) *not much, no* influence on our culture. As a result of contact with | 59. | 52 | 47 | 60 | 50 |

| | # | S | N | M | F |
|---|---|---|---|---|---|
| the Italians, the South Tyroleans have become (60) [*some undesirable characteristic*]. The Italians wish to | 60. | 52 | 68 | 54 | 45 |
| (61) *Italianize* South Tyrol; up to | 61. | 47* | 37 | 48 | 35 |
| now, they have had (62) [of those saying "Italianize"] *little, no* success. | 62. | 49* | 27 | 35 | 71 |
| The Italians very often conduct industry in South Tyrol for (63) *political, patriotic* reasons. The | 63. | 51 | 59 | 48 | 49 |
| Italian and South Tyrolean cultures are (64) *completely, in large part* different. Good traits of the Italians | 64. | 77 | 78 | 85 | 62 |
| are the following: (65) [*one or more mentioned*]; and bad ones are: (66) | 65. | 72 | 71 | 65 | 75 |
| [*one or more mentioned*]. Most of the | 66. | 78 | 69 | 75 | 73 |
| Italians who come to South Tyrol are (67) from *Southern Italy*. When | 67. | 34* | 21 | 38 | 36 |
| you see someone for the first time, you can (68) *immediately, easily, with certainty* know whether he is | 68. | 92* | 70 | 91 | 89 |
| a Tyrolean or an Italian, because (69) [of those saying "immediately," etc.: *of some genetically determined physical trait*]. Italians and South | 69. | 48 | 54 | 47 | 43 |
| Tyroleans have (70) *few, weak* contacts with each other, and | 70. | 42 | 43 | 38 | 35 |
| marriage between the two races occurs (71) *often, increasingly*. The | 71. | 36* | 64 | 25 | 59* |
| Paris (Degasperi-Gruber) Treaty of 1946 has (72) *not, not at all* been | 72. | 33 | 29 | 32 | 24 |
| carried out because (73) [of those saying "not": *some reason given*]. If | 73. | 84* | 75 | 73 | 82 |
| South Tyrol were granted full autonomy under Italy, it could (74) *quickly, alone* solve all its most | 74. | 78 | 76 | 74 | 74 |
| important problems; this autonomy South Tyrol will (75) *not, not quickly* obtain. As citizens of Italy, | 75. | 43 | 53 | 51 | 30 |
| South Tyroleans are now faring (76) *better* than they did formerly. | 76. | 44 | 42 | 53 | 43 |

Conclusions to be derived from the Credo are of course limited by the particular technique that was employed to ascertain its content: sentence completion under school conditions. In addition, arbitrary decisions were made in grouping the replies for IBM treatment and then, afterwards, for presentation in the present concise report. Still three points are perhaps noteworthy. In the first place, some stimulus patterns do have attributes which in this context are more or less universally noted or evaluated, others do not. Thus about nine-tenths of the South Tyroleans believe that people really use intensively whatever land is fertile ( # 3), but only slightly half of them consider that their agricultural products are outstanding ( # 5). Secondly, there are interesting differences in some instances between the responses of the South and the North Tyroleans and, less frequently, between the boys and the girls in the high school of South Tyrol. Some of the differences between the two areas seem self-evident on a common-sense level: more South Tyroleans refer to themselves as Tyroleans in order to avoid the designation of Italian, whereas North Tyroleans are proud of the fact that they are Austrians ( #18). Others are less obvious; do slightly more South Tyroleans consider that their country has a long history ( #6) because they would thus establish their claim to be there or because this point is emphasized more forcefully in their schools?

Finally, the variability in characterization and evaluation must be underscored. No matter how arbitrary the group of the responses for purposes of IBM and for presentation here, again and again it was not possible to find a classification used by more than 50 per cent of the subjects in the investigation. The reader must remember that the people in both Tyrols appear to be very patriotic and certainly unified; nevertheless, under these conditions, the case for disagreement seems about as strong as, if not stronger than, that for agreement. This illustrative research exercise nevertheless does reveal a kind of Tyrolean credo both similar and dissimilar to that existing in other nations and regions. Presumably such a unified and ununified portrait can be teased out of the verbal utterances of any patriotic, nationalistic group.

# 9. Justifications

People tend to justify their behavior, either past or contemplated, by invoking principles transcending the immediately observable. The description of the ethical process has been called phenomenological and, in general terms, involves such questions as the following: "How do people go about making up their minds on an ethical point?" "What sorts of appeals are accepted as relevant in ethical disputes?" (Brandt, 1954, p. 3). Unfortunately, philosophers in this area function no more concretely than they do in the general realm of values discussed three chapters back. Even a writer who states that he is about to use the phenomenological approach and make "a direct examination of the data of men's moral consciousness" (Mandelbaum, 1955, p. 30) emerges with an abstract classification of those data far removed from their actual content. The aim of this chapter and the next three is to examine in some detail the values to which nationalists appeal as they make their demands and strive to reach their goals.

## Universality

To philosophize or, for that matter, to try to be scientific about behavior is probably a universal characteristic of adults. Presumably animals respond to momentary situations with alacrity and without meditation or regret. This "eternal human need to justify action" (Tucker, 1960, p. 1) is also missing in young children but gradually acquired by them. Sometimes, when challenged, people may shrug and be unable to explain or condone what they plan or have done; and they often are willing to accept many everyday phenomena on faith and without further ado. More frequently, however, they appeal to a metaphysical principle like destiny or a physical one like climate to explain what they accomplish or wit-

147

ness. Each society has characteristic explanations to which people turn when there is a crisis, a challenge, or a frustration; and during socialization children learn the codes and the ethical principles which forever after can be invoked as justifications for conduct. Somehow, in short, men come to discover that their own behavior and that of their contemporaries do not impulsively reflect the moment, but spring from the experience they and their society have had. The experience stored within them gives rise to explanations and justifications and so produces some degree of consistency.

This universal proclivity to justify is like the similarly general tendency to evaluate the attributes of the land, its people, their culture, and corresponding foreign stimulus patterns. In both cases reference is made to important values. Indeed, the two sets of values reflect the desire to link the present to the past and the future.

### Functions

The justifications advanced in behalf of the convictions, the demands, and the actions of patriotism and nationalism, which can be thought of as their theology, are supposed to impress two different audiences—the people of the nation and relevant foreigners. In the first place, national leaders offer explanations that fortify their followers and that on occasion impel them to action. Part of what has recently been called political socialization (Hyman, 1959), consists of teaching people to respect and obey their government. The mass media and local politicians, consequently, again and again repeat communications that justify a government's specific course of action and its general policies.

Some justification can be found, it appears, for any kind of national policy and action. Among modern nations, it is necessary only to mention words like concentration camp, atomic bomb, or war itself to suggest the kinds of situations in which statesmen must display infinite ingenuity in providing intellectual and emotional support for what they and their countries do. When ordinary or extraordinary people carry out actions producing some degree of discomfort within themselves, they can be made to feel a little more comfortable by being confronted with an appealing justification. 'You must make a personal sacrifice for your country.' 'You must dislike those foreigners even though your religious creed asks you to love all your fellow men.' People prefer not to feel uncertain when a national policy is challenged by the leaders of another country. Under conditions such as these, an acceptable justification reduces the conflict within them or, in the fashionable language of the day, helps dissipate some of the dissonance they are experiencing (Festinger, 1957).

Many people in modern nations find it difficult to be completely ethnocentric because they are acquainted with alternative values or modes of behavior. They are able to admit imperfections in their own society, but then they rationalize or justify them. 'We may be a bit ruthless, but how else could we possibly survive?'

Foreigners constitute the other audience in front of which the attainment of national and international objectives must frequently be justified. As men negotiate diplomatically and as they fight other nations, they signify to neutrals and to enemies the values they claim to defend. Appealing to the conscience of the world means finding an acceptable justification for what one wants to do or to prevent others from doing. Historians usually refer to these justifications in such sweeping terms that it is impossible to know whether the phrasing is theirs or that of the people whose activities they are reporting; for example, the statement that after the Congress of Vienna "strategic reasons of national survival or security and moral reasons of cultural superiority or economic productivity were adduced to justify territorial claims and privileges of status against other nationalities" (Kohn, 1962, p. 11) seems to be an abstraction far removed from the leaders' utterances on which it is presumably based, or is it?

In international disputes, the leaders of many nations do not feel bound by international law when, as is usually the case, they can find some justification for their own unilateral decision. That justification represents a "higher" or more compelling value for themselves and in addition, they hope, for the domestic and foreign audiences to whom they communicate it as an explanation for their policy or action. The moral argument advanced in one's own behalf may be scorned officially by the opposing government, but it is possible that some nationals of that country or in some other country are affected by it. Here is a significant reason why modern governments widely publicize their publicly stated diplomatic and war aims and why therefore psychological warfare or the dissemination of information internationally is so important.

In view of the psychological and political functions served by official justifications, it is not surprising that historical records are replete with fine philosophical turns. A case in point is European imperialism during the nineteenth and twentieth centuries. The expansion then inevitably occurred at the expense of scattered and weak nonliterate or semiliterate societies in Asia and Africa and in competition with other nations, usually European. Even if they had a low moral opinion of the people they were conquering, the conquerors felt impelled to appeal to some incontrovertible value from their own standpoint, and thus either to ease their own consciences or to express their goals quite honestly. 'We must save them from sin.' 'It is our duty to help them.' 'They like to be ruled firmly.' 'We unify them and curb local wars.' In addition, such explanations were produced so that leaders could keep face, bargain, and generally negotiate with colleagues in competing nations. "Statesmen," a general treatise on international relations points out, "generally refer to their policies not in terms of power but in terms of either ethical and legal principles or biological necessities" (Morgenthau, 1948, p. 61).

No general principle concerning the justification likely to be invoked in a given circumstance is feasible other than the trite, unsatisfying one that it all depends upon the prevailing tendencies of people and upon the kinds of appeal they hear from their leaders and peers. The justification to be anticipated is the one usually associated with the demand or action being justified. 'We never declare war except in self-defense.' Missionaries have always justified the spread of nationalism to foreign countries in terms different from those employed by traders: both have had their own well-stocked kits of arguments. From another standpoint, the consciously or unconsciously wily diplomat, when arguing with an outsider, employs the justifications he calculates will make the deepest impression upon his protagonist. 'You must agree that this is a war of self-defense; also our civilization is better than theirs.'

## Truth and Sincerity

A number of ethical issues with psychological implications can be raised and, in the great tradition of philosophy, left unsettled. A really thorny question involves truth or falsity. More likely than not, most justifications cannot be dismissed as "mere" rationalizations because they reflect deeper motives within people. They usually are related to goals men and women would achieve in interaction with others and throughout their lives. They may be less truthfully employed when they are deliberate rationalizations; yet they are not likely to be invoked even cynically unless they are thought to serve their purpose effectively. People are seldom simple creatures of impulses either before or after the fact.

Then it is frequently if not usually impossible to decide whether a justification is true or not. In theory an investigation can be made to determine whether the consequences of an action being justified is the one that is proclaimed; what is then judged, though, it not the truth of the justification, rather the validity of the prediction attached to it. 'We must have more territory if we are to survive.' First, no clear-cut test is likely to be at hand to determine whether in fact survival requires the advocated expansion. Second, even if the statement could be proven in the long run, it would still be necessary to suggest why survival is valuable.

A variant of the truth-falsity issue is the motive of those who utter a justification: are they or are they not trying to tell the truth as they themselves conceptualize truth? From an ethical or a public-relations viewpoint a vast difference exists between leaders who deliberately concoct rationalizations which they then offer as justifications for their actions on the one hand and those who sincerely believe in the goodness and the truth of their explanations on the other hand; and yet either justification may be quite good or desirable, or the consequences predicted therefrom true or false. Of course we do not like intentional liars; and we tend to forgive unintentional ones, or at least we charge them with less responsibility. Similar questions, it has been shown, are raised by critics when they evaluate literary products; and it has been concluded that "by itself, sincerity in a writer never sufficed to give merit to a work of art" (Peyre, 1963, p. 339).

Sincere leaders are probably more influential and effective not because sincerity is virtuous as such but because sincere people are more likely than the insincere to reflect the prevailing and heavily reinforced principles of their society; instead of expressing rather narrow, blatantly selfish, or particular ideologies of their group, they more frequently give voice to philosophical, organized, total ideologies (Mannheim, 1936, pp. 49–53). The sincere speak the truth because they find it impossible to do otherwise and yet remain conventional. What they expound is so generally and widely acceptable that almost everyone, including they themselves, automatically consent. For this additional reason it is unwise to dismiss the justifications for nationalism or for any other group action as myths or illusions, a practice followed by those observers and writers (e.g. Shafer, 1955, pp. 15–56) who would expose the falsity of various national claims or otherwise stress the irrational elements in human conduct. On the contrary, if it be permitted to fight the fire of the economist just cited with that of an historian, "even illusions are mental facts which may have a great share in producing national solidarity, national ambitions, and national rivalries" (Hertz, 1944, p. 42). Men, in brief, guide themselves by beliefs, whether true or false, good or bad—and such psychological realities merit serious investigation.

## Beliefs

Justifications are usually accompanied by certain beliefs which, psychologically, are really justifications for those justifications. In the literature of common sense and social science other words are employed to refer to the same phenomena—such as stereotypes, ideas, convictions—but the referent is the same. The attributes of a situation or the action requiring justification are first noted before the most appropriate or satisfying justification is selected from an available arsenal. When challenged, even in difficult testing situations, people in the West explain their expressed attitudes by referring to their own values and their own beliefs. A sample of school children in St. Louis was once confronted with the boring and rather impossible task of indicating on a 5-point scale whether they liked or disliked 21 different nationalities. Most of them had definite opinions, and virtually all of those having the opinions were able to provide some kind of a reason for their feelings. In the study, for example, 12 per cent claimed they were not acquainted with, or did not know much about, the Irish. Of the remaining 88 per cent with an opinion, the most frequently mentioned reason for liking the Irish, "I am of Irish descent," was given by 22 per cent; 16 per cent considered the Irish "good," "nice," or "kind"; and only 4 per cent suggested no reason or stated frankly that they did not know why they held their opinions. The latter percentage was correspondingly low for all the other nationalities (Meltzer, 1941). It appears as if a value is not favored unless it has or can summon supporting beliefs. Or, if a bit of wild extrapolation be permitted: 'Under normal circumstances I would not kill you; I shall do so when I feel justified; I shall feel justified only when I acquire the belief that you are about to kill me. You may in fact be plotting my death; or I may be just imagining that you are doing so—but in either case the belief makes me act.'

Similarly a very general belief can restrict the use of some justifications to one group rather than another. If you believe that all men are born equal, you are more likely also to be convinced that all men have equal rights than if you believe they are born unequal—and it matters not how you define the vague terms "equal" and "rights." With a belief in equality but not with one in inequality, you probably apply the same evaluative criteria to all nations; you do not employ a double standard which maintains in effect that 'the policy is justified for us because we are superior to them, but it is not justified for them because they are inferior.'

In fact, according to a brilliant analysis of the Negro problem in the United States which was made a few decades ago, such a mechanism functions among white Americans when they discriminate against Negroes. For these Americans are faced with a "dilemma": they have "high national and Christian precepts" which frown upon prejudice and segregation, but simultaneously many of them still favor or follow a policy of segregation. Their conflict or dissonance is reduced by a belief and a justifying principle. According to the belief, "Negro Americans belong to a lower biological species than they themselves"; according to the principle, "the white race should be kept pure" (Myrdal, 1944, pp. xlvii,

102). The principle would seem psychologically untenable without the belief, and the belief has been sustained in part in order to preserve the principle. Once again another illustration of how people are caught in a Spiral.

Nationalism functions similarly. The hypothesis has been proposed, for example, that "modern Arab nationalism may be considered an effort to create a new self-conception for the Arab, a new identity." People in the Near East, this sociologist thinks, previously tended to accept Western beliefs concerning themselves as people who were "religious, indolent, patient, grave" as well as "narrow" and "unambitious." Now they are convinced that they must share some of the advances occurring elsewhere, while not abandoning critical aspects of their heritage from the past (Berger, 1962, pp. 323–24). This conviction that Arabs are not what others and hence they themselves thought they were has consequently led to the demand for independence; and it has been accompanied, if the analysis is correct, by the Spiraled hope that successful action to achieve the demand will in turn alter their beliefs concerning themselves.

Since the convictions of nationalism are complex, they are chaperoned by elaborate explanatory systems. In the two succeeding chapters, however, more attention must be paid to the justifications than to the beliefs in order to isolate the recurrent and underlying values. The justifications, moreover, will be considered one at a time, but it is well to point out that, in connection with a specific or a general issue, more than a single value is likely to be invoked. Unlike the philosopher who demands that various ethical principles be consistent with one another (Cohen, 1954, pp. 7–8), the politician and the patriot usually feel under no such compulsion: the justifications they employ are the ones they think—consciously or unconsciously, by deliberate design or by casual custom—best fit the situation at hand.

Conflicts between nations usually involve beliefs and justifications. Differences in belief can often be traced in turn to differences in fact. 'You say we are doing this, but it is not true'—here the 'we' is asking the 'you' to change his belief by appealing to the facts. On this level there can be empirical investigations by impartial third parties. But different justifications cannot be easily reconciled. 'You say your ancestors arrived here ahead of ours, but it has been we who have built up this country.' Usually no high court exists or is considered competent to decide which value is more compelling.

### Italian and Austrian Claims to the South Tyrol

Before calling the roll of the justifications pervading national-ism in general, it seems desirable to suggest why the treatment must be so lengthy by indicating concretely the complex nature of the justifications and counterjustifications, the beliefs and the counter beliefs, and the facts and counterfacts which are hurled about during an international controversy. The illustration will be the claims which two nations, Italy and Austria, make upon the South Tyrol, the patriotism and nationalism of whose German-speaking inhabitants has been frequently noted in these pages. No attempt will be made to cover the entire case presented by either side; instead, a sample of the reasoning will be given.

To try fruitlessly to avoid the unavoidable charge of bias, of-ficial sources are cited from both protagonists. The Italian position is taken from the first number of a fortnightly bulletin which began publication on January 1, 1961, in Italian, French, Spanish, Ger-man, and English (Isotti, 1961). The bulletin is called *Alto Adige,* the name used by the Italians for South Tyrol; that name, it must be hastily added, does not appear in this book (except in the pres-ent section) because the alternative derived from the German is much better known among English-speaking readers. That this document adequately represents the strongly nationalistic Italian standpoint is suggested by the facts that it appeared originally in the Italian-language newspaper of the same name in the South Tyrol and that copies of it, the editor notes, were "immediately sent to New York and distributed among delegations representing member states of the U.N.," which at the time was discussing the Italian-Austrian conflict. The Austrian viewpoint comes from a similar fortnightly publication: the first issue of *SID* (which stands for "Südtirol Information Dokumentation"), January 17, 1963, English edition (Gschnitzer, 1963). The editor-in-chief, who is also one of the publishers and owners, is acknowledged by both Aus-

trians and Italians to be one of the principal Austrian leaders supporting the South Tyroleans in their dispute with Italy. Since the
general statement about the South Tyrol in the first issue of the
bulletin is briefer than the Italian declaration and therefore does
not contain all the usual Tyrolean and Austrian claims and arguments, a small book by the same academic and political writer has
also been used: it is devoted to the South Tyrol and, though
written in German, appears interested solely in enlisting foreign
support for Tyrol (Gschnitzer, 1958). Except when a citation is
shown to come from that book, all quotations have been lifted
from the two documents, the English style of which has been polished a trifle by this writer for the sake of elegance and intelligi-
bility. Quite arbitrarily, because some choice has to be made, the
arguments are presented in the order adopted by the Italian
source.

The first Italian statement takes the form of a refutation: "The
claim that Alto Adige is 'German soil' is incorrect." In its opening
sentence, the Austrian document refers to "German-speaking South
Tyrol." Obviously a question of fact is involved: is the area Ger-
manic or not? The presumption is that South Tyrol should belong
to that nation having identical or similar ethnicity. In passing, it is
to be noted that, although the English version of both sources is
being cited, each consistently uses a different name to refer to the
region.

How then can it be determined whether the Alto Adige (or
South Tyrol) is Italian or German? Both sides agree that approximately one quarter of a million German-speaking people
lived there when Italy obtained the territory in 1919 and that the
same number are there now. In the first place, an appeal is made
to geography. "From a physical viewpoint," according to the
Italian source, "this territory, lying to the south of the Alpine ridge,
watered by the River Adige which has its source and mouth
within the boundaries, is as much a geographical part of Italy as
the land to the South of the Pyrenees is of Spain." The frontier between Italy and Austria, like the Alps and the Adige, is part of
"the natural order of things." The most important pass through
"the Alpine ridge"—because it is relatively low and can be trav-
ersed throughout the winter—is the Brenner, which, the Austrian
source maintains, has served to "join and bind together" North and

South Tyrol: "Geography shows this, history confirms it" (Gschnitzer, 1958, p. 6). The Italians, in brief, see the Alps as a barrier, the Austrians view an Alpine pass as an avenue; in either case, natural factors are believed to justify the location of the boundaries between the two countries.

Then, secondly, both sides agree that German-speaking people originally migrated from the north into what is now the Alto Adige and that they have lived there for centuries. "Tyrol has formed, for more than a thousand years," states the Austrian source, "a political, historical, and cultural entity." And the Italian statement: "During past centuries, and even in recent times, the German people moved throughout the territory for military, political, and administrative reasons and there was a spontaneous immigration movement from the north that was provoked by economic reasons." The two protagonists, however, then part drastically when they address themselves to the question of who originally had been occupying the area when the German-speaking groups first arrived:

|                          *Italian*                          |                          *Austrian*                          |
| --- | --- |
| There was, however, no question of settling in deserted localities but rather one of replacing earlier populations of Latin culture. . . . Proof of this is to be found in the Ladin population (which still speaks a Latin dialect and which still inhabits some of the valleys of the Alto Adige region) and by the fact that, in past centuries, the statutes of the ancient Bolzano Fair were drafted in Italian, this being the official language of the commercial classes and for trade across the Alps. | The Ladins: the oldest nationality in the land is Rhaeto-Romanic. . . . Recent Italian linguistics, clearly under political influence, gives the impression that the Ladin language is a dialect of Italian. That is not so; rather the situation seems to be, like Rhaeto-Romanisch among the Grisons, that these people have their own language which in pronunciation stands much closer to old French than to Italian. . . . Until the sixteenth century German culture extended farther southward. . . . In this way, in general, a clear and firm linguistic boundary was built up between Germans and Italians [Gschnitzer, 1958, pp. 45–48]. |

Clearly the Italians claim that ancestors of theirs inhabited the land before the arrival of the Germans and hence the Alto Adige has always been Italian. The Austrians, in contrast, contend that the Ladins were not Latins (rather they were conquered by the Romans) and hence South Tyrol has never really been Italian. Both sides also marshal more facts than those cited here to prove that they and their culture, unlike their opponents, have been in the area for a long time. Two related justifications are thus being advanced: priority and length of possession.

Since records exist, it is not surprising to note that both the Italians and the Austrians agree that South Tyrol was annexed in 1919 by Italy in accordance with the Treaty of St. Germain, which Austria signed with the Allies. The Italians stress that the transfer was "legally recognized" under the treaty after "the Italian victory of 1918." Legality and success are their justifying values. The Austrians concede the legality point, but deny that the Italian armies were victorious on Alpine battlefields. Then they invoke another value: the annexation, they say, was "against the will of its people and contrary to President Wilson's 14 points of January 8, 1918, which declared as basic to the peace negotiations that the future European borders should be drawn 'along clearly recognizable lines of nationality' (point 9)."

Next the Italian document features the Italian contribution to the Alto Adige: "Immigrants brought new enterprise and work, and Italy has largely industrialized an area that was once almost exclusively concerned with agriculture and trade. . . . The greater part of the commercial, banking, and tourist structure, as well as property (land and buildings), has remained unchanged, approximately 92 per cent being in the hands of the German-speaking population." These contentions the Austrians either deny or interpret differently; reference is made, for example, to "the industrial zones which have been created artificially and only for the purpose of italianizing" the area (Gschnitzer, 1958, p. 81). Both parties, consequently, agree that the contribution of Italy to the welfare of the South Tyrol is a value which should be considered in justifying her claim; but there is disagreement concerning the nature of that contribution.

Then recent history becomes an issue. The Austrians almost always recall the Mussolini era in any political discussion: "Fascism made a ruthless attempt during two decades to italianize the South Tyrolean people." For their part, the Italians usually avoid references to this historical period (which is the case in the document being cited here); less frequently, they admit that injustices and outrages were perpetrated by fascists but then immediately add that this sad and regrettable period ended with the reinstatement of democracy in Italy in 1945. Much, much more important in the present-day controversy are allegations concerning the way in which the Paris Agreement of 1946 has been executed, since that agreement set forth the treatment to be accorded South Tyrol when it was returned to Italy after World War II:

| *Italy* | *Austria* |
|---|---|
| This country again offered citizenship to more than 86,000 inhabitants of Alto Adige who opted for Germany in 1939; it has built 446 elementary and secondary schools . . . and it has not touched special Austrian legislation that impedes . . . division of land and safeguards family farms. Again "the legislative and administrative autonomy granted to Bolzano Province," which has a German language majority, tends to favor one population rather than the others. | The regional autonomy has so far not been granted by Italy. Against the will of its freely elected representatives, South Tyrol . . . was merged with the overwhelmingly Italian region of Trent. . . . South Tyrol is without legislative and executive power in the fields of farming and forestry, hunting and fishing, commerce, industry and tourism, public works, mining, utilization of public waters, welfare work and social insurance. . . . Schooling remains under the administration of Rome. |

The two sides are once again concerned with the relations between the Italian government and the South Tyroleans, since those relations are thought to justify or not to justify to a certain extent Italian jurisdiction over the region. In addition, the question is raised either implicitly or explicitly: has Italy kept the promises to which she agreed in the 1946 agreement? Both values, be it noted, involve the reputation of the Italian government not only among

Italians and South Tyroleans but also among all law-abiding, honorable nations.

The Italian document ends by stating that the people of the Alto Adige, "at a time when every effort is being made to hasten European unity," are indeed living in two civilizations and hence are "fortunate, for—while keeping their own cultural background and enjoying the protection assured by constitutional law—they may also aspire to yet another form of civilization." The Austrian spokesman likewise concludes his book by referring to the fact that "people are striving toward a higher unity in a united Europe." He believes, however, that in such "a united Europe, there will once again be a place for the historical unity of Tyrol" (Gschnitzer, 1958, p. 84). Quite appropriately, different values are being praised within the value of an internationalized Europe; the Italians say they favor the broadening of Tyrolean culture, the Austrians say they favor its preservation.

# 10. Absolutistic Justifications

Men's values reflect their drives: what they need or wish they hold in high esteem. Needs and wishes fall into some kind of hierarchy; obviously food is essential, but poetry, in spite of the fine sentiments of poets, satisfies a less insistent or a less basic urge. In a similar manner, it ought to be possible to grade values. But a difficulty arises from the fact that no agreement exists concerning the categories into which the needs and wishes themselves can be classified. For this reason, the usual distinction between primary or basic and secondary or learned drives is here only remotely related to the values behind the dichotomy being adopted: there are absolutistic and personificative justifications.

Absolutistic justifications, considered in this chapter, produce little or no controversy with respect to their underlying value: 'If what you say is true, then obviously I agree with you.' The value is not questioned, perhaps only its applicability to the situation at hand. Or else a competing mode of justification is proposed. In contrast, the personificative justifications described in the next chapter, since they are derived in effect from the attributes of personality, are much less likely to secure immediate or eventual consent. 'I am not at all sure that what you say is worth fighting for.' As ever, the line between categories as sweeping as these represents only a general demarcation and is not always clear-cut. On occasion personificative justifications are accepted without a whimper and absolutistic ones are protested.

For the absolutistic justifications the highest values of all is life itself, just as the broadest possible conceptualization of drive calls attention to a will to live. Such a general category is not useful here since an attempt is being made to phrase the justifications in a form closely resembling the one in which they actually circulate nationally and internationally. And yet most of the appeals about to be discussed remain fairly close to life vs. death, and sometimes they even refer to that cosmic issue.

## Determinism

'We must do this, we cannot do otherwise.' The plea here insists that the nationalistic demand or activity springs from an unavoidable state of affairs; it is justifiable because, being predetermined, it is unavoidable. The rains must come; God's or nature's will be done.

1. *Divine sanction:* 'What we seek has received God's blessing, we are following only His will.' That will in fact is made manifest in different ways. One or more people report a direct communication from a deity. The status quo, having come into existence gradually, peacefully, or in some other approved manner, must reflect divine approval, for otherwise He would not have tolerated the events that have produced this state of affairs.

Divine sanction is also communicated less directly. An oracle or prophet arises and conveys the wishes or commands of a deity. A divine source, such as the Bible or Koran, is consulted and, according to an acceptable interpretation, sanctions the present policy since it is the same as one once blessed in the past. Dice are rolled, entrails of animals are examined, stars are observed, as signs of divine instructions.

Under God's or the gods' guidance, then, the crusade, the hallowed crusade, begins; any action helping the cause is automatically justified by a reference to its purpose. 'We are chosen people, we march.' Without too much exaggeration, at least for the historical period in which he wrote, one observer declared that "every war is a holy war" (Partridge, 1919, p. 118). Historically the word *patria* tended in medieval time to refer to the City of God rather than to a country or some other place on earth (Shafer, 1955, p. 95). Nowadays in modern nations divine assistance in waging war is sought more modestly, without insisting that God is an ally or without holding Him responsible for the righteousness of the cause. Thus the moral-religious mode of evaluating the attributes of the land, its people, and their culture is applied to the nation's policies and activities.

'We must protect our sacred soil,' men often say when they refer to their country (Delaisi, 1925, pp. 135–53). How should such
a statement be interpreted? Obviously, the person using the precious cliché does not really believe that every square inch of his
country's land is sacred in the sense that a church or an altar is; he
would quickly agree, no doubt, that a sports field or a cesspool is
rather secular or profane. No, concealed in the expression is a symbolic metaphor of which the speaker himself may not be altogether
conscious. In effect, he is saying that 'the land which is our country
must be protected as if all of it were like a church.' The field and
the pool upon the land are details, mundane and irrelevant. Many
patriotic and national justifications resemble this one: although
they cannot be taken literally, their manifest meaning may provide a clue to powerful latent motivation.

2. *Destiny:* 'It is thus ordained,' 'It is written in the stars,' 'We
follow in the footsteps of the founding fathers.' Reference is made
not to God or to gods but to a less specific, more general type of
force having the attribute of supernatural inevitability. The notion
of destiny may simultaneously be linked to divine sanctions: God
created the universe and then, as it were, wound the clock whose
actions and movements in every or in almost every sense have been
predestined from the outset; thereafter there has been little or no
novelty, just the occurrence of the foreseeable details. Here is social determinism according to plan.

Philosophically or scientifically, the trend toward a goal can be
merely described or predicted. The description and the prediction are expressed neutrally, though their connotations or implications may be far from neutral: 'The sun will rise tomorrow,' 'All
men are mortal.' In contrast, when a statement of fact is used to
justify a patriotic conviction or a nationalistic demand or action,
its attractive connotations and implications are not left to the
chance interpretation of the audience but are explicitly stated:
what takes place is right because it must take place, there is no
alternative, this is Manifest Destiny. Reference may be made to a
broad principle. During the past century in the West, for example,
the doctrines of evolution and of the dialectic according to the
theses of Hegel and Marx and their descendants have been especially popular. The statement of any doctrine of this kind is im-

mediately considered to give rise to the policy being justified. 'It is
our destiny to lead, hence we must have a larger navy.'

Whether the referent is the country as a symbol or the nationals
who composed it, the reasoning remains the same. 'When provoked, a nation or its citizens must fight.' Why? 'It cannot be otherwise, countries and peoples are fated to defend themselves.' The
destiny of the nation is explained in terms of tradition, the destiny of its people by a reference to a combination of hereditary
and environmental factors. 'Having such a glorious past as a
model, our government is forever destined to keep its honor high.'
'Being human and also proud, we as individuals can tolerate no
insult.' The argument that groups or persons must carry on in a
specific manner because they are powerless to do otherwise is comforting. In fact, on the non-national level of murder or falling in
love, similar justifications can be invoked: under some circumstances impulses are said to be uncontrollable and so the resulting behavior may be excused or condoned.

3. *Nature:* 'What we want is perfectly natural.' That which is
allegedly natural is very often a set of boundaries. The "natural"
frontier is said to be a river, an ocean, a mountain, a pass, or a
climatic zone. Likewise, an offshore island is likely to be considered an appendage of the closest mainland rather than some
more distant place. It may be speculated that the basis for postu-
lating natural boundaries must be perceptual; one's land ends, as it
were, at a line that can be easily observed. These observable lines,
moreover, may also have or, at least before air and nuclear warfare, they may have had some justification in actual fact: foot soldiers find it difficult to cross a river or a mountain pass, and hence
a frontier employing one of these natural features may be, may
have been, more defensible. For the same reason, natural features
have determined the actual lines of demarcation between different
cultural groups. Often, perhaps usually, there are so many different features of this kind to which reference can be made in justifying a policy or action that the choice itself must be considered
either cultural or just arbitrary.

Then nature obviously also includes human nature. People have
innumerable impulses which they are supposed to be compelled
to express as inevitably as a river flows down and not up a hill.

'Men cannot live . . .' And because they are men, what must they
have in order to continue to live? They cannot live 'by bread
alone,' 'without security,' 'without honor,' 'without religion,' 'in
uncertainty,' 'with strangers,' 'in the absence of beauty,' etc. With
little or no modification similar claims are made for the nation as
a whole. At this point, the absolutistic justification shades over
into the kind of personificative justification discussed in the next
chapter.

4. *Humanitarian responsibility:* 'We must do this for the good
of mankind.' The good that mankind will allegedly gain as a result of the proposal can include almost every conceivable human
or political goal. People in foreign countries are helped when
disaster strikes them, such as a flood or a drought; when they are
being ruled by outside oppressors, as in the various wars of libera-
tion; when they are being exploited by their own leaders, as communists justify their own subversive activity in every capitalist
country; when they are threatened with attack from the outside,
as in many so-called preventive wars; when they are outstandingly
poor and ill, as occurs so often in many of the less-developed countries.

Whoever uses this fairly sophisticated justification is probably
self-consciously aware of his own goals and of his culture. In many
instances the plea seeks to impress outsiders, including those who
will benefit from the proposal. The values involved in the responsibility are not necessarily considered superior, rather the view is
advanced that something immortal will either perish or fail to
come into existence if the proper policy is not formulated or action taken. Obviously this justification contains only a touch of determinism: the duty may be predetermined but its acceptance involves considerable voluntarism.

Imperialism of any kind is usually justified by at least one reference to humanitarian responsibility. The example par excellence
is the missionary who is convinced that he has a real duty to con-
vert the heathen to an acceptable religion. In more general terms
it has often been said quite literally that 'we carry the White Man's
burden.' Or 'we have a mission to perform: these people need our
help, we must not stand aside and allow them to suffer,' 'remain
unchanged,' or 'endure too much economic misery or political

chaos during their first years of independence.' The objective observer may have real difficulty deciding whether the crusaders from outside or their willing or unwilling beneficiaries are correct, since that judgment requires a careful appraisal of the values that are involved. The values of the missionary and the imperialist can be very basic: religion, health, material progress. Another value that is closely related to freedom and sovereignty, however, often appears in modern times: is any intrusion from the outside, no matter how sincerely motivated, to be considered desirable in the short or the long run?

The objective for which humanitarian responsibility is felt may be phrased in very general terms: an ethical or political creed, such as Christianity or communism, is propagated so that more people or all people can benefit. In national or international communications, the creed need only be mentioned, it is assumed, for more or less universal acclamation to ensue. Its value is self-evident. "Democracy" is perhaps the only word actually receiving such approbation on both sides of every curtain in the modern world, although the trite, the telling, and the sad point must immediately be made that its precise referent varies with the communicator and the audience.

In the West for more than a century reference has frequently been made to the goal of "progress." The high-sounding term can be reasonably well defined in a particular situation, but usually its converts dislike being confined by the specific instance; rather they are interested, they say, in the trend. To stand in the path of whatever is progressively determined is immoral, in the manner of cutting off the supply of oxygen from a beautiful child gasping for breath. People invoking the justification must have, as has been concisely stated, "the faith in the possible and necessary amelioration of the human condition" (Kohn, 1962, p. 43); they must believe that traditions do not simply unfold but can be altered by intervention which, if it be the right kind, merits only high praise. Thus this discussion of deterministic justifications introduces yet another voluntaristic note.

'They dare not do that, such action is inhuman.' In considering the other side of the coin being called humanitarian responsibility, it is necessary merely to recall that every society has taboos against some form of behavior: people are not supposed to commit certain acts under specified circumstances. The killing of another human being, for example, is never tolerated in the way that sneezing is; usually it is permitted only in defense of oneself or one's family or in behalf of one's country. "The world public order," as the authorities and organizations struggling to maintain peace have been called, seeks first of all to prevent nations from going to war; then, when war breaks out, an effort is made "to minimize the inevitable destruction of values"; finally, if "the laws of war" are not followed and such values are damaged, reprisals are sanctioned. Humanitarian impulses function in this way to reduce some of the horror and evil of war, or at least to keep them to a minimum. They find expression in formal and informal attempts to regulate war with respect to such matters as the treatment of women, children, and other special classes of combatants and noncombatants; surprise attacks; the territory of nonparticipating countries; the use of particularly shocking weapons (e.g. poison gas); the inviolability of certain areas, such as hospitals; the handling of prisoners; the occupation of enemy territory, etc. (McDougal and Feliciano, 1961, pp. 71–91). Or, from another standpoint, a shotgun is believed to be more moral than an atomic bomb, provided of course the gentler weapon can attain the objective.

It is simple and perhaps justifiable to feel cynical toward much humanitarianism and likewise to smile indulgently at many codes of chivalry. Modern nations help less prosperous countries not for idealistic reasons alone, but to keep them as allies or to prevent them from joining the side of a potential enemy. The rules of war are obeyed to some degree not always to spare the enemy some brutality but to induce him to behave humanely toward one's own side or to avoid reprisals from him. Simultaneously, however, such humanitarian activity also merits approval on its own terms. For when the leaders of a nation justify policies and activities by invoking the apparently finer motives of mankind, at the very least they are giving additional currency to them. They may even be making them so conspicuous that eventually they will affect more of human behavior and of international relations than they do at present.

## Transcendental Values

The trio of justifications under this heading refer to values which, it is believed, are always present within people and hence may be said to transcend the usual limits of time and culture. They involve, in effect, the conditions which are the prerequisites to the satisfaction of numerous significant needs and drives. Naturally the precise meaning of the terms varies, but only in the way that cuisine fluctuates while always serving to reduce hunger.

5. *Peace:* 'Only thus can war be averted, only thus can there be peace.' Whatever the real causes of international conflict may be—and they undoubtedly range from the economic to the psychological—they are not likely to be referred to publicly or unabashedly by the leaders of modern nations. For angels in good standing are on the side of peace, not war. No one, except the hopelessly insane or perhaps professional warriors in the privacy of their own caste, justifies a policy because it leads to war or labels war a desirable value. Rather the policy provoking war or the act of war itself must somehow be considered a blow for peace in the future or a valiant defense in response to the hostility of some other nation or group. 'We love peace, really we do; they are the warmongers.' The justifications for war are so important that they receive short shrift here and instead are discussed and copiously illustrated in Chapter 12.

The ubiquity of war and aggression unquestionably reflects the basic nature of the drives that are ready to be evoked in their support. But that men usually are also ashamed of the ease with which the impulses can be tapped and of the havoc that is wrought after their arousal suggests equally forcefully the conflict within, perhaps, every man. At any rate, justifications for peace are more respectable than those for war.

6. *Freedom:* 'We must control our own lives.' The oft-repeated justification contains clear and unclear concepts. The "we" obviously refers to people of the nation, the land, the region with which the welfare is identified; it is a way of calling attention to members of the ingroup. "Control" may or may not be specific: when people are struggling for independence, that is, when they seek to replace one kind of power with another which they believe

springs from themselves, the meaning is quite apparent. But the exact scope of the control that is sought or that has been obtained may vary considerably, just as the functions and services of government do.

The "lives" to be freely controlled is a similarly ambiguous concept. In some senses, to be sure, people are never free: they inherit certain habits from their earliest training, and they most certainly find themselves in a web of human relationships in which they must assume some responsibility and from which consequently they cannot be liberated. They would probably reject complete freedom, furthermore, if all its details were operationally defined for them. A moment of free reflection usually produces the insight that freedom is not desirable beyond certain limits. Sometimes, for example, competent advice or commands from without are "better" in the long run than incompetent, free decisions from within. When freedom is employed as the justification, the conclusion must be, reference is probably being made to self-control or national control only in certain spheres of existence.

But in these spheres the conviction can be very strong. People believe that their own decisions or ones coming from respected leaders to whom they have delegated power are likely to be wiser and better than any imposed from without; and such decisions, they also are convinced, add to man's dignity and worth. Although the number of alternatives in front of them is always limited, they like and are eager to justify those they think to be available to them. A cross-section of Englishmen were asked, at a dreary point in World War II, June 1941, "What do you think we are fighting for?" "Freedom, liberty, and democracy" were named by 46 per cent; "to stop fascism, Hitlerism, Nazism, aggression" by 14 per cent; the equivalent of "it's them or us" by 8 per cent; "for a better world" or "for lasting peace" by 7 per cent; and only 7 per cent of the group had no opinion. Mere words? Probably not. Then the percentage among those mentioning the values of freedom and democracy who also believed that Britain was "going about war the right way" was significantly higher than among those subscribing to the value of survival: the figure for the former was 73 per cent, for the latter 54 per cent (Cantril and Strunk, 1951, p. 1077). Naturally, the slogans of freedom, etc., had been used and heard again and again, but their reappearance in response to a pollster's question must indicate that they had been internalized and hence were functioning as a labeling process with some psychological priority and as possible goads to action.

Similarly, the leaders in control of countries that have just achieved independence and many of their followers feel less restrained because they are impressed by the new symbols with which they surround themselves and, in the case of African and Asian countries, because in fact they are able to make more day-to-day decisions affecting their own lives. An outburst of energy and planning is observable as well as activity directed toward the changing of the country's internal economy and the establishment of relations with other nations. The experience of freedom, at least to men valuing some version of it, is indeed exhilarating.

Perhaps the demand for freedom and hence its utilization as a justification are cultural artifacts peculiar to the Western world and to other societies. For it can be argued that people ought to be satisfied when their basic drives are reduced and when they also secure satisfaction beyond or above the bread-alone level, provided that no other important impulses are prevented from reaching their goals. Clinically some men are happier when they obey than when they command, but has there ever been a nation of really contented slaves? Is basic contentment in fact unattainable unless people make some of their own critical choices? Even if men and women reject or have never known freedom for themselves they nevertheless are likely to favor it for their nation as a whole, that is, for those who make decisions for them vis-à-vis foreigners.

The freedom of the nation to act can be reduced to freedom for a specific few, but the freedom of that minority in turn may involve the welfare of almost everybody. When leaders demand "freedom of the seas," in effect they are defending the right of their merchant marine or their navy to navigate in certain waters. The journeys of these private ships, however, may affect the entire economy; domestic production, for example, often depends upon international trade.

7. *Security:* 'They are a threat to us and our way of life; we must protect ourselves.' This justification obviously refers to peo-

ple's needs and hence ought to be classified in the personificative category of the next chapter. It is included here, however, because its referent is the nation from a cultural standpoint. While a realistic analysis again suggests that it is people, in this instance at least a small clique, who seek the security, in fact it is also necessary to think in superindividual terms. The resources allegedly required for the sake of security, for example, at the moment benefit everyone only to a minor degree, but they can quite significantly affect the government's ability to wage war in the future.

In resorting to this justification, the presumption is that the way of life to be made secure is a way worth preserving. Ordinarily the presumption is not challenged. For only by radically criticizing the practices of another nation and by believing that other values are higher or better can the audacious thought be expressed that an outside culture should go, that it is not worth preserving. Even the missionary hesitates to change completely the culture of a heathen tribe; he would have them come to the Lord, his Lord, and alter some of their customs but, in all probability, not their entire way of life. The idea of completely exterminating European Jews, the "final solution" attempted by Hitler and the Nazis, did not arise completely de novo: for years Germans had had, as a result of many historical circumstances and of Nazi doctrine, a series of beliefs and assertions concerning the incompatibility of Jews and Gentiles and concerning an alleged Jewish menace.

Indeed, in general terms, if the presumption concerning the desirability of 'our' way of life 'for us' is accepted, then it is also alleged as an empirical fact that outsiders or foreigners are behaving, or are about to behave, in a manner which actually interferes with 'us.' On a biological level, intermarriage or miscegenation may be feared; 'The distinctive qualities of our race will disappear.' Culturally, reference can be made to any aspect of the traditional heritage, but it would seem that in the modern world language, religion, and general standard of living are most likely to be singled out as the practices that are in danger.

The action being justified may also involve military considerations of a direct or indirect sort: a frontier is fortified or occupied, or strategic materials are demanded. And then again a more general note is sounded: 'We cannot feel comfortable, we cannot sleep well at night, we cannot plan for the future unless we have what we want.' Obviously considerable personification occurs when this justification is invoked: just as the individual requires certain essentials if he is to go about his daily existence happily and healthily, so the nation has its own requirements. 'The nation will feel as exposed as the man who has lost the lot in front of his house if you take away that strip of land' or ' . . . as the man who has lost his fence if you don't protect home industry with a tariff.' The same argument, moreover, may be extended to one's friends and allies: 'You and we have this common enemy and what we are doing will therefore help you by threatening or weakening him.'

The cry for security reflects, in all probability, people's conservative tendency to retain what they know or have. What they know or have, however, must have been satisfactory, or otherwise they would be quite willing to abandon it. Under nationalism great emphasis is placed upon the connection between people's welfare and the nation-state, with the result that defending the motherland is considered both essential and ennobling.

Defensiveness of this kind and an accompanying, appropriate justification may be an essential ingredient of nationalism, or at least they are as universal as the existence of an outgroup. Such a group, it will be argued subsequently, is probably in fact always at hand or on the horizon. Hostility toward its members, like every form of prejudice, is easily engendered when they are made to appear to pose a threat, and they appear threatening by virtue of the fact that they evoke hostility. Round and up, round and up goes the Spiral.

## Legality and Semilegality

Every society has some kind of legal system to enforce and interpret its regulations. Consciously or not, people realize that social life would become impossible if the basic assumptions of that system were constantly violated. When identical or similar justifications are employed in connection with national policies and activities, consequently, approval is easily obtained.

8. *Sovereignty:* 'Our rights dare not be violated, our privileges cannot be tampered with.' In effect, it is maintained that each na-

tion is fated to possess its own legal system with which there should be no outside interference. The most sovereign right of a modern nation, the one which it is most loath to have abridged, is that of declaring war (Engelbrecht, 1937, pp. 311–12). This right carries with it certain corollary privileges. After war begins, a sovereign government believes it may fight and also treat or try to treat the enemy more or less as it wishes; it may offer or sue for peace terms; and it does not delegate such power to other nations, not even to its allies. At all times, moreover, sovereignty includes the obligation to protect nationals and often property abroad. In brief, any of the characteristic and cherished values of the nation are to be defended from foreign interference or encroachment; invoking sovereignty is usually a very serious matter.

The justification of sovereignty, consequently, contains a touch of almost every other absolutistic justification. That each nation has its own integrity and individuality which it must defend has doubtless received divine sanction; it is in accord with destiny; it is natural; it is a responsibility that the keepers of the faith must assume; and it is virtually a synonym for freedom on the national level. If every nation achieves and then shields its own sovereignty, it was popularly maintained at the end of World War I, all nations will be self-respecting and respected within the community of nations, and there will be peace. Sovereignty and security have especially close ties. According to a summary of one very typical and influential view of national sovereignty, that of Friedrich Meinecke, "unless the nation could defend its existence in the given environment by means of its own resources and organization, it could not call itself political" and hence such sovereignty becomes "the indispensable foundation for political nationhood" (Sterling, 1958, p. 41).

Actually sovereignty is a useful justification because its legal or extralegal meaning is vague. 'If you agree that each nation has a right to preserve its sovereignty, you must also give approval to whatever we consider our sovereign right.' The prevailing view in the West, moreover, would suggest that no one sovereignty is to be considered superior to another: a small nation or a large nation is equally entitled to defend its integrity. Some portion of the magical prerogative is in fact always associated with any nation.

In theory what is done within the national boundaries is of concern only to the nationals of the area and their leaders. In practice, however, limits to the exercise of sovereignty have been set. Some repercussions beyond the national frontiers, for example, may be considered undesirable. The persecution of a minority group within one nation is often believed to be not the private affair of that nation alone but to concern outsiders. Those outsiders, be it noted, usually try to justify their interest or interference on other than humanitarian grounds: 'They are our brothers,' 'They speak the same language as we,' 'Their skin color is like ours,' 'Our own security is threatened when any group on this continent is oppressed.' As the civilized movement to strengthen peace gains headway, more and more sane people challenge the state's assumption that it may grant its own citizens, in the perversely felicitous phrase of one observer (Rostow, 1961, p. 107), the "right to kill people of other nations" in war.

9. *Justice:* 'Right is on our side, justice will triumph.' Any appeal of course can be considered just or unjust in the sense of being reasonable, well-founded, correct, fair, or the reverse. Justice as a justification presumes the existence of some formal or informal code through which the merits and demerits of a policy or action can or could be determined by impartial judges who may or may not actually exist. The reference, consequently, may be to agreements, treaties, or laws which men can consult, or to general ethical principles or "natural" laws which exist only in their minds but which the just and the honest believe to be true or good. The appeal to justice, therefore, assumes that qualified judges, when faced with the facts in the situation, must unanimously agree that the policy or action is morally and ethically right or wrong.

The most explicitly formulated regulations which nations are supposed to follow in their relations with one another are embodied in international law. Such law may be not unambiguous and the decisions of the International Court of Justice in The Hague may not always be prompt or popular, but leaders in the West often seek to prove that they have been following its principles. "When national governments are themselves accused of violating international law," it has been observed, "they rarely deny the existence of that law, but generally seek to interpret it in their favour" (Cohen, 1954, p. 81).

In the absence of a code determining standards of justice, the belief in the righteousness of a cause can easily become an expression of self-righteousness. 'When they were our masters, they mistreated us; hence it is just for us to seek revenge now.' The eye-for-an-eye type of retributive justice is a form of justification that will be discussed again in the next chapter, under the blunt heading of revenge. Another slippery expression of justice is associated with what is often called disinterestedness or idealism: 'We lose rather than gain by expanding; it is our duty to expand, nevertheless; the purity of our aim proves its justness.' Any policy or action that apparently is against one's self-interest, in short, is praiseworthy. Whether idealists of this kind delude themselves or try thereby to delude others is an ethically relevant issue; but their so-called idealism is likely to strengthen their motivation.

Crusading, whether sincere or not, whether disinterested or not, involves some conception of justice. The infidel must be given the true faith, the downtrodden must be freed either because justice demands truth or freedom or because good men cannot live with their consciences until there is justice everywhere. At this point lily-white justice joins ranks with pure humanitarian responsibility, the combination of which produces a justification almost too good for this world.

10. *Contract:* 'We agreed to do it, we must do it.' In effect people must keep their promises, whether embodied in a formal contract or not; the expectations they now share with one another (Lasswell and Kaplan, 1950, pp. 21–22) must be valid guides to what they will later experience. Otherwise all relations between people, beginning on a simple, personal level and ending with the most complicated international organizations, are reduced to anarchy or chaos. In fact, when justice is invoked, a very specific document, agreement, or treaty may be mentioned, and then the policy or action in question is claimed to be only implementing what already has attained consent. The sacrosanct or acceptable status of the original source employed to establish legality is assumed. This theme of legality resulting from a contract with which

all parties have been previously acquainted is part of a doctrine closely associated with Western civilization: the judgments of those in power must not be arbitrary or impulsive, they should be predictable in advance so that people can accurately estimate whether they will be doing right or wrong, and they must stem from laws to which governments as well as individual people conform.

The efficaciousness of a contract depends upon the good will of the parties who sign it and also upon the sanctions that can be applied against those not fulfilling its terms. The "binding force" of international law in settling significant disputes between nations, and especially in avoiding war, has been weak in the absence of a "minimum consensus" among the participating countries and of adequate modes of enforcement (McDougal and Feliciano, 1961, pp. 275–78). And so again and again the enemy in modern times is accused of breaking a contract or making a treaty into a scrap of paper; the charge justifies one's own cause and discredits his.

11. *Majority:* 'We outnumber them; therefore we should have our way, not they.' This justification really harks back to one of the bases for law, the will of the majority. Obviously here is a value that has not always held the highest priority either historically or cross-culturally; and yet the majority cannot be utterly disregarded even by the most dictatorial leader who is dependent upon them in some ways for material assistance or spiritual support. *Vox populi, vox Dei*—the ancient proverb succinctly reflects the democratic faith and suggests why the theme appears so prominently in the theology of nationalism.

The majority has this almost sacred status in the West, in spite of at least three important circumstances under which the larger group does not triumph over the smaller or in which its triumph is likely to be deplored. First, children in a large family and all children in school, though they outnumber the adults, are submerged and not permitted to be the authorities or rulers in most situations. Then in all societies it is a minority and not a majority of the people who possess the skills and talents which are admired and which bring both prestige and power. Finally, according to another tradition, the rights of the minority must also be protected. In a free society they are permitted to express their view-

point and to try to win converts; in the Security Council of the
United Nations, they may cast a decisive veto. Perhaps, therefore,
in view of these exceptions, the foundation for using the majority
to justify policy or action must be not ethical cogency but the potential or actual ability to exercise power.

A minority is probably tolerated when it does not appear to
threaten the majority. Competition and combat are stimulating
and joyful when you are reasonably sure of winning or, if you lose,
when you will have enjoyed the battle and have not been too se-
verely punished. Insecure majorities prefer to crush the opposition. National leaders often demand conformity along cultural
lines in order to avoid being influenced by a smaller group: 'If you
would remain here, you must become like the rest of us.'

The operational definition of majority and minority may depend
upon the region in which the noses are counted. One group can be
in the majority in a small area but in the minority in a larger one
which contains another group or additional groups. The German-
speaking South Tyroleans, it has been shown in the previous chapter, are in the majority in the province where they have lived for
centuries, whereas they are in the minority within the region created by the Italian government after World War II. In this instance, the location of the area in which the majority should rule
has become the controversy, and not the validity of the justification.

12. *Superiority:* 'We are better than they, hence we do what
we wish.' At this point the discussion has fairly definitely shifted
from a legal to a quasi-legal level. Instead of determining who is
superior in numbers, some other criterion of superiority is invoked.
The tendency to make comparisons, invidious or not, is probably
another universal human tendency, stemming from the ever-
present fact of individual variability. Quickly children learn to
perceive disparities based upon age, and then they know that the
differences are correlated with variations in strength, prestige, and
demonstrated ability. In like manner adults assume roles com-
patible with the social structure of their society, indeed may com-
pete for a limited number of statuses; they are literally surrounded
by inequalities that are constantly evaluated. The attributes being
compared, on the basis of which superiority is asserted, can pertain

to every imaginable stimulus pattern or human quality. Eventually the differences, having been noted and evaluated, serve as the basis for justifying policies or actions. The existence of ethnocentrism in all or most societies suggests that people consider themselves superior in some respects when they contemplate outsiders, and such superiority justifies pride in oneself and the condemnation of others.

Explanations for the perceived differences and for superiority are usually offered either implicitly or explicitly. 'He is stronger than I, because he is older.' 'I have more cattle than he, because I am a better herder.' Among nations one belief is particularly prominent: 'We are superior because we were born that way, because of our race.' Like any genetic explanation, this one carries with it the atmosphere of finality associated with divine sanction, destiny, and nature. 'Our superiority is as undeniable as the color of our skins.'

A variant is the explanation of superiority through what is assumed to be national character. That character can be traced in large or small part to the race allegedly composing the nation, but it can also be ascribed almost completely to past and present deeds: 'We have always worked hard, and hence we are eminent.' In this sense national character becomes an environmental counterpart of race. Sometimes a much looser form of determinism is offered, that of luck or good fortune. 'We are leaders in the world just because our country is rich in natural resources'—even here a touch of inevitability is added—'and we were born with the wit to take advantage of those resources' or 'we have developed the will' to do so.

Shifts in beliefs concerning differences are accompanied by changes in evaluation and in the use of superiority as the basis for justification. 'I could treat him this way when he was a child, but he is no longer a child; hence I must now behave differently in relation to him.' During this century and especially since World War II, leaders and others in the West have altered their conceptualization of nonliterate peoples in Asia and Africa, at least on the surface. Imperialism and colonialism could formerly be justified for reasons other than moral, religious, and economic by pointing to the superiority of white people. In contrast, Asians and Africans were then considered biologically inferior or to possess the minds of children or apes. Today these people are acclaimed equal in fact or potentiality. Then the assumption is made—and vindicated —that they can manage their own countries with skill and beneficence. Obviously, as noted in the previous chapter, another Spiral is visible. The belief in the equality of mankind did not by itself cause the colonial powers to withdraw, but it facilitated or hastened their actions; and now that the withdrawal has occurred, Africans and Asians can further demonstrate their ability and thus reinforce the conviction of their equality.

The most blatant, brutal basis for superiority is that of power or force: 'We are stronger, nobody can stop us.' Whether the strength stems from numbers, skill, or chance, it is paraded as a justification in the sense that might makes right or can prevent wrong from being perpetrated. The deterrent of strength, like any other value, can be effective because usually past experiences have offered evidence of its importance. Any person can remember his earlier years when he was actually weaker than most other people and was continually reminded of the fact; he has seen instance after instance in which force triumphs; and both recorded and orally transmitted accounts provide illustrations of the same sad fact.

In the affairs of nations some forms of justification gradually atrophy, even disappear altogether. The notion of destiny, for example, seems to be slowly departing from the Western repertoire, in spite of being revived by the Nazis and receiving more than a lukewarm nod of approval from communist theorists who predict the ultimate and certain triumph of their social organization. The invocation of superiority, however, is likely to endure if only because, as already suggested, nationals always are able to find that their country is distinctive in innumerable respects. And the leap from a feeling of distinctiveness to one of superiority is very short.

At the same time there are indications that superiority in some respects is becoming a less impressive justification. Most religious creeds and many political philosophies favor sympathy with the underdog, with the less powerful, with the inferior. The genius of course is more intelligent, but the moron needs help. On a national level, an anthropological viewpoint has pervaded a large portion of Western thought: nations differ, it is clear, but each has its own way of life which need not be considered superior or inferior. The use of force in fact or the appeal to it as a justification, finally, is frequently condemned, unless the goal involves another value that secures approval. There is little virtue left in having a large army as such—rather it must be shown that the army deters an enemy. The ethical goal seems to be the legal dethronement of avoidable superiority.

## 11. Personificative Justifications

In an earlier chapter attention has been called to the tendency to use symbols to personify the nation. The country's name is especially convenient for that purpose. Here the value of such symbolization must again be strongly emphasized. For after a nation has been personified, it is said to merit the treatment accorded a real person. Just as an individual has feelings which, when injured, lead him to take appropriate action; just as he has a point of honor beyond which he permits no transgressor to go; just as he has ambitions which must be achieved and which lead to anger and neurosis under conditions of interference, so the nation allegedly also reacts under analogous circumstances. Nations must avenge insults or demand some retribution; to cast a slur on the honor of a country—either by speaking ill of it or of its ancient heroes—is to invite attack; and some expansion of territory seems as necessary to a nation as a new suit of clothes to a needy person. In fact personification on the national level is usually so complete that it probably affords as good a basis for predicting national policy as personality traits on the level of the specific individual. It is useful to know that a person can endure many or few insults for a long period of time before losing his temper and engaging in overtly aggressive behavior; similarly, it may be possible to discover or guess that a nation has a high or a low tolerance for what "it" believes to be insulting and hence a corresponding readiness or reluctance to declare war.

It would be foolhardy to assume that personification of the nation is only a figure of speech. Eventually, like all expressions that are frequently utilized, this one becomes concretely meaningful. The leaders of a nation do in fact demand an apology because the national honor has been insulted; they seek reparations when their sovereignty has been infringed upon. For they know that, unless they obtain the apology or the reparations, they will lose the support of their followers, who are also imbued with the same mode of thinking; consequently they in turn demand the appropriate actions per se and for symbolic reasons. In addition, their diplomats may feel psychically uncomfortable when they confer with the representatives of other nations or meet them socially if they have failed to bring home the symbols. 'You cannot bargain with me, you are not worthy of my confidence because you come from a country which has lost its self-respect.' That these sentiments have become deeply embedded in people is suggested by the strong emotions that can be evoked when one of their symbols is violated by an outsider; let someone deliberately trample upon the national flag under insulting circumstances and the battle may be on.

If these personificative values can arouse intense feelings and if they are related to reality, why does it appear that people in the West, perhaps everywhere, accord higher respect to absolutistic values? Perhaps, one hypothesis could be, the absolutistic ones are more readily reinforced over long periods of time since they function in so many different kinds of situations. Children in the schools of South Tyrol, for example, are taught that stealing is bad. Why is stealing bad? Because it is "against God's will." Then later they are provided with a legal explanation and still later with the principle that "stealing is something decent people just don't do." The appeal to religion is doubtless more intelligible to them at first than one to legal or ethical principles because they already possess a conception of religious morality. Eventually, since they remain devout, they are likely to be impressed with similar justifications learned early in life. Then, too, people everywhere do not always view their actions in broad perspective; it is easier to react to momentary pressures and offer the kind of broad, platitudinous justifications embodied in the absolutistic ones. And it is sometimes embarrassing to express homespun, personificative values.

### Family

Surely it is not necessary to belabor the point that the human family is important: every person experiences his own family; some form of the family "exists as a distinct and strongly functional group in every known society" (Murdock, 1949, p. 2). The amount of cultural variability in the human family, it must be added, is considerable. The nuclear family, consisting of a husband and wife together with their children, is expanded in many societies. There may be more than one spouse. Several nuclear families form an extended family: married adults with their children are attached to one set of parents. In addition, nonliterate societies often have larger kin groups, such as phratries, moieties, and clans, which affect markedly their social structure; and these groups in turn, through rules of exogamy or endogamy, influence the formation of the nuclear family.

Symbols from this critically important, omnipresent institution are used again and again to describe nations, and patriotism and nationalism are almost always extolled through the use of some sort of familial metaphor. In fact almost anyone who has ever written on patriotism and nationalism contends that much of their strength can be traced to such symbolism, which in turn exists because of a close connection in fact between nation and family. This observation has been made, for example, by people as diverse as a brilliant journalist (Delaisi, 1925, pp. 154–57), a semipopular and perspicacious writer (Ward, 1959, p. 15), an early student of nationalism from a psychological standpoint (Pillsbury, 1919, p. 6), a thinker very distinguished in many disciplines (McDougall, 1920, pp. 225–26), Freud himself (1922), and one of Freud's recklessly imaginative disciples (Róheim, 1959, pp. 14–15).

13. *Birthright:* 'We were born here, this is our home.' "Home" is generally used in the same very broad and ambiguous senses as the German word *Heimat:* it can mean literally the house in which one was born or raised or the general region in which the earlier years were passed. Almost always such a site is precious for two reasons. People associate it with their earliest and most profound satisfactions. And usually they expect to remain at or near home throughout their lives; hence significant goals, especially those involving compatriots, continue to be centered there. Even the geographically mobile people in modern nations are sentimentally attached to their birthplace and usually conceive of such "roots" as being desirable.

A reference to birthright, consequently, is likely to draw some sort of sympathy, since almost everyone has had similar experiences in his own home. Only a cruel villain will prevent another person under "normal" circumstances from remaining in, or visiting, his birthplace. Other considerations making the claim of birthright both likely and appealing lurk near the surface. The infant, it is clearly recognized, has not selected his place of birth and so, even though his parents may be considered interlopers, he himself in all innocence has some important claim to remain. Perfectly obvious, too, is the fact that people must live some place, and hence a birthplace appears to be the sensible site, or more sensible than most others.

This appeal to birthright occurs most frequently when a group of people is about to be dispossessed or dispersed and when they wish passionately to remain where they are. Their ancestors, they are told by those who would have them go, did not have the right to settle where they themselves now are. But then the sincere, tear-jerking reply can be: 'We are not responsible for the bad deeds of our ancestors; even if they did wrong by coming, we did not select our birthplace, we cannot be held responsible for the fact that we were born here.' Birthright includes another right, that of being raised in the culture of one's parents; and so the entire national group must remain where it is. Here is one of the psychological reasons why a long-standing dispute over the occupancy of a territory is so difficult to settle: the new generation genuinely does not wish to move out.

14. *Consanguinity:* 'We are a family, we must remain together, they are strangers.' Members of a family, any civilized person is supposed to agree, should not be separated; they must never be prevented from inhabiting their own homestead. The appeal to consanguinity may be technically a metaphor, but on a psychological level nationals may believe that they are reporting a fact or at least not merely personifying. Members of the nation are really considered to be a family, or they are viewed as though indeed this were the actual situation.

South Tyroleans have very strong feelings of consanguinity with one another. From time to time, in an effort to shed light on the structure of the sentiments, this writer has dug as deeply as he could into the conscious convictions of well-educated, highly verbal, and secure Tyrolean friends. He has said: "Stop misusing

words; you are not a large family, you are a nation." And the reply
which undoubtedly appears in a similar form wherever patriotism
is intense has been, in effect, the following:

> These people are my brothers, we cannot be separated, we
> must forever live together not anywhere but upon our land,
> our property, our home. If you are my brother or if you are
> my son, then clearly I am hurt when you are hurt and I shall
> always come to your rescue: you are intimately a part of me;
> I respond to any difficulty you experience in the way I do
> when the same thing happens to me or to a member of my im-
> mediate family; and I would be spiritually poorer without
> you. I am much less disturbed when harm comes to a stranger;
> in fact, I may not hear of his misfortune or, if I do, I feel only
> the kind of vague sympathy I have for any human being who
> suffers. Outsiders ask me why I am so profoundly and deeply
> concerned with the fate of my countrymen. After all, I am
> told, they are not really my relatives. And I reply by agreeing
> that strictly speaking, of course, they are not relatives, but
> this fact does not and cannot alter my feelings: they are like
> me, we live together as if we were a family, an injustice to
> one affects us all.

Men and women everywhere are accustomed in their daily lives
to perceive family relationships and to employ the terminology of
the family in common speech. The perception and the symbols can
be easily extended to include one's contemporaries who in fact do
have some of the attributes of real relatives. They usually share
the same culture and speak the same language. They often belong
to the same race. And they almost always inhabit the same land.

Likewise the older internationalist movements of Europe, such
as pan-Slavism and pan-Germanism, have often based their claims
for unity not on racial or biological arguments but on decidedly
cultural facts which point to some aspect of consanguinity. 'We
Slavs [Germans] speak the same language, hence all peoples outside our boundaries who use that language belong to our family
and consequently should be under our state.' Consanguinity, moreover, may be accompanied by other forms of justification. European irredentism has appealed not only to a need to unite a common family but also to military necessity and security. Before

World War I, the land in which the term originated sought to embrace all who were "Italian in speech and feeling"; but afterwards Yugoslavs and Austrians were included. Since consanguinity obviously could not be applied to such culturally different peoples, Italy claimed that "she was heir to the old Venetian empire and that the new frontiers were necessary for her military defence" (Hayes, 1937, p. 138).

A variant of the justification of consanguinity is one involving ethnicity: 'We belong to a race that is different from theirs.' Racial or ethnic ties are considered to be very similar to those associated with the family but, though they also involve "blood," the relationship is believed to be a little less intimate. On occasion, people who think they belong to the same race treat one another like distant cousins. Marriages in the West are not supposed to occur between members of the same family in the slightly extended nuclear sense, but they are usually encouraged among those within an ethnic group. For this reason ethnicity as a plea often seems not only more realistic but also less incestuous than consanguinity. It is not necessary to assert that the race forming the nation is superior to other races in order to employ this form of the justification, but the assertion is often implied and certainly strengthens the argument.

15. *Culture:* 'The customs and the institutions here are ours, not theirs.' People who share a common culture are similar to one another, it is thought, not quite so similar as members of the same family or race but sufficiently so to have deep and significant ties. The basis for cultural similarity may be considered purely in learning or historical terms, the way anthropologists do; but inherited, biological, or racial overtones may also be introduced. Some attributes of the culture and of the land subject to human control are perceived, as has been indicated previously, to be distinctive; their distinctiveness is attributed to, or associated with, the nation; and so a phenomenologically unified national culture emerges. 'Our tradition, or culture, must continue; it needs this particular change, however, to do so.'

When culture is the justification, the assumption is usually also made that a people's happiness and a nation's destiny depend upon having the components of that culture fit harmoniously together. Such an assertion is not out of line with modern anthropology, but it may be recklessly employed in the service of nationalism. 'We have our own culture; to retain our way of life, foreign intrusions must be halted; one little change can bring grave consequences.'

The cultural justification can be invoked to evict strangers or foreigners who do not share the same culture as one's contemporaries: 'Basically different people cannot live together.' Whatever the explanation of the differences, it is believed that at a given point in time they cannot be eliminated or mitigated. For their existence inevitably gives rise to incompatibility, and incompatibility brings evils: miscegenation, fusing of cultures, social conflicts. The incompatibility can be reduced and eliminated only through separation, which can mean segregation in social or ecological spheres or the outright expulsion of the outsiders from the land they share with the ingroup. In a few instances, people who feel keenly about incompatibility, like the Boers in South Africa at the start of the nineteenth century, themselves trek away.

It is perhaps easier to understand the psychological and social reasons for considering differences incompatible and disastrous than it is to appreciate exactly why the use of this justification is effective. For at least on the surface men seek both the customary and the novel. Basic accommodations occur automatically and without interruption, but diversity and the unexpected can often be alluring. Innovation results, of course, from many circumstances, including contact with outsiders. People from heterogeneous backgrounds stimulate one another, produce changes, prevent monotony and stagnation. These and other advantages from the excitement of change, however, are quickly discounted when the allegedly incompatible groups dwell in the same area, the psychologically meaningful unit of which is usually the neighborhood. Then it is thought desirable to have only people with similar cultures associate with one another under everyday conditions; the exotic is tolerated, if at all, on Sundays or holidays, or overseas.

## Temporal Factors

A distinctively human attribute is the ability to peer backwards and forwards while engaging in the activities of the moment. Nations always have a background that can be glorified as a set of traditions; and they presumably, too, will continue into the future. In this realm of time, therefore, a number of justifications can be found. Often the controversy is provoked by the question, 'Does this land belong to us?' The query is one not likely to be raised unless someone challenges the right to own or use the land; but, having been raised, it usually receives a prompt reply. For in the previous experience of each person someone has viewed skeptically his claim upon objects or human beings he has cherished, and he has then had to defend his preference or his practice.

16. *Primacy:* 'We were here first.' Such a claim by itself is supposed to be sacrosanct. Two sets of arguments are advanced. First, there is the implication that 'our getting here has been an achievement involving risk and sacrifice on our part'; continued possession is, consequently, a legitimate reward for past achievement. Then, 'since our arrival here, we have further established our claim by what we have accomplished.'

The "we" who arrived first, when primacy is featured as a justification, usually refers not to the present generation but to one's ancestors, who have important roles to perform in the present. Some connection between the past and the present can always be assumed, since everyone has had to be descended from groups of people now long dead. More specifically, ancestors are an extension of the self, or the self is descended from ancestors—whichever way the relation is phrased, the living person as their representative assumes that he himself has the same rights they once had. If they were the first to occupy the land and secured the privileges of possession, then he is justified in remaining where they were merely because of his relation to them.

The principle of primacy as the basis for justifying possession and retention is usually not questioned in a dispute, rather doubts are raised concerning the factual foundation for assuming that one's ancestors were the first or original settlers. Here the discipline of history may become a weapon. The historical record is often not easy to establish in the absence of written documents among non-literate peoples; and so in the present era the artifacts uncovered by archaeologists are put forward as evidence. Folklore and mythology may not provide data in the scholarly or scientific sense, but in suggesting how the land originally came to be inhabited by the ancestors of the present inhabitants they buttress emotionally the conviction that those ancestors were there first.

The claim of primacy may have to be defended against counter-claims. 'All right, you were here first, but now we should have a turn.' Such a simple maneuver may be successful among children in a playground where some other notion of equity prevails, but it runs counter to many highly reinforced preferences among adults. 'Why should I turn over my property to less fortunate neighbors?' 'Of course those people are poorer, but why should our country give them a piece of our land?' Descent leads to possession, and possession has a high priority.

17. *Duration:* 'We have been doing this for a long time and therefore expect to continue.' Or else, when land is in dispute, those who were not the original inhabitants maintain that 'we have been here longer than they.' The justification of duration derives its prestige from two sources: people's inevitable experience and the value of tradition to society. Long established patterns are usually known to be, if not exactly satisfying, at least comfortable and requiring no strain or risk. Also age-grading must be discovered at an early age: older people have higher status, younger ones acquire such status by growing older—you have to wait a while before you are respected. Socially, moreover, modes of acting and thinking that have endured over generations are held in high esteem: the fact of their longevity is assumed to reflect their soundness or goodness. Such modes have been originated, moreover, by ancestors who, like parents, allegedly were 'greater and wiser than we,' at least in some respects.

Since the plea of duration tends to be accompanied by an overtone of sanctity, here is still another reason why patriots and nationalists are prone to point up the antiquity of their traditions. The attempt of some modern nations, such as Greece and Wales, to revive the classical form of a language or a fading language suggests an interest in establishing respectability and distinctiveness with respect to lineage. In a time of crisis, nationals may seek outside friends by stressing their antiquity. During World War II, for example, the Basque Government in Exile appealed for American support with the following arguments:

> But some of you may ask: Why do the Basque people wish autonomy? Euzkadi (the name of our country in our own lan-

guage) is the country of the Basques with as much right to exist independently as a nation as Poland or Ireland. The Basques are a very ancient people, whose origin is still shrouded in mystery, but who have kept alive for centuries their own national personality, their language, laws, and customs and, except for brief periods in the history of Europe, even their independence. They have always fought for their political liberty and their democratic conception of life whenever it has been menaced. In fact, the Basques are admittedly one of the oldest and healthiest democracies on earth, and their forms of freedom have developed, not through revolution, but by a natural evolution of the Basque temperament [Anonymous, 1943, p. 3].

18. *Status quo:* 'So it is and that's that.' A touch of the *fait accompli* is usually detectable when the present arrangement is justified simply because it is the one now in existence: 'We are here, we are not going to move, nobody can force us to do so, we have a right to what we have.' Probably a conviction stemming from naturalistic ethics explicitly or implicitly sustains such thinking: whatever is, is right, for otherwise the present would not have come to pass the way it has. The plea of status quo, like that of duration, moreover, is based upon elements in the past; if a custom has functioned well or sufficiently well, why risk the unknown components a change in the future is likely to add? The principle of arguing from precedent, *stare decisis,* which plays such an important role in the legal thinking of some countries in the West, reflects in part confidence in the past as a guide to the present and future. People, in a glib but valid summary, become accustomed to the customary. Over generations, moreover, what has existed for a long time is hallowed by tradition and hence, it is believed, should not be disturbed.

The suspicion must be expressed, nevertheless, that justification via the status quo can often be far from satisfying. Some other chord must be sounded before people feel righteous. Possession is said to be nine-tenths of the law—presumably the remaining tenth produces disquietude which can be dispelled only by filing an additional claim.

19. *Posterity:* 'We must do this—for the sake of our children' or

'to keep our culture alive.' The orientation toward the future is clear: 'We must keep the torch lit, our descendants must survive and thrive.' Presumptive evidence suggests, more usually than not, that the appeal stems from genuine motives. For people seldom wish to die, and they are certain only of achieving one kind of immortality—that of having their children become heir to some of their accomplishments and prerogatives. Everywhere, consequently, formal provision is made to bequeath property and titles to succeeding generations. Just as the present generation links itself to ancestors in the past and consequently may invoke the justifications of primacy and duration, so it contemplates the future as a continuation of the self through sons and daughters. By simple extension the society, too, survives because the young learn its culture during socialization. The plea of posterity affects deeply the very people who use it. Some of its urgent quality rubs off upon the outsiders to whom it is addressed, since they recognize within themselves the same urge to stay alive vicariously. Again, however, the justification seems compelling only after a connection is established between a particular policy or action on the one hand and posterity on the other.

At a tribal meeting during World War II, a member of the Navaho nation opposed the Federal government's plea to give up the uneconomic practice of raising sheep in favor of industries more suitably adapted to their resources:

> Give us our sheep, give us our mutton, let us have our herds as our fathers and our grandfathers had. If you take away our sheep, you take away our food, and we have nothing. What then will become of our children? What will we say to our young men who have gone to war? What will they eat and how will they come back to us? They are fighting now for our homes and our land, and these things will be useless if you take away our sheep. This is not right. You must let us keep our sheep or we die [Kluckhohn and Leighton, 1946, p. 41].

*Human Justifications*

At this point personification reaches its peak: the nation is thought to have the same human needs as people. The needs in both instances are considered legitimate. Interference with them, consequently, is deplored. The suggestion of inevitability, associated with the absolutistic justification of human nature, may or may not be added.

20. *Need:* 'We must have this foreign market if our industry is to prosper.' A need to retain a custom and especially a territory may be vaguely expressed, and it can stem from a large variety of motives involving equally diverse military, economic, political, and social objectives. At the top of the hierarchy of motives is the absolutistic need to continue to live: injury and death are to be avoided, at least for members of one's own nation. Any policy or action promoting life, consequently, wins approval, except perhaps one benefiting the enemy during war.

A recurrently expressed need of modern nations has been for land: 'Our resources are limited, our population is too big, we need more space.' This geometric appeal is intended to be understood literally; it would justify expansion in terms of very basic drives. Obviously all objects and living organisms occupy some position in space. The latter, moreover, require some indefinite quantity of land in order to survive satisfactorily. Overcrowding means, first, inconvenience and, eventually, disaster.

The need for a quantity of land, consequently, if only for eating and sleeping, must be acknowledged by everybody. And land in most societies is scarce, or is considered scarce, so that, as previously indicated, the use and the inheritance of property is always regulated. People who are convinced that they do not possess either the minimum or the optimum quantity of land are likely to search for more, even when this means dispossessing a distinguishable outgroup heretofore occupying it. 'That space belongs to us, we need it.'

Much further down in the hierarchy than land are needs which, though less basic and insistent, have important implications for people and hence are highly relevant to policy and action. "National honor," "national pride," and other well-worn symbols dare not be injured, though they are far removed from the goals of shelter and protection. On suitable occasions the need is phrased in terms of one or more of the ten values with which nationals judge the land, its people, and their culture (as described in Chapter 6).

Even subtler, as has often been noted (e.g. Kohn, 1962, p. 57), is an article of faith in the Western world during the last hundred years: 'People are able to improve their lot, and they must be encouraged to do so.' Misery or underdevelopment is no longer accepted as a divine and unalterable mandate. Nations not possessing whatever it is they would like to possess, therefore, can justify their present deeds as forms of self-improvement.

Imperialistic policies and actions were once vindicated by references to the unfulfilled needs of the colonizing powers. 'Our population is so dense, we need more land for ourselves.' 'Our industry will perish unless it can be assured of a steady supply of raw materials' or 'unless it has foreign markets in which it can profitably dispose of its surplus goods.' Implied again is an appeal to human nature: 'We must do this, we are powerless to curb ourselves.' Or 'unless we do this, we shall perish, the way people perish who are deprived of food and drink for too long a period of time.'

The justification via need is a tempting target for scholars and counterpropagandists who can assemble facts to puncture either the need itself or its connection with a policy or action. Claims for colonies are discredited by showing that they do not solve the very problems that are supposed to have given rise to the need to expand. Between the two World Wars, for example, many German nationalists clamored for the return of the four African colonies that Germany lost in 1920, in spite of the facts that before World War I (a) only 20,000 Europeans had settled in those areas, (b) more Germans had actually been living in Paris than in Africa, and (c) German imports from, and exports to, Africa in the very last year before the outbreak of war constituted only one-half of one per cent of her total import-export trade (Morgenthau, 1948, p. 66). When examining the exposé of a justification, two psychological points must not be overlooked. First, the justification, regardless of its truth or falsity, gives a lift to national propaganda; cynically or not, the plea is made because people respond favorably to it. Then the justification is effective because it satisfies some unsatisfied needs within the audience. In Germany during the twenties and thirties there was real economic stress, and the idea of colonies looked subjectively inviting.

A note of desperation often is sounded in connection with unfulfilled needs: 'No alternative is possible, we must, we must, we must.' The appeal is neither to natural conditions nor to human nature—rather the claim is made that life has simply worked out in a particular way, no other possibility has come to be conceivable. 'We must remain where we are, we have no other place to go.' 'We must migrate elsewhere, that is the only place left open to us.' 'They are interfering with our internal affairs, we must stop them.' Usually, in addition, reasons are supplied for the desperate state. 'Here is our home, we would not be welcome elsewhere.' 'Only here [or there] can we feel secure or happy.' Desperation is expressed because logically possible alternatives do not appear to provide adequate opportunity to achieve important goals.

One well-publicized need requires special mention: 'We would perish if we left our country, so great would our homesickness be.' Obviously the phrase varies, as does that for every other justification, but the sentiment is clear: the land and its people are considered so important that life outside the nation must be intolerable. The craving to return home from exile or from travel is recognized linguistically as being potentially deep within people. In English, reference is made to "homesickness" as though this were a special form of disease like measles; in German the word *Heimweh* suggests the kind of hurt which comes from the lasceration of the skin, and one of the words for "misery" (*Elend*) is derived from "foreign country" (*Ausland*). Just as no one would condemn a people for contracting a fatal illness, so presumably help must be given them to avoid the plague of homesickness. On the positive side, moreover, nationals are thought to possess the legitimate right to live in their surroundings; 'It is inhuman to drive them out.' Great is the attachment of the patriot to his land and its people. In fact, the voluntary exile or expatriot is an unusual person: he is willing and able to reject his homeland for some other kind of life, since he finds elsewhere, it must be presumed, sufficient compensation. More usual is the banal statement of thanksgiving traditionally uttered—or at least thought—by the traveler who has enjoyed the exotic offerings of other lands: "There's no place like home." And, as the dissection of distinctiveness in a previous chapter has shown, the man, though unoriginal, is right—at least for himself.

'We like it here, we want to remain, we don't want to go.' Such an unabashed claim is not linked to a specific need; it seems connected with a general combination of needs usually suggested by some phrase such as "way of life." The hedonistic plea is not likely to be openly and frankly expressed at international gatherings of modern diplomats. Or else, if expressed, it is accompanied by justifications concerned with references to other needs, to space, to duration, or to posterity. Except in private, some concealment of underlying hedonism appears necessary since apparently the bald plea does not sound respectable: deeper or subtler values than happiness or joy are supposed to be invoked to justify political action. A hedonistic cry may be branded as cynical or selfish, but it can often come closer to the real human motives behind much of nationalism than other pleas possessing very elaborate façades. 'We do this because we jolly well want to do it, and thus we attain the kind of joy we associate with the good life.' Crude and shocking yes, but one nonpuritanical, sentence cannot be restrained: maybe the attainment of a selfish goal can also have altruistic consequences!

21. *Achievement:* 'We have developed this area, we deserve to own it.' According to this plea, achievements satisfying human needs should benefit the individuals responsible for them. It matters not, as indicated in connection with primacy, whether those invoking the justification or their ancestors have been the actual agents producing the gains; the present generation lays claim to them. What has been accomplished, moreover, is presumed to embody approved values. Natural resources have been exploited; disease has been controlled; roads and schools have been constructed; art has flourished—these deeds in the past establish people's right to the land they now occupy. Colonial powers have been prone to stress their own accomplishments among the peoples they rule whenever their domination is challenged. 'We have converted this wilderness into a civilization, why should we leave?' Then both capitalists and communists are convinced that capital investments, either when permitted, encouraged, or forced upon a country, carry with them the right to receive certain returns and also to protect the investments. Confiscation of the plant or the business of foreign investors, consequently, usually produces howls of anger.

The value of efficiency can also creep into this justification. People praise themselves or others for taking full advantage of the opportunities offered by the environment: they are skillfully extracting the minerals; they are conscientiously cultivating the land; they are, in brief, acting in the best interests of themselves and, by implication, of others. This belief can usually be accompanied by an array of facts, for efficiency is a concept to be tested by performance or by production. Other forms of assessment can be put forward: people ascribe to themselves virtues or talents which enable them, they say, to exploit the land and to organize and operate a good society. They may likewise think that they achieve intangible values efficiently. When they proclaim themselves or their institutions to be important, they may be only thinly disguising their own very egocentric goals. Or importance per se can be defended most variously. 'Any sane person can see that we have an important contribution to make.' Or 'what we contribute may not seem important to you, but let it not be forgotten that diversity itself is desirable; hence ours is a contribution which under all circumstances must continue.'

22. *Public opinion:* 'Not just we, but very influential people want us to do this'; 'What will they think of us if we do it?' These other people are considered important for a variety of reasons: they are allies, they have prestige in the group to which the justification is offered, or they are people whose favor for any reason is sought or cannot be avoided. The opinion of such outsiders, in a word, is respected. 'Visitors from that country bring us joy when they say that they like the way we serve cheese' or 'the way we administer justice in police courts.' People show concern for what other people think of them; hence a favorable public opinion is one of the national needs which can be mentioned to justify a policy or activity.

Policies ostensibly pursued only for the glory of the state may in fact be geared to outside public opinion. Often, though, the real communicator is only a small clique at home which seeks to affect not all the inhabitants of the opposing nation but an equally small group therein. Members of the foreign office may literally be trying to raise their own status in the estimation of another foreign office so that they themselves will be accorded more respect during diplomatic conferences. But the policy must be clothed in terms appearing to include almost everyone. In modern nations, moreover, the communications embodying a policy can reach the mass media which then in turn create the impression that all people and not just the cliques are involved in the maneuvering. On the other hand, the concept of world opinion is not an empty symbol since either unilaterally or through various international organizations, including the United Nations, sanctions may be applied against those nations whose leaders violate what are considered to be civilized, honorable, or respectable principles.

23. *Revenge:* 'We are doing this because they started it.' Primacy, a justification previously discussed, is claimed for desirable values but disclaimed for undesirable ones; and so the morally wrong activity of an opponent permits or demands similar activity for the sake of self-defense or justice. In each instance factual and ethical questions must be raised concerning whether the foe was actually the first to engage in the specified activity and whether the reason for the second party's countermeasures has been validly depicted. 'They have a tariff against our goods, now we must have one against theirs.' Did they in fact begin the tariff war? If they did, was that tariff a reaction to an earlier measure of another kind that had been adopted by the side now justifying its counter-tariff? Had the second party been searching for an excuse to enact its tariff?

Revenge occurs, in brief, in connection with actions not otherwise to be tolerated and consequently, however psychologically sweet, is very rarely admitted to be the primary objective. Many horrors of war, including declarations of war, are justified by asserting that the enemy has been the initiator. In fact, a quasi-legal argument states that "unlawful violence gives a right to respond in self-defense with counterviolence" (McDougal and Feliciano, 1961, p. 37). Thus "self-defense" is the value stressed, not the damage done to the enemy. Or else some other value is invoked: 'If we begin torturing their prisoners, then maybe they will stop torturing ours.'

In the sphere of feelings, where factual evidence is difficult to gather and where the projection of one's own impulses cannot easily be detected, revenge frequently is admitted but again in the company of other justifications. 'They hate us and therefore we must protect ourselves.' Or counterhatred is uttered with a note of sadness: 'Unfortunately we must hate them because they hate us.' In many societies, especially in the West, hatred is not permissible on religious, moral, aesthetic, and social grounds; its manifestation against the ingroup obviously cannot be tolerated; and so, too, its expression against an outgroup must be carefully regulated, lest it spill over or be displaced upon the ingroup. But if an outgroup is held responsible for the hatred in the first place, then counter-hatred can be viewed as another form of self-defense—'deplorable, yes, yet what else can we be expected to do under the circumstances?'

Counterhatred of this kind is often involved in conflict extending over generations. 'We must avenge the wrongs perpetrated upon our ancestors.' 'They are seeking revenge upon us because our ancestors, they think, once wronged their ancestors.' Obviously, although people do not personally experience the pain inflicted upon a dead ancestor, they can be mightily disturbed when the experience is recalled vicariously or partially re-enacted in the present.

'We must do this, otherwise they will.' Here the revenge is anticipatory: it is asserted that the intentions of the opponent must be frustrated before he has a chance to act. If those intentions had been executed, revenge would have been justified. Such reasoning can be made to appear valid when it is accompanied by evidence concerning the intentions: 'We know they planned to do it, we intercepted a message showing just that.'

Finally, semantic and psychological nuances are sometimes deliberately neglected and the ancient hymn of an "eye for an eye" is trumpeted unabashedly. 'They have been cruel, they have committed a crime, they deserve to be punished.' Or nations whose leaders have caused them flagrantly to transgress international law or the rules of warfare are considered outside the pale and hence subject to sanctions, nonrecognition, or attack.

## 12. War and Peace Aims

Toward the end of the eighteenth century an Italian jurist attempted to improve Machiavelli's reputation by publishing a collection of maxims derived from his writings. In that publication fifty of the maxims fall under the heading of "peace and war." Many of them, as might be expected, are obnoxiously platitudinous; for example, the first states that "a good and wise prince should love peace and avoid war." The ninth and tenth, however, are noteworthy:

> That war is just which is necessary.
> The people will complain of a war made without reason [Detmold, 1891, p. 439].

The first bit of wisdom raises the question of a just war, the second suggests that psychologically a war must appear either just or reasonable if people's cooperation is to be obtained. The present chapter considers both questions.

Indeed a most difficult task faced by any government is to command its citizens to go to war. For then men are called upon to risk their lives, and ordinarily death and the possibility of dying are avoided by all save the most neurotic, the very desperate, and the hopelessly ill and aged. In addition, the killing of other people which war requires is also an activity most normal human beings prefer to shun.

But there have always been wars; in fact prolonged periods of peace, especially in the West, are unusual. Obviously, therefore, men are also willing to fight, or at least can be induced to do so. No attempt here will be made to cover the well-covered topic of why they do fight. Clearly some of their motivation has little to do with patriotism or nationalism: heavy sanctions are applied against those recruits failing to join the ranks and against those in the armed services refusing to obey. Professional warriors or, in a traditional nation, almost all males are trained to expect to perform the duty of fighting for their nation, and no alternative seems possible. Sadism, masochism, or sheer fury are respectable motives in some societies, idiosyncratic ones in others. Certainly, too, most men—and women—are willing to seize the opportunity offered by warfare to displace and project their own aggressive impulses (Durbin and Bowlby, 1939; May, 1943). Only one point, however, is of interest here: regardless of the underlying economic, political, and psychological background of war, men must be offered reasons to fight.

Evidence on this last point comes from American soldiers. About three-quarters of a group which had fought against Franco in Spain were convinced later that "belief in war aims" helped them overcome fear in battle, and close to one hundred per cent subscribed to the view that "discussing the war aims and their importance in the personal lives of the men makes better soldiers" (Dollard, 1943, pp. 54–57). Two psychiatrists reported during World War II that "not all Americans have been able to develop a range of identification large enough to include the nation and thus to develop strong feelings of loyalty and obligation." Such men resented the sacrifices they had to make; they complained constantly; when they became fliers, they failed to develop "adequate combat personalities" and they also affected adversely the morale of their unit (Grinker and Spiegel, 1945, pp. 40–41). In the American army during the same period "conviction about the war" —as measured by responses to questions concerning whether the war was "worth fighting" and whether the fighting should stop if the Germans and Japanese were to agree to "give up all the countries they have taken over"—was found to be "associated with a favorable motivational picture," even though "any talk of a flag-waving variety" was strongly taboo (Stouffer et al., 1949, pp. 150–56). The really ardent warriors of the present day appear to belong to two groups: guerillas who are convinced that their country is being invaded or ruined by outsiders or by ingroups with an alien philosophy; and rebels who believe that they will be able to lead appreciably better lives than they now do if they violently over-throw a society from which they have never obtained many sweets.

This chapter is concerned in large part with statements of war aims that represent the justifications for waging war. Such justifications are not mere façades for underlying greed or pathology. They are needed, the discussion above suggests, to provide men, or at least the conscious part of them, with a rationale for submitting to the dangers and the horror and the glory which actual fighting brings. In fact, so great is the problem of maintaining the morale of soldiers in a modern army whose country is not actually being invaded that it is tempting to wonder whether the convictions of nationalism have been either superseded by convictions concerning internationalism or simply weakened by the cynicism which comes from frequent wars and from the puncturing of old values.

Modern wars must also be justified because their successful prosecution depends not only on the fighting forces but also upon virtually the entire population. The morale of the civilian population must be kept high for a number of reasons. All except professional soldiers are recruited from civilian life. There is constant communication between members of military groups and their families and friends through the mail or during leaves. The complicated machinery and weapons of war come almost entirely from civilian factories. The enemy, moreover, includes ordinary men and women among his targets: he bombs industrial as well as nonindustrial sections of towns and cities; he directs his psychological warfare to everybody. Total war, in brief, means that everyone must be interested in winning and hence in the reasons that are advanced for the struggle.

Justifications for war, like most other justifications with international implications, moreover, are served to other audiences besides the home side. They seek to strengthen the morale and the will-to-fight of allies and friendly nations. They may attract neutral countries or at least prevent them from joining the enemy. And in some instances they may help demoralize the enemy. For these reasons, war aims constitute one of the most important weapons in the arsenal of all branches of psychological warfare.

Finally, war aims affect a nation's own policy and actions. Obviously there is some relation between the publicly expressed or the privately circulated aims of a country and the peace terms it offers a conquered enemy. Then the conditions under which the leaders of a country believe that war is justified can have a profound effect upon the readiness with which they are morally and politically willing to declare war; thus the American belief that war is justified only in self-defense or as a form of collective defense against an armed attack has been shown to influence the kind of war in which this country is willing to engage as well as its general foreign policy and its armament program (Tucker, 1960, pp. 11, 20, 26, 68, and 114).

In view of the importance of the publicly stated and promulgated war aims, it is surprising to find, after quite a diligent search, no systematic treatment of this subject. Historians and students of war very naturally turn their attention to the causes of war. By implication, the war aims of a nation must be related to its reasons for getting embroiled, but the relationship is imperfect on at least two counts. First, the reasons may come from a scholar's analysis and may not be the ones that preoccupied the nation's leaders and their followers during the conflict. Secondly, although such reasons may in fact have induced leaders to formulate a set of war aims, they may not have been featured in public statements. In either case, some of the arguments justifying the war for the benefit of large domestic and overseas audiences are usually far removed from its real or imagined causes.

The two students of international law being cited frequently in this book, for example, deliberately raise the question of war aims, which they rephrase as "the objectives of coercion":

> The objectives of states participating in this process of coercion may, like those of any actor in any system of action, be most broadly characterized in terms of a maximization postulate: any particular participant acts to maximize certain or all of its values in relation to the other participants in the world arena. Such objectives embrace, in most general statement, all the characteristic value demands of nation-states, including the demand to protect and expand their own bases of power and other values and to weaken or disintegrate the bases and values of those defined as enemies or potential enemies.

On another level of abstraction, the objectives of any participant may be generalized as a demand that the enemy accept certain terms with respect to specified policies and accordingly alter its previous behavior—for instance, withdrawal or abstention from a hostile policy or projected policy, affirmative adoption of some policy demanded by the acting participant [McDougal and Feliciano, 1961, pp. 14–15].

The above summary is admittedly abstract, as it should be when declarations of war are analyzed from a legal standpoint; but it is far removed in most instances from the declaration of aims which reaches people. The same authors also indicate types of specific objectives:

> More concretely, the spectrum of particular demands asserted through coercion may range from such limited ones as the payment of a debt owed by the target state or its nationals or the temporary passage of troops through its territory, through the relinquishment of the target state's control over a specific portion of its territory or acceptance of certain limitations on its freedom of decision-making, to the complete absorption of the target state, the annihilation of its people, and the establishment of a universal empire [ibid., pp. 16–17].

Objectives such as the above may be proudly admitted and claimed, but then they have to be justified or they must automatically carry along with them their own justification if they are to win support.

Anyone who addresses himself comprehensively to the subject of war must become aware of the problem of justification. Here, for example, are three quotations from an attack on war by one of the most competent of the pacifists who wrote during the 1930s:

> In all the welter of claims and counter-claims, of accusation and justification, the economic basis of modern war is becoming clearer and clearer. Faced with the necessity of aligning their populations on their side and of creating enthusiastic support for themselves, the governments advance all manner of idealistic defenses of war, such as "upholding national honor" or "protecting national rights." . . .
>
> The possessor of colonies is supposed to occupy a position

of superiority in the world and the so-called "have-not" nations insist that they too must have colonies. . . .

   If many of the traditionally acceptable excuses for going
to war have lost their appeal, unfortunately at least one
other has arisen—the fierce hatred of Fascism on the one
hand and Communism on the other [Engelbrecht, 1937, pp.
237–38, 249, 315].

The writer believed that the economic objectives of war had to be
clothed in fine phrases; that colonies were claimed on the basis of
superiority; and that people then found war acceptable if it
were directed against the two forms of totalitarianism he mentioned. These contentions may have been true enough, but they
do not provide systematic insight into the ways in which wars in
general can be justified.

   What has now been asserted concerning the significance of
war aims applies equally well to policies and activities in behalf
of peace. Peace itself requires no justification; in fact in the list
presented during the last two chapters it itself is a justification, the
fifth among the absolutistic justifications or the first among the
transcendental values. But procedures for attaining peace must be
proposed and then implicitly or explicitly justified if the threat of
war is to be reduced or eliminated. For this reason, the present
chapter also contains documents on the theme of peace.

   What kinds of documents should be employed to analyze justifications for war and peace? In fact, any realistic description of
warfare or of yearning for peace offers a relevant illustration. The
reports of anthropologists, for example, often contain very adequate data on war aims. A chief of the Comanches, previously
cited many chapters ago, justified the deeds of his warriors by invoking the claim of protective revenge and, to a minor degree, that
of security and need:

   My people have never first drawn a bow or fired a gun against
   the whites. There has been trouble on the line between us,
   and my young men have danced the war dance. But it was
   not begun by us. It was you who sent out the first soldier and
   we who sent out the second. Two years ago, I came upon this
   road, following the buffalo, that my wives and children might

have their cheeks plump and their bodies warm. But the soldiers fired on us. . . . So it was in Texas. They made sorrow come in our camps, and we went out like the buffalo bulls when the cows are attacked. When we found them, we killed them, and their scalps hang in our lodges [Wallace and Hoebel, 1952, pp. 282–83].

It is impossible, therefore, to try to offer a comprehensive survey of war aims. Instead attention is concentrated first upon selected, not necessarily typical, summaries and then upon documents which have played an important role in international affairs since the end of World War I. The exercise is supposed to serve three purposes. First, the reader will be plunged into concrete materials. Exact quotations are employed to try to convey without distortion the precise flavor of the values invoked in behalf of war or peace. Then, the twenty-three justifications described in the last two chapters are informally illustrated. Finally, the adequacy of the list to cope with these materials can be informally tested. No generalizations are made to emerge from this empirical survey because none seem possible beyond those implicit within the classificatory scheme being employed and a few summarizing sentences.

It is not always easy to decide in connection with a statement the precise justification being invoked by its author; admittedly the reliability of the twenty-three categories has not been determined in this preliminary survey. In addition, a problem of presentation arises. It would be annoying to interrupt the summaries and the quotations in order to point out the justification which, in the best but more or less subjective opinion of the present writer, appears to be the one that is being mentioned. The most unobtrusive method would be to enclose the name of the justification in parentheses at the appropriate spot. But such a device would interfere with the smooth flow of the declaration. And so a compromise has been adopted: the number of the justification is placed in parentheses: the reader's eye can skip hastily over a number, or it can halt if he wishes. A convenient list of the justifications follows herewith—roman numerals are employed since, it is hoped, they create less confusion when embodied in the quotations:

I. Divine sanction
II. Destiny
III. Nature
IV. Humanistic responsibility
V. Peace
VI. Freedom
VII. Security
VIII. Sovereignty
IX. Justice
X. Contract
XI. Majority
XII. Superiority
XIII. Birthright
XIV. Consanguinity
XV. Culture
XVI. Primacy
XVII. Duration
XVIII. Status quo
XIX. Posterity
XX. Need
XXI. Achievement
XXII. Public opinion
XXIII. Revenge

*The Causes of Nationalistic Wars*

A few pages back it was pointed out that the scholar's analysis of the causes of war has no one-to-one relation with the justifications employed to enlist people's cooperation. The strong probability of some relationship, however, demands that more than perfunctory consideration be given to the problem of causes. There is no easy and certain way, of course, to ascertain those causes. Deliberately one source is tapped—a very eminent one (Wright, 1942). In what is probably the most definitive study of war that has emerged in the twentieth century, the "wars arising from nationalism" are thus characterized:

a. *Self-determination and irredentism.* Wars have arisen from demands of "nationalities" to be organized in nation-

states [VI, VIII]. . . . So also existing states have fought to in-
corporate irredentas, or foreign areas deemed to have their
nationality [XIV, XV]. . . .

b. *Solidarity and prestige.* Wars have arisen because of
the utilization by governments of military preparedness [XII],
fear of invasion [VII], pride in national prestige [XXI], and
expansionism [XX] as instruments of national solidarity. . . .
Balance-of-power wars have often originated from an exalta-
tion of national honor [XX], prestige [XXII], and power [XII]
above all values. . . .

c. *Self-sufficiency and isolation.* Wars have arisen because
of the tendency of states seriously afflicted by nationalism to
seek security from attack [VII], stability of the economic life
[XX], and development of a distinctive character by economic isolation and self-sufficiency [XII, XV]. . . .

d. *Mission and expansion.* Wars have also arisen because
of the tendency of a people affected by nationalism . . . to acquire an attitude of superiority to some or all other peoples
[XII], to seek to extend its cultural characteristics throughout
the world [IV], and to ignore the claims of other states and of
the world-community [XXII] [Wright, 1942, pp. 987–91].

It appears as if these causes of war can be related to both absolutistic and personificative justifications. Among the absolutistic,
determinism is mentioned with relation to humanistic responsibility; stress is placed upon the transcendental values of freedom
and security; and from a legal standpoint sovereignty and superiority are invoked. Among the personificative justifications, consanguinity and culture appear though not birthright; needs and
public opinion are featured; but temporal factors as well as all aspects of revenge seem altogether neglected.

### The Just War

From the very beginning of historical records it appears that
men, especially those with juristic leanings, have been attempting
to distinguish the just from the unjust war. Their principal problems, according to one competent survey, to which all page references in this lengthy paragraph refer except one, have been to de-

termine the groups with which it is proper to carry on war, the significance of a formal declaration of war, the circumstances under which it is right to resort to war, the policy to be pursued by neutrals, and the time and place of the actual combat (Ballis, 1937, p. 2). In classical Greece, for example, warfare was prohibited during religious festivals and was regulated by treaties (X) (p. 16). Aristotle believed war to be justified only in order to defend the city-state (VII), to establish a hegemony over people for their own good (IV), and to control nations deserving to be enslaved (XII) (p. 19). In Rome, Cicero considered wars just whose objective is revenge (XXIII) or self-defense (VII) (p. 28). The Catholic Church in the Middle Ages gave its full blessing only to the Crusades against the infidel (IV) (pp. 33–36). St. Augustine believed a war to be just when injustice is avenged: either a city or people should be punished when its citizens have not previously been punished for doing wrong (IX); or stolen properties should be restored (X) (pp. 42–43). In fact, as two jurists have pointed out, in that period the Papacy effectively regulated and controlled warfare between local European rulers (McDougal and Feliciano, 1961, p. 133); hence the conflicts could be to some degree interpreted as having divine sanction through the Pope (I). Later Sir Thomas More gave his approval to wars fought in defense of oneself (VII) or one's friends (X) and to offensive wars in behalf of those friends, provided that, in spite of a previous effort to settle the issue peacefully (V), war has become unavoidable (IV) (pp. 73–75). A legal war, according to the Dutch jurist Hugo Grotius, is one that has been formally declared (X); but a war not formally declared may also be legal if it is in a just cause (IX). For him a war is just when it is fought to right an injury received; hence he recognized self-defense (VII), the recovery of property (X), and the inflicting of punishment (XXIII) as just causes (p. 113).

In an eighteenth-century classic on "The Laws of Nations," Emer de Vattel, a Swiss jurist and once a diplomat employed by the King of Saxony, discussed what he called the "justificatory reasons" for carrying on war. In the first instance and in the last analysis, he strongly insisted that a right of so momentous a nature—the right of judging whether the nation has real grounds of complaint, whether she is authorized to employ force, and justifiable in taking up arms, whether prudence will admit of such a step, and whether the welfare of the state requires it—that right, I say, can belong to the body of the nation, or to the sovereign, her representative [VIII].

Before and especially during and after the Renaissance, virtually every jurist similarly ascribed the ultimate decision to the ruler of the nation. Vattel, however, limited the right to wage war. Such a right, he said, "belongs to nations no farther than is necessary for their own defence [VII], and for the maintenance of their rights" (VIII). He clearly stated that "the just and lawful object of every war, which is, to avenge or prevent injury" (XXIII, XX) is authorized by "the right to security" (VII). A proposition that "requires no proof" he believed to be the following: "Defensive war is just when made against an unjust aggressor" (IX, XXIII). He extended this justification as follows: "It is lawful and commendable to succour and assist, by all possible means, a nation engaged in a just war; and it is even incumbent on every nation, to give such assistance, when she can give it without injury to herself" (IV). Finally, he directly noted the nonlegal functions served by justifications when, following Grotius and many others before him, he wrote that the "responses alleged as justificatory, but which are so only in appearance, or which are even absolutely destitute of all foundation" must be called "pretexts" (Vattel, 1865, pp. 292, 301–05, 324).

This last distinction, appearing in various forms in analyses of wars, also suggests that some justifications are more likely to recur and to be more effective than others. The reasons for carrying on war that are approved ethically by Vattel and other writers are the very ones likely to be employed in order to win the approval and cooperation not of people like themselves but of ordinary citizens. Justifications that are mere "pretexts," on the other hand, can be more easily exposed and ridiculed; but on occasion they, too, have some appeal if only as passing rationalizations.

Abruptly and arbitrarily attention is now shifted to an American general and lawyer, H. W. Halleck, who conscientiously reflected the viewpoint current in large sections of British and American jurisprudence during the nineteenth century. In his general statements he deliberately followed Vattel: "The justifiable causes of a war are injuries received or threatened" (VII, XXIII). Such justifiable wars have three objectives: "to secure what belongs or is due to us" (IV, IX); "to provide for our future safety [VII, XIX], by obtaining reparation of injuries done to us" (XXIII); "to protect ourselves and property from a threatened injury" (VII, XX). In addition, Halleck's classification of wars, quoted verbatim in the following list, suggests, if considerable Risky Stimulus Inference be permitted, the justifications that are likely to accompany each: wars of insurrection and revolution (VI); wars of independence (VI, VIII); wars of opinion, subdivided in turn into political and religious wars (XV); wars of conquest (XX); civil wars (IX); national wars, "those where the great body of the people of a state take up arms and join in the contest, like those of the Swiss against Austria and the Duke of Burgundy" (VI, VIII); and wars of intervention (IV, X) (Halleck, 1861, pp. 313–15, 328–34).

In this quick historical survey the emphasis seems to be on absolutistic justifications, with the most frequent references being to transcendental and legal values. Among the personificative justifications, that of revenge as here broadly defined is heavily stressed. On a verbal level, the impression is unavoidable, there seems to have been little progress. Article 1, Convention III, of the second Hague Conference only repeated what Grotius had written almost three centuries earlier:

|                    *1907*                    |                    *1625*                    |
| :--- | :--- |
| The Contracting Parties recognize that hostilities between themselves shall not commence without previous and explicit warning, in the form either of a reasoned declaration of war or of an ultimatum with conditional declaration of war. | But to make a war legal . . . it is not enough that it should be carried on by sovereign powers on both sides, but it must also . . . be declared so publicly as to constitute a notification of the event by one party to the other. |

Grotius, however, was a mere legal scholar and minor official expressing his own viewpoint, the Hague Convention a document to which the representatives of forty-four governments gave at least nominal consent. Learned treatises have been replaced by specific treaties and international organizations seeking, however vainly, to declare certain kinds of war (though not war itself) illegal.

## Wilson's Fourteen Points

Although all the powers stated their war aims as they entered World War I, attention is concentrated on only one document issued toward the end of that conflict: the fourteen points which President Wilson mentioned in his address to Congress on January 8, 1918. He was responding to the request of the Central Empires (Germany and Austria-Hungary) to indicate, in his words, "the possible basis of a general peace." In addition, the new Russian government at that time was actually negotiating a peace with representatives of those states at Brest-Litovsk. How did each point justify the President's basic contention that he and his allies were planning a desirable world which their foes could enter by surrendering forthwith?

1. Open covenants of peace, openly arrived at [X]. . . .
2. Absolute freedom of navigation upon the seas, outside territorial waters, alike in peace and in war [VI]. . . .
3. The removal . . . of all economic barriers and the establishment of an equality of trade conditions among all the nations [XX]. . . .
4. Adequate guarantees given and taken that national armaments will be reduced to the lowest points consistent with domestic safety [VII, X].
5. A free, open-minded, and absolutely impartial adjustment of all colonial claims, based upon a strict observance of the principles that, in determining all such questions of sovereignty [VIII], the interests of the populations concerned [XX] must have equal weight with the equitable claims of the government whose title is to be determined [X].
6. The evacuation of all Russian territory and such a settlement of all questions affecting Russia as will secure the best

and freest cooperation of the other nations of the world in obtaining for her an unhampered and unembarrassed opportunity for the independent determination of her own political development and national policy and assure her of a sincere welcome into the society of free nations under institutions of her own choosing [VI, VIII, IX]. . . .

7. Belgium . . . must be evacuated and restored, without an attempt to limit the sovereignty which she enjoys in common with all other free nations [VI, VIII]. . . .

8. All French territory should be freed and the invaded portions restored [VIII], and the wrong done to France by Prussia in 1871 in the matter of Alsace-Lorraine . . . should be righted [IX], in order that peace may once more be made secure in the interest of all [V].

9. A readjustment of the frontiers of Italy should be effected along clearly recognizable lines of nationality [XV].

10. The peoples of Austria-Hungary . . . should be accorded the freest opportunity of autonomous development [VIII].

11. . . . international guarantees of the political and economic independence and territorial integrity of the several Balkan states should be entered into [VII, VIII, X].

12. The Turkish portion of the present Ottoman Empire should be assured a secure sovereignty [VIII], but the other nationalities which are now under Turkish rule should be assured an undoubted security of life [VII] and an absolutely unmolested opportunity of autonomous development [VI]. . . .

13. An independent Polish state should be erected which should include the territories inhabited by indisputably Polish populations [XV], which should be assured a free and secure access to the sea [XX], and whose political and economic independence [VI] and territorial integrity [VIII] should be guaranteed by international covenant [X].

14. A general association of nations must be formed under specific covenants for the purpose of affording mutual guarantees [X] of political independence [VI] and territorial integrity [VIII] to great and small states alike [V] [Shaw, 1924, pp. 468–70].

These aims clearly emphasize absolutistic values of the transcendent and legal type; personificative ones are employed only as principles to guide the relocation of boundaries.

## World War II: The Declarations

The need to make a formal declaration of war before the onset of hostilities is an ethical tradition which in the West has been discussed and to some degree followed since antiquity. Surprise attacks in recent times are followed by declarations. In either case governments make known their war aims. Unquestionably among modern nations the declarations are widely publicized; hence their explanations come very close to revealing the underlying justifications that are supposed to affect the target audiences. Documents galore from the onset of World War II are available, inasmuch as many of the important leaders of that era were conscious of the problem of communicating with their people and with friends and enemies, and all of them knew that for the first time their words were likely to reach millions of people everywhere through radio. Salient sections from some of the most important are presented here in chronological order; whenever possible, the one statement from each country has been selected which is likely to have received the widest dissemination.

*Germany, September 1, 1939,*
*Hitler's Address to the German Reichstag:*

I am resolved to remove from the German frontiers the element of uncertainty, the everlasting atmosphere of conditions resembling civil war [VII]. I will see to it that in the East there is, on the frontier, a peace precisely similar to that on our other frontiers [V]. . . . I will continue this struggle, no matter against whom, until the safety of the Reich [VII] and its rights are secured [VIII]. . . . There will be no hardships for Germans to which I myself will not submit [XX]. . . . My whole life has been nothing but one long struggle for my people, for its restoration, and for Germany [XV]. . . . The sacrifice that is demanded of us is not greater than the sacrifice that many generations have made [XVII] [Royal Institute of International Affairs, 1951, pp. 508–11].

All of the absolutistic and personificative values in this speech are ethno- and egocentric: Germany and Hitler must fight in behalf of themselves. Poland's immediate reply naturally stressed self-defense and attacked Germany; it sought also to bolster domestic morale by invoking deterministic and transcendental values regarding an ultimate victory.

*Poland, September 2, 1939,*
*Address of Prime Minister Slawoj-Skladkowski*
*to the Polish Parliament:*

War has been imposed on us [XVI]. We accept the challenge. We have been attacked and we are fighting [XXIII].

We shall win this war [II] because Josef Pilsudski taught us how to win liberty [VI] and how to defend it [XII]. . . .

We are in the second day of the war. The tremendous rush of historic events does not hold any terrors for us [II]. We know that the fortunes of war are changeable; but the unconquerable Polish Army [XXI] will defeat the historic enemy of our country [III] and crush Teutonic arrogance [XV] [*New York Times*, September 3, 1939, p. 14].

Poland's allies agreed with this interpretation of events as they declared war on Germany.

*France, September 3, 1939,*
*Premier Daladier's Radio Address:*

Since dawn September 1, Poland has been the victim of one of the most brutal and most cynical aggressions [XVI]. . . .

Future peace was in Hitler's hands; he chose war [XVI]. France and England multiplied their efforts to save peace [V]. . . .

In aligning ourselves against the most despicable of tyrannies [VI], in honoring our word [X], we are fighting to defend our land, our homes, our liberty [VII, XV, VI, XX]. . . .

The cause of France is the cause of justice [IX]. It is the cause of all peaceful [V] and free [VI] nations. She will be victorious [II].

Frenchmen and Frenchwomen: we are waging war because it is forced upon us [XXIII]. Each of us will be at his

post on French soil [XIII]—on that soil where respect and
human dignity finds one of its last refuges [XXI].

You will all unite your efforts in the deep feeling of union
and fraternity to save France [XV].

Vive la France! [*New York Times,* September 4, 1939,
p. 8].

The Premier's indignation is shown by the large number of
arguments he advanced in a short statement to justify his country's
declaration of war; he mentioned at least one value in each of the
main categories beginning with determinism and ending with
need. Somewhat in contrast, the British Prime Minister, who had
perhaps greater reason to feel indignant, expressed his wrath
with more emphasis upon absolutistic justifications.

*Great Britain, September 3, 1939,*
*Prime Minister Chamberlain's Radio Address:*
You can imagine what a bitter blow it is to me that all my
long struggle to win peace has failed [V, XVI]. . . . We and
France are today, in fulfillment of our obligations [X], going
to the aid of Poland, who is so bravely resisting this wicked
and unprovoked attack on her people [XXIII]. We have a
clear conscience [XXII]. We have done all that any country
could do to establish peace [V, XII]. The situation in which
no word given by Germany's ruler could be trusted [X] and
no people or country could feel themselves safe [VII] has become intolerable. And now that we have resolved to finish it,
I know that you will all play your part with calmness and
courage [IV]. . . . Now may God bless you all. May He defend the right [I]. It is the evil things that we shall be fighting against—brute force [XII], bad faith [X], injustice [IX],
oppression and persecution [VI]—and against them I am
certain that the right will prevail [II] [Royal Institute of
International Affairs, 1951, pp. 522–23].

After the German armies had occupied Denmark, Norway,
and the Low Countries and as they were invading France, Italy
joined the war in Western Europe.

*Italy, June 10, 1940,*
*Address by Premier Mussolini:*

We take the field against the plutocratic and reactionary democracies [IV] who always have blocked the march and frequently plotted against the existence of the Italian people [VII, XXIII]. . . . We are taking up arms, after having solved the problem of our continental frontiers, to solve our maritime frontiers [VII, XX]. . . . This gigantic conflict is only a phase of the logical development of our revolution [II]. It is the conflict of poor, numerous peoples who labor against starvers who ferociously cling to a monopoly of all riches and all gold on earth [IX] . . . Italians, in a memorable mass meeting in Berlin, I said that according to the rules of Fascist morals when one has a friend one marches with him to the end [X] [*New York Times,* June 11, 1940, p. 4].

Mussolini's declaration covered a wide range of justifications beginning with the destiny of Italy and ending with revenge against the plots of his enemies; Hitler's justifications for invading Russia a little over a year later were similar, except that he used no legal arguments.

*Germany, June 21, 1941,*
*Statement by Hitler:*

The penetration of Russia into Rumania and the Greek liaison with England threatened to place new, large areas into the war [VII] . . . A few days later [Russia] concluded the well-known friendship agreement which was to incite the Serbs against Germany [XXIII]. . . . Now the moment has come when I can no longer look at this development [XX]. Waiting would be a crime for Germany [VII]. . . . The task is to safeguard Europe and thus save all [IV] [*New York Times,* June 22, 1941, p. 1].

The Soviet Union, the target of the German attack, acknowledged a state of war by ascribing responsibility to her enemies and then by affirming faith in her own values and in ultimate victory.

*Soviet Union, June 22, 1941,*
*Radio Address of Foreign Minister Molotoff:*

This unheard of attack upon our country [XXIII] is perfidy unparalleled in the history of civilized nations [X]. The attack on our country was perpetrated despite the fact that a treaty of nonaggression had been signed between the U. S. S. R. and Germany and that the Soviet Government most faithfully abided by all provisions of this treaty [X]. . . . This war has been forced upon us [XXIII], not by the German people, not by German workers, peasants and intellectuals whose suffering we well understand [IV], but by the clique of bloodthirsty Fascist rulers of Germany who have enslaved Frenchmen, Czechs, Poles, Serbians, Norway, Belgium, Denmark, Holland, Greece and other nations [VI]. . . . The Red Army and our whole people will again wage victorious war [II] for the fatherland, for our country [XV], for honor [XX], for liberty [VI] [*New York Times,* June 23, 1941, p. 10].

Less than a half year later, the Japanese launched attacks against the United States, Great Britain, and their allies.

*Japan, December 8, 1941,*
*The Emperor's Imperial Rescript:*

To insure the stability of East Asia [IV] and to contribute to world peace [V] is the far-sighted policy which was formulated by our Great Illustrious Imperial Grandsire and Our Great Imperial Sire succeeding Him [XVII] and which we lay constantly to heart. To cultivate friendship among nations and to enjoy prosperity in common with all nations has always been the guiding principle of Our Empire's foreign policy [IV]. It has been truly unavoidable and far from Our wishes that Our Empire has now been brought to cross swords with America and Britain. . . . Eager for the realization of their inordinate ambition to dominate the Orient, both America and Britain, giving support to the Chungking regime, have aggravated the disturbances in East Asia [XXIII]. Moreover, these two powers, inducing other countries to follow suit, increased military preparations on all sides of Our Empire to challenge us [VII]. They have obstructed by every means Our peaceful commerce, and finally resorted to a direct severance of economic relations, menacing gravely the existence of Our Empire [VII]. Patiently have We waited and long have We endured, in the hope that Our Government might retrieve the situation in peace [V, XXIII]. But our adversaries, showing not the least spirit of conciliation, have unduly delayed a settlement [V]; and in the meantime, they have intensified the economic and political pressure to compel thereby Our Empire to submission [VII]. This trend of affairs would, if left unchecked, not only nullify Our Empire's effort of many years for the sake of the stabilization of East Asia [IV], but also endanger the very existence of Our nation [VII]. The situation being such as it is, Our Empire for its existence [VIII] and self-defense [VII] has no other recourse but to appeal to arms and to crush every obstacle in its path [XXIII] [Foreign Affairs Association of Japan, 1943, p. 222].

The Emperor emphasized that not Japan but her enemies were responsible for this new war and that his country was in fact defending ideals important to her and to all East Asia. In his brief reply, President Roosevelt pointed to the most recent event, the attack on Pearl Harbor, and to the peril in which the United States consequently found itself.

*United States, December 8, 1941,*
*Message of President Roosevelt to Congress:*
    Yesterday, December 7, 1941—a date which will live in infamy [X]—the United States of America was suddenly and deliberately attacked by naval and air forces of the Empire of Japan [XXIII]. . . . Hostilities exist. There is no blinking at the fact that our people, our territory, and our interests are in grave danger [VII, XX] [Goodrich, 1942, pp. 116–17].

Mutual recrimination was the principal theme in the declarations of war by Germany and the United States.

*Germany, December 11, 1941,*
*Foreign Affairs Minister Ribbentrop to*
*American Chargé d'Affaires at Berlin:*

The Government of the United States having violated in the most flagrant manner and in ever-increasing measures all rules of neutrality in favor of the adversaries of Germany [XXIII] and having continually been guilty of the most severe provocations toward Germany ever since the outbreak of the European war [XXIII], provoked by the British declaration of war against Germany on September 3, 1939 [XXIII], has finally resorted to open military acts of aggression [V, XXIII]. . . . The Government of the United States has thereby virtually created a state of war [XXIII] [Goodrich, 1942, pp. 118–19].

*United States, December 11, 1941,*
*Message of President Roosevelt to Congress:*

On the morning of December eleventh, the Government of Germany, pursuing its course of world-conquest [VI], declared war against the United States [XXIII]. . . . Never before has there been a greater challenge to life, liberty, and civilization [VI, XX]. . . . Rapid and united effort by all of the peoples of the world who are determined to remain free [V, VIII] will insure a world victory of the forces of justice and of righteousness [IX] over the forces of savagery and barbarism [IV] [Goodrich, 1942, p. 121].

The last declaration in World War II came from the Soviet Union, which maintained, in effect, that the Russians had decided to fight Japan for the good of the Japanese people.

*Soviet Union, August 8, 1945,*
*Address by Foreign Minister Molotoff:*

After the defeat and capitulation of Hitlerite Germany, Japan became the only great power that still stood for the continuation of the war [XXIII]. . . . Loyal to its Allied duty, the Soviet Government has accepted the proposal of the Allies and has joined in the declaration of the Allied powers of July 26 [X].

The Soviet Government considers that this policy is the only means able to bring peace nearer [V], free the people from further sacrifice and suffering [XX], and give the Japanese people the possibility of avoiding the dangers and destruction suffered by Germany after her refusal to capitulate unconditionally [IV] [*New York Times*, August 9, 1945, p. 3].

All the public declarations of war that have been examined in this section are in agreement on one point: war is justified only when the enemy has begun, or threatens to begin, the conflict. Faced with a potential threat or with actual aggression, leaders then consider war necessary to protect rights, privileges, and values whose importance and significance for the nation are declared beyond debate. Nobody really wants to fight, if the public statements of leaders can be believed.

### Peace?

After so many thunderous documents, it is well to turn to the postwar world and examine some of the notable attempts to promote peace and limited forms of international cooperation. The following are "the purposes of the United Nations," according to Article 1 of the United Nations' Charter.

*United Nations, June 26, 1945:*
  1. To maintain international peace [V] and security [VII], and to that end: to take effective collective measures for the prevention and removal of threats to the peace [X], and for the suppression of acts of aggression or other breaches of the peace [XXIII], and to bring about by peaceful means, and in conformity with the principles of justice [IX] and international law [X], adjustment or settlement of international disputes or situations which might lead to a breach of the peace [V];
  2. To develop friendly relations among nations based on respect for the principle of equal rights [VI] and self-determination of peoples [VIII], and to take other appropriate measures to strengthen universal peace [V];
  3. To achieve international cooperation in solving inter-

national problems of an economic, social, cultural, or humanitarian character [IV, XX], and in promoting and encouraging respect for human rights and for fundamental freedoms for all without distinction as to race, sex, language, or religion [VI, IX]; and

4. To establish a center for harmonizing the actions of nations in the attainment of these common ends [V] [Hudson, 1950, v. 9, pp. 330–31].

Representatives of the Soviet Union, six Eastern European countries with communist regimes, France, and Italy issued a declaration as they founded an alliance which sought to counteract the Marshall Plan in Western Europe and to become the successor to the Comitern and to the other communist internationals which functioned between the two world wars.

*The Cominform, September 23, 1947:*
Fundamental changes have taken place in the international situation as a result of the Second World War and in the postwar period [XX]. . . .

To frustrate the plan of imperialist aggression [XXIII], the efforts of all the democratic anti-imperialist forces of Europe are necessary [IV]. . . .

The nations of the world do not want war [V]. The forces standing for peace are so large and so strong that if these forces be staunch and firm in defending the peace, if they display stamina and resolution [XX], the plans of the aggressors will meet with utter failure [V]. [Royal Institute of International Affairs, 1952, pp. 122–24].

*North Atlantic Treaty, April 4, 1949.* The entire preamble to the Treaty which established NATO reads as follows:
The Parties to this Treaty reaffirm their faith in the purposes and principles of the Charter of the United Nations [X] and their desire to live in peace with all peoples and all governments [V].

They are determined [IV] to safeguard the freedom [VI], common heritage and civilization of their peoples [XV], founded on the principles of democracy [XVIII], individual liberty [VI], and the rule of law [X].

They seek to promote stability and well-being in the North Atlantic area [XX].

They are resolved to unite their efforts for collective defense [XX] and for the preservation of peace [V] and security [VII] [Royal Institute of International Affairs, 1953, pp. 257–58].

*The Council of Europe, May 5, 1949.* Ten countries in Western Europe, five of which eventually formed the European Common Community, subscribed to the following preamble as they set forth the rules governing their Council of Europe.

The Governments [of the ten countries];

Convinced that the pursuit of peace [V] based upon justice [IX] and international cooperation [X] is vital for the preservation of human society and civilization [VI, XX];

Reaffirming their devotion to the spiritual and moral values which are the common heritage of their peoples [XVIII] and the true source of individual freedom [VI], political liberty [VIII], and the rule of law [X], principles which form the basis of all genuine democracy [XXI];

Believing that, for the maintenance and further realization of these ideals and in the interests of economic and social progress [IV], there is need of a closer unity between all like-minded countries of Europe;

Considering that, to respond to this need and to the expressed aspirations of their peoples in this regard [XX], it is necessary forthwith to create an organization which will bring European States in closer association [Royal Institute of International Affairs, 1953, p. 348].

If the common elements in these four declarations are extracted, a rather unified message emerges: It is our responsibility (IV) and deeply felt need (XX) to preserve the peace (V) through some kind of international agreement. A similar message pervades most of the declarations of war, except that regret concerning the ending of peace and hope concerning its restoration are also expressed. Mankind's universal, constant reference to peace must indeed reflect profound impulses.

## 13. The Facilitation of Nationalism

This chapter and the next seek to answer the same question: what psychological conditions facilitate the existence and persistence of nationalism? Again in terms of the purposes and limitations of this book, attention is drawn not to historical factors but to their psychological consequences. More specifically the question can be referred to the original Diagram of Chapter 1: What kinds of conditions or stimuli must exist or come into existence for the prevailing media to be able to transmit communications which can convince men that their own welfare and that of the groups they consider significant are intimately linked to a nation? When do patriots then become nationalistic by voicing demands on the basis of such convictions or by engaging in appropriate activity? The two questions, as emphasized in previous chapters, are interrelated: nationalism is more likely to appear when patriotism is strong and hence the conditions promoting strong patriotism directly increase the probability of nationalism in some form.

The factors believed to facilitate nationalism have been derived from two sources. The first and more frequent of the two stems from the experience and knowledge of scholarly writers and authorities on these subjects: each usually believes and asserts that a particular factor or set of factors isolated or detected by himself is crucial. Such wisdom, though it is not fortified by systematic documentation, merits respect in the manner of any kind of clinical judgment: here at least are first impressions or hypotheses. The difficulty is the lack of agreement among these scholars and observers, or at least the use of apparently different language to describe what may be basically identical or similar phenomenon. Two excellent summaries of existing literature, the one British and the other German, for example, both seek to indicate the essential characteristics of a nation. The British source is cited in

English, and where possible what is guessed to be the equivalent phrasing in the German source is offered immediately afterwards in parentheses: "the idea of a common government" ("gemeinsamer Staat"); "a certain size and closeness of contact between all the individual members"; "a more or less defined territory" ("gemeinsamer Wohnsitz"); "certain characteristics (of which the most frequent is language) clearly distinguishing the nation from other nations and non-national groups" ("gemeinsame Sprache," "gemeinsame Kultur"); "certain interests common to the individual members"; and "a certain degree of common feeling or will" ("Bewusstsein und Wille"). The German list fails to produce two characteristics found in the English list; and it contains two not directly represented in the British source, viz., "gemeinsame Rasse" and "gemeinsame Religion" (Royal Institute of International Affairs, 1939, p. xx; Fels, 1927, pp. 73–74).

The lack of agreement among these observers, it must be emphasized, is highly significant. In our present state of knowledge there is no mathematical formula for assessing the factors contributing to patriotism and nationalism. The independent variables have not been identified, and for those on which there is some high degree of agreement no consistent method of weighting exists. In fact, no formula seems applicable to all kinds of nations or to one nation at different stages of its development. The components of patriotism and nationalism, as the German analyst cited above has noted, are "different in each individual nation and are not operative in the same number and strength" (Fels, 1927, p. xiv). An astute analysis of the growth of nationalism in Africa necessarily places great emphasis upon "aspects of the colonial situation and colonial policy" there (Hodgkin, 1956, pp. 55–59). Colonial factors as such, however, played no role or virtually none in the development of European nationalism, and indeed they functioned somewhat differently in each African territory and in colonies elsewhere. The number of situations in which they are relevant could be increased by considering them the concrete manifestation of a more abstract concept, such as the presence of any alien outgroup, but thereby some of their specific incisiveness is lost. Generality yes, but also singularity.

Then, in the second place, a handful of studies approach nationalism quantitatively and share a common procedure: they would determine through empirical data the kinds of statistical relations existing between nations and a particular set of factors, without necessarily exploring the reasons for, and the consequences of, whatever associations emerge. Quantitative measures of certain national characteristics (e.g. population density, standard of living, number of Nobel Prize winners) or of certain naional attitudes (e.g. "radicalism-conservatism," "tough- and tender-mindedness") are obtained and then subjected to scrutiny by means of a statistical tool such as factor analysis. Some factors are found to be more closely related to one another than others; and hence the emerging clusters are considered to reflect, or to be symptoms of, a more general, basic factor. The studies usually produce stimulating but limited hypotheses: stimulating because they suggest some of the factors associated with, perhaps even giving rise to, patriotism and nationalism; limited because the data are likely to be rather specific for the situation or country at hand (e.g. Cattell, 1949 and 1950; Deutsch, 1953; Eysenck, 1954).

What is really needed on a correlational level is a genuine cross-cultural study, such as one relating some measure of nationalism to other social or psychological factors. An analyst primarily interested in religion has conscientiously rated various cultural traits in 50 carefully selected societies throughout the world. Among his variables is "sovereignty" which is applied not only to nations and states but also to groups, such as the family, which have "original and independent jurisdiction over some sphere of life." Sovereignty so defined is found to be related to, or associated with, other ascertainable traits in the sample of societies. The greater the number of sovereign groups, for example, the greater the tendency toward monotheism rather than polytheism (Swanson, 1960, p. 20, 65). Such an approach, however, cannot be utilized at the moment because adequate measures of, or specific data concerning, some aspect of nationalism are not available in a sufficiently large sample of societies. The Human Relations Area Files, to which reference has been previously made, contains relevant categories (ethnocentrism, ingroup antagonisms, behavior toward nonrelatives, political movements, warfare, etc.), but too few data appear under them to calculate any kind of meaningful correlation.

In this chapter, then, an effort is made to leap or creep forward by utilizing both the wisdom of scholars and available quantitative studies. In addition, the clinical procedure associated with the literature on nationalism is followed: private intuition, derived from experience in Africa, Jamaica, the South Tyrol, and Germany in 1930–1932, is liberally invoked. The admission is made for the sake of disarming candor and not at all shamefacedly, because the state of the art produces no certainty.

## A Common Culture

Patriots and nationalists, since they live together in a society, by definition share a common culture to some extent; their bond is strengthened as the number of culture traits they share increases. This matter-of-fact generalization has some important implications. In the first place, the emphasis is upon cultural and not biological homogeneity. Then it immediately follows that nation-building can occur or at least can most effectively occur among people with a similar culture. When there is cultural diversity—for example, in all African countries—political leaders face the task of trying to produce some degree of unity.

A common culture comes into existence and also is promoted by the interaction of people, and interaction occurs most readily when people occupy the same land. For this reason, nationalists inhabit a particular region which they would protect from other peoples and whose size and influence they frequently would expand. If the land is a recognizable geographical unit, its inhabitants are able more easily to appreciate and value its distinctive attributes or to ascribe such attributes to it; transportation and communication within a somewhat geographically homogeneous area are facilitated and hence national unity is further promoted. People with a common culture who do not live together, on the other hand, either lose their common heritage over time, or else they must deliberately strive to become geographically united.

The case of the Jews is unusual. Though scattered throughout the world, they have always shared important elements of a common culture which existed in ancient times and which has persisted to some extent ever since. The elements pertain not only to religion but also to other values and modes of behaving. Very crucial has been a "mental orientation" which consists of "a knowledge and awareness of an historical past different from that of the non-Jewish environment" in which they happen to have been living (Patai, 1953, pp. 118–19). They have lacked, however, a common land; and so the Zionists and other Jewish groups sought and finally obtained Palestine as the physical site for a Jewish state. Prior to the establishment of Israel, Jews could be nationalistic, but only in spite of the fact that they had to transmit symbolic communications at a distance; prominent Zionists feared that, without a state of their own, Jews everywhere would lose their distinctive culture and be assimilated in their countries of residence.

Likewise any form of detachment from the land of one's nation is likely to create difficulties in retaining the national culture and hence in remaining both patriotic and nationalistic. The general tendency, for example, is for immigrants to a country to become assimilated and gradually to lose their identity with, and hence their patriotic feelings for, their native land. Clearly that land still exists, but the ties to it gradually weaken unless people have the conscious determination that they will return after obtaining some limited objective, such as wealth, or unless they continually visit their birthplace. The old culture does not lapse or lapses less quickly if they are able to acquire, as it were, an annex for their nation abroad; for example, they live together and perpetuate the old ways by segregating themselves or by being segregated in a section of a city or country. Of course contrary tendencies appear; the oldest generation, the one that originally migrated, is likely to abandon the traditional ways with great reluctance; and all generations may wish to continue some emotional tie to the homeland in order to demonstrate to strangers in the new land their pride in their own background and a determination not to be completely absorbed. Without land and surrounded by an alien culture, people's patriotism and nationalism can survive only when they make a very deliberate effort to do so.

In contrast, cultural homogeneity and hence nationalism are likely to be promoted by geographical or cultural isolation, for then people have ample opportunity to interact without being appreciably affected by outside influence. Isolation can be even more effective when nationals know, as they usually do, that outsiders exist who are quite different from themselves and perhaps also hostile. In the present day most of the inhabitants of a prominent Ladin community in the South Tyrol oppose the construction of a modern road from the main highway to their village. They seem worried less about its cost than about its probable effects. They tolerate the inconvenience and the time it takes to climb and descend on foot for the sake of their cultural independence and the feeling of being relatively self-contained. Few outsiders visit them now, and they are willing to forgo a profitable increase in tourists, who, they know, would come in larger numbers if motor transportation were to become feasible for average drivers—at the moment only a few Ladins have the skill and courage to drive on the existing rocky, narrow, steep, spring-breaking trail. These people cling all the more to their geographical isolation because they are so few in number and because they realize, however unconsciously, that eventually their way of life and hence their nation are doomed to be changed radically by modern influences.

Enclaves separated from the outside world because they are located on islands or upon not easily accessible mountains or mountain passes have their destiny largely determined by geographical factors. Isolation can also be achieved through cultural devices; thus people virtually make the decision to insulate themselves from their surroundings. They may dwell in a large city, but they then deliberately congregate in one section. Or they may monopolize one area of a land and therein zealously promote their own culture and reject innovations from neighbors. In some instances the larger or host group takes the initiative and elicits within the minority a feeling of isolation through informal discrimination or formal legal ordinances.

Isolation of either type is permanently possible only when there is a high degree of economic self-sufficiency, a factor which therefore also may promote a common culture and hence nationalism. For if people are able to satisfy their needs without engaging appreciably in international trade, they can easily conceive of themselves as distinctive and they can appreciate, too, the connection between their own welfare and the economy. It is also true, how-

ever, that the inability to be self-sufficient may produce nationalistic demands for expansion in order to obtain the necessary
supplies or raw materials; the rare elements required in the twentieth century to prepare for and to wage war, for example, frequently must be sought overseas. The nationalism of insular societies, consequently, stresses preservation, whereas that of modern
nations is more likely to feature expansion.

In passing it is well to note that the close relation between nationalism and the exclusive possession of land by a society with a
homogeneous culture may characterize modern nations of the
West but not necessarily countries with other forms of social organization. For some peoples have been able to live side by side
without affecting one another appreciably and allegedly without
losing their sense of national identity. This is the situation reported to have existed in the Middle East, especially in Turkey
under the Ottoman Empire. For Islam permits such relationships
and does not require its adherents to follow the principle of "territorial nationalism" which diffused from Europe after World War
I (Cahnman, 1944, pp. 525–26). Such harmony, however, was
perhaps only a variation of the postulated relation between culture
and nationalism and not an exception to it. Two nations in close
physical contact but with little or no interaction could have valued very highly their own nationality. Orientation primarily toward their land within a circumscribed sphere and toward
their compatriots did not necessarily preclude loyalty in some respects to Turkey, the dominating power. Or part of their loyalty
could very well have been only on the surface and have resulted
from a show of force and other compelling measures by the Turks.
It may be surmised, therefore, that this type of alliance or limited
internationalism is weak, or at least contains within itself the possibility of discord between the different national groups. Certainly
modern nations seem to operate most efficiently, if efficiency be
measured by the power to wage war, by economic growth, or by
ingroup stability, when a single, somewhat homogeneous group
occupies a territory exclusively. Even the author just cited, who
believes that "the principle of the French Revolution—one nation
and one territory—has wrought havoc in the East" with its mixture of nationalities, has also referred to the "frequent strife, con-

flict, and friction" of various "populations that have lived side by side for centuries" (Cahnman, 1944, p. 529).

## Language

If a common culture greatly facilitates nationalism, then it becomes necessary to identify the cultural components shared by people. One component is perhaps more outstanding and more frequently noted than any other: a common language. Even an historian breaks the written or unwritten rule of his guild and emerges with a universal statement: "All major works on nationalism stress in details the significance of language" (Snyder, 1954, pp. 20–21). A sociologist makes a similarly cosmic sweep: "A common written language and literature is a necessary condition of overcoming separatism of local and regional collectivities with different folk cultures" (Znaniecki, 1952, p. 30). For language, as previously suggested, provides an efficient way to create awareness within people of their own distinctive attributes. Those using the same language immediately have an important bond almost equivalent to that provided by kinship; in fact, such a feeling is thought also to be "sometimes found between people who speak closely related languages" (Chadwick, 1945, p. 113). According to one writer, language was assigned a really profound meaning in nineteenth-century Europe: "All men speaking the same lagnuage were alleged to belong to the same race . . . and should be united within the same Nation" (Delaisi, 1925, p. 207). Without subscribing to such a biological view, people do say in effect that 'whoever talks the way I do is like me; we think and act similarly.' In spite of some notable differences in pronunciation, spelling, and vocabulary, a common language facilitates contacts and even promotes friendships between the people of Britain and the United States as well as their leaders.

Other advantages of a single language within a nation can be briefly mentioned. Most societies have proverbs that embody rules of behavior and political aspirations and that usually lose most or all of their flavor in translation. The communication of a message in one language is more economical than in several. The audience perceiving a communication can probably more easily imagine that others are similarly reacting to its content when only one language is employed. Necessary communications from and to government are transmitted and received with dispatch. Just as members of a family can remember the past and confront the present and future with identical words and phrases because they speak the same language, so nationals immediately have some feeling of communion because they can be emotionally pleased and disturbed by the same verbal apparatus. The speakers of a language, finally, are likely to resemble one another in fact by virtue of that language. They have learned and been impressed by a cultural heritage which has reached them in large part through verbal media. The language they share has its own more or less unique vocabulary and grammar and hence exerts, as modern psycholinguistics has not very adequately demonstrated, some influence upon perception, memory, and value judgments. English makes finer discriminations in color terminology and cruder ones in kinship terminology than most Bantu languages; in these respects speakers of English are more likely to resemble one another than the speakers of Bantu languages. Similarly, the leaders of the French Revolution, whose self-conscious aim was to have the state dominate the church and hence command the "first and paramount loyalty" of all its citizens, included among its demands "linguistic uniformity" (Hayes, 1937, pp. 46–47).

Language is so important that it comes to be personified. The language, it is said, accepts or rejects foreign words; it makes men think in particular ways. People also praise their language in the way they extol other customs and themselves. "We Germans can be very happy," Hitler stated just a year before he started World War II, "to possess a language that is both beautiful and rich but also difficult. To learn to be master of it is a wonderful task" (Florstedt and Stieber, 1943, p. 1).

From a negative standpoint, the strength of language is shown by the reluctance with which people living permanently in a foreign land abandon their mother tongue and substitute completely the language of the new nation. Every dictator has experienced resistance when he sought to impose his own language upon the people he has conquered. People want to use their own language, and they are seldom willing or able to learn another language with any degree of skill. It is not strange, therefore, that many of the pan-nationalistic movements of modern times have been based upon nations having the same or similar languages. When the name of a language is the rallying point for such a movement but when differences in pronunciation and vocabulary exist, an effort is made to produce or revive some standardized form of the language. It has been suggested, for example, that a modernized version of classical Arabic must replace the colloquial dialects of the uneducated in Arab countries if pan-Arabism is to be successful (Nuseibeh, 1956, pp. 74–76).

The importance of a common language, however, must not be exaggerated. Reference need only be made to the unity within Switzerland in spite of the existence of three major languages and a minor one. Swiss unity, it must be quickly added, has not been fortuitously achieved. Each section of the country possesses a high degree of self-determination; tolerance and mutual respect are recognized as virtues; and the Swiss in general have a strong determination to preserve their country intact (Weilenmann, 1951, pp. 340–41). More specifically, each language group is guaranteed certain rights by the federal constitution; but within a canton only one language is used as the vehicle of instruction, while the other two major ones are taught as regular school subjects. About three-quarters of the Swiss live in areas where one language is dominant; still a linguistic minority within a canton has the right to establish its own churches and associations (Ammann, 1955). Most of the internal migration involves the movement of German-speakers into French-speaking areas where they become "rapidly assimilated to the new language" (Mayer, 1951, pp. 159–61). There is unity, therefore, in Switzerland in spite of linguistic diversity and certainly not because of it. The same conclusion must also be reached whenever some degree of nationalism is achieved in nations, such as the old Austrian-Hungarian Empire, with linguistic and hence also cultural diversity.

In many nations, furthermore, one language exists only formally, for in reality numerous dialects are spoken. Such linguistic variations are often treasured in the manner of local patriotism, which, as will be subsequently suggested, makes its contribution to the common weal. Finally, a common language by itself does not necessarily promote nationalism or pan-nationalism; German-speakers in Alsace and in Switzerland, for example, have never appreciably responded to pan-German appeals.

### Intelligibility

Another aspect of culture which facilitates nationalism involves people's comprehension of their own culture. If they are to cooperate efficiently and easily with the state and if they are to be more than mildly patriotic, they must find the beliefs, the convictions, the policies, the justifications, and the actions of their country sufficiently intelligible; there must be "a common well-defined purpose present to, and dominant in, the minds of all individuals" (McDougall, 1920, p. 195). Faith in a nation and its purpose has to be widespread, and to be widespread it cannot be utterly blind. People always have a general tendency, no matter how weak, to build or change institutions in their own image or at least to change them in a manner they believe will make them more satisfactory. Sometimes when a peasant laity does not fully comprehend the formal sacraments of the Catholic Church, folk customs have been added to the usual procedures (Bauer, 1959). Such additions gratify other needs and may indirectly serve nationalistic ends by linking church practices to nationality.

Attention has already been called, in Chapter 3, to the role of the mass media in transmitting and clarifying the psychological components of patriotism and nationalism; there, too, the importance of a somewhat coherent credo linking the past to the present and the future has been emphasized. Nationalism may well require a very specific tradition or custom to reinforce the conviction that the society is essential for the individual and the significant groups to which he belongs. That end can be achieved in many ways; and it is for this reason that the scholarly writers on nationalism have emphasized different ingredients of nationalism. One custom seldom mentioned, for example, involves a recurrent problem in rural societies where cultivable soil is scarce: the distribution of land to a peasant's heirs. If holdings are so small that further division of the land would result in nonviable plots, then only a single heir is prescribed either by custom or law. Under these conditions, the sons not inheriting the land migrate to another region or a foreign country when they grow up or marry. They are almost always reluctant to go and their families share the sadness. The cry for more land or for local industry is then likely to arise; hence the demand for expansion can be heard in insular nations. Whether the actual system of inheritance is based upon primogeniture or upon the independent decision of the father, the prevailing practice is perceived as part of patriotism and nationalism and also as a symptom of the preciousness of one's country—for how better can a way of life be appreciated than when it must be abandoned?

Almost any institution can facilitate cultural homogeneity by providing people with a common understanding, and so may well be included among the essentials of nationalism. Consider, for example, religion, which so often is conspicuously present on scholarly lists of those essentials. Clearly a common religion, if deeply experienced and accorded prestige, produces uniformity among people with respect to very significant beliefs and behavior. Then, when the religious institution is also subservient to, or at least not in conflict with, the state, it provides officials with a very effective means of social control. Some unified nations, nevertheless, possess several or many different religions. Unity may not be disrupted under such circumstances for reasons to be found within the nation itself. In nonliterate societies, religion and government are usually intertwined; hence in nations containing many tribes the differences are viewed in a broad cultural rather than in a religious sense. The diverse religions in the developing nations of Asia and Africa are often the result in large part of missionary work from the outside: they may be valued less than indigenous religions would be and hence lead to less friction. Most important of all, even though the discrete rituals, theology, or even ultimate beliefs differ, diverse religions can be in general agreement concerning basic ethical principles, with the result that social cooperation is possible. Finally, the religious groups may live in separate districts of the same country or, as is now not too unusual in the modern world, some are actually able to dwell together in peace and mutual respect.

What is needed in any nation is some kind of efficacious appeal which will create the intelligible conviction that men's welfare is linked to the society and will induce them to take appropriate action. If patriotism is strong, the state does not have to invoke religion. But if, as in the case of "ordinary" as contrasted with educated Arabs today (Berger, 1962, pp. 343–44), that conviction is not strong, then a fiercely compelling religion can be utilized. Nationalism, therefore, does not require religious support but clearly thrives when such support exists.

## Temporal Factors

Both the passing of objective time and the readiness of people to make subjective temporal judgments concerning the past and the future facilitate nationalism. Objectively, as various writers have suggested (Muir, 1916, pp. 46–51), many generations must usually live together before patriotism can become intense and nationalism overpowering. Gripping traditions take time to establish: effective ways of adapting to, and interpreting, the environment are learned through trial and error. Eventually, as nationality becomes distinctive, these traditions are transmitted during early socialization and hence are so thoroughly reinforced that they are not abandoned lightly or easily. It seems probable, then, that there is a direct relation between the length of time a society has had the principal ingredients of its culture (including its political system) and the strength of people's convictions concerning the need to preserve that culture. Finally, some optimum time period elapses before expansion is demanded: the culture must be sufficiently stable to have enabled the appropriate modes of behavior to be firmly established, but not so well established that people are prevented from feeling the insecurity and lack of contentment which leads them and their leaders to seek more land and power. For this reason, so many formal definitions of nations and so many analyses of nationalism single out the "community of interests developed in [the] course of time" (Oakesmith, 1919, p. ix) as an essential characteristic; and likewise the point is frequently made that "national" or "folk" characters only slowly evolve (e.g. von Fieandt, 1953).

As ever, however, the above generalizations must be inter-

preted with care. Nationalistic countries may be old, yes, but they
may also be young. Again and again, outside and inside this book
references are made to the feeling of brave adventure and enthusiasm of people during the early days of a nation. Youth, consequently, may also be important. In behalf of age this qualification
must in turn be immediately qualified: the adventure and enthusiasm may facilitate nationalism initially but eventually over time
they must give rise to conserving traditions if the nation is to survive.

One attribute of the land, its people, and their culture seems
especially crucial for patriotism and nationalism: noting their development from the past. Here the subjective aspect of time is
dramatically emphasized. When this attribute is part of people's
response repertory, they are able to appreciate their nation's past
and hence also to anticipate its future. They have a sense of history and, in all probability, some confidence in what is to come.
The sense of history is derived not necessarily from a set of systematically collected facts in the scholarly tradition of the West,
but from traditional narratives embodied in folk tales and myths,
which for each generation not only illuminate the past but also
help sustain contemporary rituals and customs (Raglan 1936, pp.
121–45). People effortlessly feel that they share a common culture
when it can be demonstrated to them that they have evolved from
a common past. Modern scholars and leaders in Africa, as previously suggested, must deliberately reconstruct such a past if their
countries are to possess the pride and the prestige of their models
in the West. By and large, this temporal attribute is frequently
ascribed to the land and its people; through literary and historical
tradition, nationals become acquainted with their country and
hence justify their own efforts to preserve or extend it.

Another factor facilitating nationalism, especially when expansion rather than preservation is the demand, involves time in a
forward direction: the convictions of people come to have a utopian tinge. Such a tinge indicates that they are enduring a frustration but that simultaneously they are able to conceive of the
possibility of eliminating it. The frustration may result from a
threatening outgroup; and then the utopian element refers to the
preservation of the vanishing status quo. Or, toward the other

end of the continuum, people are indignant that they do not now have national independence, which they assume is inevitably accompanied by economic prosperity. Unless nationals look toward the future to some extent, a future which they actively wish will resemble or not resemble the past and the present, they are not likely to act or incite others to action. A relevant but unresolved issue is whether this utopian component provides strong motivation in the presence or the absence of specific, detailed plans and promises. For if the details are present, it has been argued, then people strive to attain what is thus foreshadowed. But if they are absent, the counterargument goes, people are able to supply them in fantasy, and fantasy is happily unrestrained by reality or contradictory proposals.

As this section slowly concludes, the advantages of relying upon the abstraction of cultural homogeneity must be reiterated and amplified. First of all, the approach avoids the intellectual embarrassment arising from being compelled to retract a generalization. One German philosopher has considered "a common domicile, common ancestry . . . , a common language, common spiritual life, membership in a confederacy or federation of several similar states" to be "important and definitive criteria of nationhood," but then he has added that "this is not to say that every nation must have them all in order to be a nation" (Sterling, 1958, pp. 35–36).

Then, any probable or improbable factor linked to nationalism is likely, upon analysis, to be found to be a reference to one of the conditions promoting cultural homogeneity. Earlier writers, for example, had to address themselves to the question of whether "unity of race is . . . an essential, perhaps the one essential, element in nationhood" (Muir, 1916, p. 39). Today race is never mentioned in such broad terms; rather it is considered to furnish a clue to some more basic factor.

In terms of the analysis presented here, race is relevant to nationalism only when its by-products affect people's psychological reactions. Skin pigmentation and other attributes of people's appearance, as indicated previously, are employed as indices of race, but they are in fact perfectly commonplace devices through which people feel that they are distinctive and hence have common ties.

Pigmentation may effectively suggest common experiences in the past; Africans, in spite of cultural differences, feel close to one another because they know that until recently men and women with dark skins were ruled by colonial powers and relegated to a subservient status.

The conclusion must be that the sharing of a common culture, no matter how it has come about, is significant because people with such a culture are likely to have similar personality traits. These traits in turn produce inclinations toward a similar personality, and hence the previously indicated possibility of a basic personality type or national character. When people are similar, they understand one another more easily. They cooperate relatively easily. They can believe they have a common origin and then employ the compelling, absolutistic justifications of the family. They are able to subscribe, as one writer has phrased it, to the myth of the "National Genius" (Delaisi, 1925, pp. 172–73).

### Leaders

Leaders play such an important part in achieving and sustaining loyalty to the state that their role must now be examined in some detail. They contribute ideas and plans which lead to nationalism and to its continuation and perpetuation. The beginning of the growth of modern nationalism in Europe during the eighteenth and nineteenth centuries, and hence eventually throughout the world, is usually traced to "a relatively small nucleus whose influence slowly spreads until it eventually reaches millions of people" (Znaniecki, 1952, p. 24). This "eminent company of 'intellectuals'—philologists, historians, anthropologists, economists, philosophers, and litterateurs" (Hayes, 1937, p. 62)— evidently expressed some of the unexpressed aspirations of their time and consequently inspired many contemporaries to strike out for independence and for the other rights now associated with national sovereignty. Intellectuals, writers, and artists have repeatedly been in the vanguard of nationalistic movements; in a few instances—as in the case of Ireland (Figgis, 1916, pp. 94–134)—it is claimed that they alone virtually originated the very idea of creating the nation. In fact, an outstanding conviction of this century—that peace can be attained by allowing nations to form and then to guide their own existence (Kohn, 1962, pp. 27–28)— undoubtedly can be traced not to the masses of people but to outstanding leaders. Much, perhaps almost all, of the nationalism in independent African countries began when African leaders became acquainted with nationalistic ideas in the course of being educated in the tradition of the West under the colonial powers (Wallerstein, 1961, p. 45); more specifically, they absorbed "the Christian idea of human brotherhood," "the traditional democratic belief" in self-government, and "the Socialist . . . conception of a society in which economic exploitation, poverty, and unemployment are abolished, and rewards are related to work" (Hodgkin, 1956, p. 170).

It seems likely that ordinary citizens, concentrating as they must upon the normal challenges of their existence, have relatively little time or inclination to conceive of nationalism or to dwell upon it after its establishment unless they are induced or compelled to do so. Nationalism may perform many psychological functions, but many or most people must be encouraged or persuaded, as it were, to utilize the services. Somewhere in the society are men who do just that and who are, in fact, professional patriots—the hackneyed phrase is resurrected not to convey its antiquated slur but to call attention to the deep motives that impel such men to present the nation in the most favorable possible light. It is not necessary that they be leaders with political power; they may be organizers or clergymen whose interest in the promotion of nationalism is avocational. In fact, research in the West suggests, informal leaders who lack formal status in a society are often the very people having greatest influence upon groups of followers (e.g. Berelson et al., 1954, pp. 93–117).

Leaders are considered so important that perhaps everywhere and at all times mankind seems to have faith in the ability of a Great Man or Messiah to solve any conceivable problem. Responsibility is thereby avoided: 'Since I know full well that I myself can bring about no miracle, it is comforting to think that others can; I surrender myself to a great father who can do what I cannot do, and indeed who can do it for my sake.'

When there is such faith and when the leader occupies the traditional and the respected seat of power, he is likely to be obeyed almost unquestioningly. Even very devoted proponents of freedom and individual initiative admit that under some circumstances obedience is necessary and desirable: the captain must be in command or there will be chaos. During a crisis and in a strongly nationalistic state the leader is expected to speak with authority.

In addition to prestige, the successful leader has at least one other essential attribute: like the nation and the culture, he must have meaning to people and be intelligible. While elevated, he is human: he has his own joys but he also has sorrows; he is successful but he also makes errors; he is very important but he is also mortal. His traits in fact may be different from those ascribed to him, since he, though a person, is personified.

An inevitable accompaniment of nationalism and hence part of the common culture is pride in one's ancestors. The founding fathers are considered great and unusual for a variety of reasons. They may have been gods or demigods. They possessed virtues which are much scarcer nowadays. They were heroes. Or they had no unusual qualities except for one: although humble and ordinary people, they managed by dint of good character to perform the superhuman feats for which they are remembered. Regardless of the reasons for their fame and for the veneration they receive, they serve the concrete function of linking people to their common heritage in a personal way; often, too, they can be pointed to as models to be followed in the present day.

All ancestors may merit and receive respect, but particular heroes are singled out for special veneration. The attributes of these heroes vary from society to society and from epoch to epoch within the same society; for example, the aristocratic king, the self-made success from the middle class, and the little man ascending to great heights from a humble origin are asserted to have reigned successively in the Western world (Wecter, 1941, p. 71). The national and biblical heroes portrayed in third-grade readers published in the thirties and forties in the United States were generous and kind characters (Child et al., 1946, p. 53); rather than draw a Risky Stimulus Inference, it is to be wondered skeptically whether the children of those decades were in fact inspired by cowboys and bandits and the adults by millionaires and Don Juans. Heroes can even be selected from another society; thus a psychologist, employing a version of a conventional projective instrument (the Thematic Apperception Test) among Africans in Southern Africa, has found that the interpretation of the results requires the addition of a "need to emulate White men," among others, to the list ordinarily employed in the West (Lee, 1953, p. 21–22).

From the existing pantheon of heroes, it might be asked, which one is likely to be selected at a given moment for special praise and veneration? Some heroes are routinely remembered or worshipped, for example, upon the anniversary of their birth, their death, or their important contribution; others, however, seem suddenly to become fashionable or unfashionable. The explanation for the routine or the shift must be found in the singular combination of events and circumstances within the society. The hero raised to new prestige probably satisfies people's existing moods, and the dethroned hero no longer does so. After the Germans were driven out of the Netherlands toward the end of World War II, for example, the inhabitants are reported to have paid considerable attention to the history of their country, particularly to one incident in 1652 when the Dutch fleet under Admiral de Ruyter defeated the English. A reproduction of a painting depicting the battle was widely displayed. According to one psychoanalyst, the Dutch were provided in this manner with "some compensation for the, largely unconscious, resentment which was felt against the Netherland's liberators" (Gess, 1950, p. 346). Is it possible to find another case of resurrecting a hero in order to express hostility resulting from the shame of having to be dependent upon another country, albeit a friendly one ordinarily well liked and respected? There is no reason to think that such compensation on a national scale is frequently observable. If the psychoanalytic interpretation is valid, here indeed is a unique event.

Even mythical heroes are made to appear human and hence intelligible by accounts which describe at a very minimum their birth, accession to power, and death (Raglan, 936, p. 190). In addition, some of the significant events in their lives may be associated with specific sites inside the nation, which people are able to visit. In ancient Greece, the birthplaces of most gods and the sites of their supernatural exploits were ascribed to local areas in Greece or neighboring countries; hence they must have seemed more real and meaningful. The figures in the world's great religions such as Christianity and Islam, on the other hand, spent their lives, from the standpoint of most believers, in foreign, "holy" countries; they are perhaps thus rendered less human and understandable but also more mysterious and impressive.

After their death, ordinary people acquire to a lesser degree the same kind of prestige associated with extraordinary leaders and heroes. In the first place, their departure cannot go unnoticed in any society: some sort of ceremony takes place, if only—as the Ganda in East Africa treated the corpse of a suicide (Roscoe, 1911, p. 20)—to rid themselves of the body and its traces as efficiently as possible. In fact, funeral rites and mourning are among the universal institutions of mankind (Murdock, 1945, p. 124). Then, in many societies ancestors are considered spirits able to influence men's present actions; among the Akan peoples, for example, "the dead are regarded virtually as small gods, able to send either bane or blessing to their survivors or descendents" (Field, 1960, p. 48). These ancestors, being kinsmen, are associated with the nation, therefore, and so the land on which they lived and are buried assumes a sacrosanct character. If their posthumous influence is not so directly experienced, an effort may be made to utilize the fact of death as part of the system of beliefs embedded in patriotism; for example, Memorial Day and similar rituals in a New England town are believed "to integrate the whole community" and, through a burst of patriotism, to provide people with feelings of "well-being" and of "triumph over death" (Warner, 1959, pp. 248–49).

The invocation of myths and history not only serves the psychological functions just indicated but also performs nonpsychological roles within the society. In traditional nations references to the past constitute the legal basis for land rights, the way written deeds do in the West. During international negotiations, as has been previously pointed out, they provide the personificative justifications based upon family and temporal factors.

The recurrence, in widely scattered societies, of similar myths and symbols concerning leaders and ancestors is an interesting phenomenon subject to two interpretations. Diffusion from one society to other societies is the more parsimonious explanation when there are available facts to show that such has been the case. In their absence and especially when the distances are very great, the feeling arises that there have been independent but parallel inventions. These discoveries have been thought to arise because of a racial or collective unconscious within all people (Jung, 1959), but such a postulate is generally found to be much too complicated and hence, tentatively, unnecessary. Rather it is felt that in the light of common problems men spontaneously arrive at similar solutions. People everywhere are faced with the phenomena of birth and death and hence come to know, to their sorrow, that they are mortal. To live with the fact of mortality constantly pervading one's thoughts is unpleasant, perhaps impossible; for this reason some kind of cosmic, metaphysical explanation is always sought; the number of possibilities is limited; and so similar solutions can be independently achieved. Still some of the parallels that have been uncovered look on the surface so complicated that the hypothesis of fortuitously similar solutions to common problems may be mathematically improbable; hence the Jungian speculation cannot be altogether discarded. At any rate, the existence of some universal myths and symbols, whatever their origin, may promote internationalism by providing common experiences and feelings which transcend cultural and national boundaries.

Usually but not always, nationalistic leaders include government officials. Obviously such officials appear whenever there is a formal state with its executive and administrative machinery. It is possible, however, to have a strong sense of nationalism in the absence of government; a conquered people seeking to re-establish independence constitutes a good example (Znaniecki, 1952, p. ix). If it served any purpose, in fact, a typology of nationalism based on land and government could be established: both factors present (any modern nation); government present, land absent (refugees from France during World War II who lived in England and took orders from a Government-in-Exile located in London); government absent, land present (Poland before World War I); government and land absent (Jews outside of Palestine until the establishment of Israel). In the absence of government, leaders function in less formal groups, such as political parties or voluntary associations and clubs.

In government or in other organizations, then, leaders are able to transmit the communications which are so important for the establishment and preservation of patriotism and nationalism. It is not surprising that in diverse countries—for example, the Soviet Union and Czechoslovakia after World War I, Nazi Germany, and Burma and Ghana in recent times—the political party through which an elite has been able to obtain power is utilized later to perpetuate the newly established regime by continuing to function as an educational or communication agency. In other ways, too, leaders employ groups to prepare for nationalism; associations in African countries veering toward independence provided their members with the "valuable experience of modern forms of administration—the keeping of minutes and accounts, the handling of records and correspondence, the techniques of propaganda and diplomacy" (Hodgkin, 1956, p. 84).

How can the originality and the contributions of leaders be accounted for? The talent of such people, the unconventionality of their creations, or their own personal frustrations force them into social positions different from that of their provenance (Mannheim, 1936, pp. 136–46). By changing their status, they acquire knowledge of another social group or class and they are able, consequently, to survey society with greater perspective. As individuals they are motivated to be successful not only in terms of the conventional coin of the realm but also, more importantly, through their original creations. They seek change for the society since they themselves have been compelled to change. It is noteworthy, too, that many national leaders have first shown an interest in traditional forms of artistic expression within their own societies and that they sought at the outset either to preserve or revive handicraft, folk dancing, or the vernacular language. In these ways they selected already existing but perhaps fading cultural forms likely to be popular among large segments of the population and to be utilizable as distinctive attributes of a new nation, while they proceeded to the task of creating the nation-state.

For national leaders to function effectively certain optimal conditions are essential: they seem to require an opportunity within their own society to interact with one another, so that they can co-operate, produce new ideas, and indeed provide the communications so essential for the formation and maintenance of nationalism. In modern societies, such conditions are to be found only in urban areas where a small group, usually an elite, can be free from the pressures of having to produce directly the means of surviving and hence can concentrate upon the tasks of communicating and governing. Cities, consequently, must be included among the indirect requirements of nationalism.

Whenever leaders are singled out as a source of social change or stability, there is the danger that their role can be overemphasized. On the one hand there seems to be no doubt, as has been indicated, that the ideal of self-determination associated with nationalism has become widespread throughout the world and that the leaders of newly developing countries deliberately seek to adopt the forms and sometimes even the spirit of the highly industrialized countries. The same process occurred in Europe almost a century earlier when, according to one analysis, Germans sought national unity because "the nation-States of Great Britain and France had been a success in the world" (Royal Institute of International Affairs, 1939, p. 35). On the other hand, leaders cannot function independently of their followers. At the very least they must persuade or force them to cooperate, and eventually they must establish organizations which can resocialize them and hence compel or persuade them to conform to the pattern of nationalism. More importantly, it is not unreasonable to believe that followers are ready to adopt only certain types of change, never all types. Leaders, in brief, are important in spreading nationalism, but their importance is limited to some degree by their culture or, rather, by the people whom they must change.

### Strong Patriotism

Over and over again it has been asserted in this book that strong patriotism probably promotes nationalism: he who loves his land dearly seeks ways to preserve and perhaps also to expand its culture and power. If this relation does exist, then an understanding of the conditions promoting patriotism ought to provide insight into those affecting nationalism. But no miracle should be expected: the two interact in the manner of the Spiral, and hence factors mentioned in this section can only closely parallel factors already isolated on the preceding pages.

Strong patriotism, as was made clear during a discussion of measurement in the introductory chapter, means that this predisposition is frequently exercised, that people on numerous occasions see a connection between their workaday activities and their country. When is patriotism not a holiday phenomenon?—that is, when is it evoked without the stimulation of an orator, a tune, or a flag? An easy answer is to say that nationals are consciously patriotic when the media of communication often remind them of their country. Such a Stimulus Inference is particularly Risky. People may not be affected by the martial music they obviously hear because it is within earshot. In general, the modern media are so numerous and strident that they also can be deliberately ignored or discounted.

The nation must be genuinely associated with profound gratifications if patriotism is to be strong. For this reason emphasis has already been placed upon the components of a common culture; psychologically, being the ingredients of people's lives, they can produce such satisfactions. Culture here is not an abstraction: patriotism is reinforced when people constantly feel patriotic in their homes, in their occupations, and during their leisure time. Those living in tribal and insular nations are likely to relate so-called leisure to their society: the ceremonial celebrates the achievements in the past and propitiates relevant powers for the sake of the future. In contrast, people in most modern nations divorce leisure-time activity from patriotism: the national anthem is played perfunctorily, and then the game or performance begins.

Paradoxically, not only the attainment but also the nonattainment of important goals, or at least their attainment with difficulty, can cause people to think about their country and to feel grateful toward it. The peasant who tills unfavorable or mountainous fields, for example, and who also knows that life need not be so arduous is likely to perceive the distinctiveness of his existence and hence of his nation. Tentatively, in fact, the conclusion may be drawn that a touch of adversity is a requirement of nationalism.

With more confidence it can be said that strong patriotism springs from doctrines and policies that are sufficiently broad to stir up innumerable significant emotions and impulses; or, in the words heading a previous section of this chapter, they must be psychologically intelligible. Here is no Risky Stimulus Inference, though the means for achieving these responses is not indicated. Men do not go into battle willingly or cheerfully to defend foreign markets or if they think they are at the mercy of a leader's whim; they must believe deeply in the righteousness of the cause according to the values they consider important. You regret that you have but one life to lose for your country only after that country has rewarded you and has convinced you that one, two, or more transmigratory existences would be sterile if it ceased to exist; and that you may have to make the Supreme Sacrifice for your country to remain immortal. Modern nationalism has been powerful because its paraphernalia and articles of faith are clearly or symbolically important; and in previous chapters the list of justifications which can be invoked in behalf of policies and actions has been shown to touch the very core of people's existence. Patriotism is not exactly a religion, but it can contain some of its components and hence possess some or most of its compelling power.

This type of strong patriotism seems especially evident when there is insular nationalism. In a small French-Canadian community during the thirties the educational system is reported to have functioned as follows:

> The explicit purpose of the parish school is to make the children into good Catholics and good citizens, the two being synonymous in the local culture. . . . Study in the schools is organized so as to produce Catholic farmers. Concepts and values which have no place in such a life are omitted or attacked. . . . The schools give the children the material they are expected to learn and believe. Pupils would no more question the veracity of the history the teacher presents than the catechism she teaches. The rural culture can have schools which teach concrete reactions to life's problems, for the so-

ciety is based on one acceptable way of life [Miner, 1939, pp. 184–85].

Such coherence is attainable in a relatively stable community. When forces enter from the outside, people are less unified: the curriculum can no longer combine the teaching of skills and values without conflict, doubts arise, patriotism grows less absolute, and nationalism correspondingly changes.

It is well to end this chapter with the reminder that not all patriotism is genuine, that mere lip service can be paid to the shibboleths and goals of a nation. For the power that governments possess may or may not be voluntarily and periodically granted to them by their nationals; and it may be used to compel internal support and to foster nationalistic policies among foreigners. To win respect or to strike terror either inside or outside—or both—concrete evidence of the power must be observable or publicized. The police and the military forces serve that function in fact and in symbol. At any rate it seems probable that to some extent both patriotism and nationalism require such conformity-producing agencies to supplement the not always gentle pressures of public opinion.

## 14. The Enemy

Perhaps since the beginning of man but certainly in modern times it has been repeatedly observed that the presence of an out-group, especially one evincing hostility, promotes the loyalty of people to their own group. The most famous declaration, at least in the West, has come from a sociologist: "The relation of comradeship and peace in the we-group and that of hostility and war towards others-groups are correlative to each other. . . . Loyalty to the group, sacrifice for it, hatred and contempt for outsiders, brotherhood within, warlikeness without—all grow together, common products of the same situation" (Sumner, 1906, pp. 12–13). The same point has been made a bit more vividly by H. G. Wells as he describes a botanist:

> He has a strong feeling for systematic botanists as against plant physiologists, whom he regards as lewd and evil scoundrels in this relation; but he has a strong feeling for all botanists, and, indeed, all biologists, as against physicists, and those who profess the exact sciences, all of whom he regards as dull, mechanical, ugly-minded scoundrels in this relation; but he has a strong feeling for all who profess what he calls Science, as against psychologists, sociologists, philosophers, and literary men, whom he regards as wild, foolish, immoral scoundrels in this relation; but he has a strong feeling for all educated men as against the working man, whom he regards as a cheating, lying, loafing, drunken, thievish, dirty scoundrel in this relation; but as soon as the working man is comprehended together with those others, as Englishmen —which includes, in this case, I may remark, the Scottish and the Welsh—he holds them superior to all other sorts of Europeans, whom he regards, &c. [Wells, 1905, p. 322].

249

In this chapter the implications of the dictum about the out-group must be carefully examined. First, it is necessary to decide whether the existence of an enemy is another sine qua non of patriotism; and, secondly, the discussion must prepare the way for internationalism, the problem of the next and concluding chapter. Let the suspense be lifted: the dictum appears to be vindicated. And yet Wells' snobbish botanist, according to the psychologist who brought him to this writer's attention, demonstrates at least that "in-group memberships are not permanently fixed" with respect to the groups to which he belongs (Allport, 1954, pp. 35–36). For his loyalty to a particular group to be evoked, nevertheless, he has to feel temporarily contemptuous toward the next larger group. Could he have farther extended himself beyond England to the still bigger circles of NATO, the Common Market, the UN?

## Local Patriotism

At the start of the analysis the point must be made that probably no society of any size is ever completely unified. Some form of rivalry appears, whether it be between members of different classes, associations, sects, or regions. Such local groups can command fierce loyalties; they consider themselves distinctive; in short, they have all the attributes of a nation with one exception: the members recognize that they share a common culture with their rivals (though they differ on small points) and that they live in the same society. Also in the face of a common threat, whether from nature or from one another, they are able quickly to forget their differences and to unite against the common enemy. These loyalties have of course some kind of historical foundation. Before the French Revolution, for example, men everywhere in Europe tended to associate their welfare to a greater degree with the community or the region than with the emerging or emerged nation (Shafer, 1955, p. 95); and these feelings persist today to some degree when they are sustained by local customs. At the same time the factor of sheer distance, which used to separate and isolate peoples and which therefore gave rise to the existence

and perpetuation of differences, has now diminished in importance as a result of improved modes of transportation. Some of the
regional differences (clothing styles) tend to disappear relatively
rapidly, but others (dialects) linger on.

The stubborn intensity and longevity of local patriotism in enclaves and in rural communities can be traced in part to the circumstance that in smaller units people are able to become intimately associated with one another and thus to see a significant
connection between their culture and way of life on the one hand
and the local society on the other. In one sense, therefore, some
form of local patriotism is inevitable; at the very least people are
proud of their neighborhood or their home town. Paradoxically it
appears that the unity of most societies is somewhat disrupted by
local loyalties and simultaneously thereby also strengthened. The
noxious effect of petty rivalries is clear enough, but why may a
beneficial result be achieved? It would seem that the modes of behaving learned with reference to the smaller unit can be extended to include the larger one, the nation itself. The local bonds,
being more intimate and meaningful, may well be stronger, but
the national bonds can also be extremely important if the conviction exists that local life depends upon the preservation of the entire nation.

Obviously the strength of local patriotism varies, and the variation depends upon the attachment nationals feel both to the section of the land they occupy within the nation and to their contemporaries living there. In countries where geographical mobility is
great, therefore, the feelings about one's birthplace must become
weaker, local patriotism is correspondingly diminished, and hence
other means are employed to strengthen national unity. According to one observer, the role of heroes in producing a sense of continuity from the past into the present is more important in America than in Europe. Americans, he thinks, move about too much
to feel loyal to a geographical area; they attach themselves to traditions through symbolic heroes, such as the Founding Fathers,
Washington, Franklin, Jefferson, and Lincoln, whose genius is not
geographically limited and who "have grown into talismans with
a strong emotional tone." Europeans, being less mobile, do not

have to "invoke the spirit of Charlemagne, of Pitt, of Danton, of Garibaldi"—all national figures of course—to strengthen their love of country (Wecter, 1941, pp. 2–3).

Sometimes local patriotism is much more disruptive than unifying. A minority with a really distinctive culture of its own—and the distinctiveness may be based upon language, religion, skin pigmentation, etc.—is able seriously to interfere with the conviction of the majority that the nation is homogeneous and strong, especially if its loyalty at a time of crisis appears doubtful. In addition, schisms within the strata of a society, such as those between peasants and nobles or between intellectuals and workers, can produce serious strains unless they are brushed aside or diminished when on occasion loyalty to the nation is required.

Since some diversity is inevitable in any nation, it would be useful to know just when it produces unity or disunity. Unquestionably many variables must be involved. In the absence of adequate research on the subject, one somewhat but not completely germane study of 165 nonliterate societies in all parts of the world may be cited. An index of political diversity can be derived from a measure of "political organization" which is categorized in terms of whether sovereignty ("the normal unit under whose authority criminal justice is administered internally and war is conducted") resides in the clan, the village, the tribe, or the state; thus greatest diversity may be said to be exhibited by a society in which the clan is sovereign, least by one in which the state has that power. As an index of unity, the character of warfare waged in each society may be used; the societies are classified under the headings of defensive, social, economic, and political warfare. The presumption can be, with the indulgent permission of the reader, that the unity required within a society progresses from the defensive end of the continuum and reaches its maximum in political warfare. The analysis of the data, then, shows a marked tendency for degree of unity so defined to be greater with a decrease in diversity measured by the size of the sovereign political organization; in less formal and accurate language, defensive wars are likely to be fought by clans and other small units, political wars by states and other large units. Even this statistical association, however, fluctuates with other social factors (type of occupation, social organization, contacts with other groups) as well as with various geographical and climatic factors (Wright, 1942, pp. 527–59).

## The Joys of Hatred

Whether the outsider comes from another group within the nation or another nation, he seems to provide people with a number of satisfactions. They can find in him an explanation for many of their ills. Any person, let the sad fact be recalled, inevitably passes through periods of misery. No child ever has his needs reduced as rapidly or as frequently as he wishes. Conformity in a society is never utterly pleasant. Most important, during a period of rapid social change when countries everywhere are likely to feel the impact of strangers and of strange customs, the more or less comfortable existence so vital to retain seems to disappear. This is especially true in rural areas as they begin to move in the direction of modern industrialism. How convenient, how meaningful it is to ascribe the pain of change not to abstract forces but to some identifiable, distinctive outgroup. 'The smoke of the factories comes not from us, but from them.' An accompanying assumption is that people always succeed in explaining why adversity strikes them; or at least they seek some explanation, they do not merely react blindly and stupidly.

For this reason nationalistic movements among nationals living under what they consider to be foreign or alien domination are likely to grow strong when conditions are bad and can be ascribed to the colonial or alien power. In Africa some frustration of the elite and their followers has been a by-product of benefits bestowed by the very colonial powers from whom independence has been sought. A taste of the material and nonmaterial values from outside has quickened the desire to secure larger quantitites of these advantages, and then the inability to do so has been a source of profound or superficial annoyance. Communist states have supported independence movements which have often been composed of middle-class Africans and which have been striving for middle-class goals, because they have observed that anticolonialism is the only available feeling that can be tapped for revolutionary purposes.

When people possess an explanation that pins responsibility upon outsiders, they are better able to appreciate the benefits granted them within their own society. Ordinarily they are surrounded by symbols, artifacts, and modes of behavior they consider distinctive only when they self-consciously react to them. Outgroupers can induce this very self-consciousness: 'They always eat their meals in the kitchen, which we never do.' By observing others patriots come to the conclusion that their own society is better not only because it is different from what they think they perceive out there, but also because they can then believe or continue to believe that it has been gratifying in the past. A threat from the outside makes the inside seem much more precious; certainly at the very least it can be maintained that patriotism and nationalism are facilitated by misery of alien origin.

In addition, sure-fire ways exist to produce the miserable feelings that lead to indignation against outsiders and to appreciation of insiders. One is to issue restrictive regulations concerning a people's language or to require that a foreign language become the official vehicle of communication or of instruction in the schools. The Italian government under Mussolini prohibited the use of German in South Tyrol on public notices (including tombstones), in government, and in most schools (Ritschel, 1959, pp. 57–62); decades later Tyroleans still complain about that practice, assert their hatred for the Italians, and obviously love their own country. Interference with a people's language not only is a symbolic insult but also creates difficulties of a realistic sort in simple communication. The emergence of a martyr likewise facilitates patriotism and nationalism: if people feel that someone with whom they identify themselves has been killed, tortured, or otherwise deprived of some value, their indignation is likely to be great and perhaps long enduring.

The ability to label the ingroup as distinctive and then to obtain joy from perceiving the attribute may require that some outgroup be not only perceived but also disliked. For to consider other people different it is always necessary to disregard their similarities. To deny, minimize, or de-emphasize the basic similarities common to all mankind demands the kind of blindness that hatred or fear can provide.

Evidence of a restricted sort for these assertions comes from a study of Californians conducted during the 1940s. There local patriotism could take the form of prejudice against Negroes, Jews, and other ethnic groups. In the research prejudice against Negroes, for example, was ascertained by asking samples of people whether they agreed or disagreed with items such as the following: "Most Negroes would become officious, overbearing, and disagreeable if not kept in their place"; "There is something inherently primitive and uncivilized in the Negro, as shown in his music and his extreme aggressiveness." An American brand of "patriotism" was scaled by means of other items, such as: "The main threat to basic American institutions during this century has come from foreign ideas, doctrines, and agitators"; "America may not be perfect, but the American Way has brought us about as close as human beings can get to a perfect society." As indicated in an earlier chapter, patriotism so measured was found to correlate not only with attitude toward Negroes (.76) but also with attitude toward Jews (.69) and toward other minorities (.83). Such correlations, though reasonably high and hence statistically significant, obviously stem from the particular modes of measurement being employed (Adorno et al., 1950, pp. 105, 113, 117, 122); but they do show that stigmatizing an outgroup was associated with a chauvinistic love of country.

Some years earlier a group of American college students was able to carry out the following instructions: "I want you to mark these sheets as you think a typical German would mark them. Try to imagine yourself as a German citizen, living under the conditions they are living under today, and indicate the way you think he would feel." In obeying these instructions and identical ones relating to "an English citizen," the subjects tended to project their own beliefs upon the two national groups (Stagner and Osgood, 1941); they thus revealed that even under artificial conditions they could utilize an outgroup as a form of self-expression.

A similar mechanism presumably functions in less intellectualized spheres whenever nationals are encouraged to fear or hate some other nation. Then, after learning to feel antagonistic, they are likely to seek modes of expressing themselves and to feel purged when they are able to do so. The thrill attached to destruction, actual or symbolic, is considered respectable and praiseworthy. It is good to be provided with a scapegoat, and then to use him for that purpose.

In the presence of a threatening outgroup, the crucial question must be: What satisfying solution is adopted by people in the short and long run? They may value their nation all the more, but what do they actually do to express their feelings? All the reactions of people as individuals reappear on the national level: they are overtly aggressive when they wage war, they displace anger upon innocent bystanders, they may perversely cry *mea culpa.* Any particular solution for the national group springs, as ever, from a host of circumstances. The wandering bands of the Siriono of Bolivia, when they come in contact with Indian or white outsiders, do not take a stand but instead "retire deeper and deeper into the impenetrable jungle." It may be assumed that, in the face of the enemy, they value their own heritage all the more; but why do they retreat? According to one observer, they have suffered "punishment" in the past as a result of waging warfare; they lack, he also states, the organization, the weapons, and the numbers to fight (Holmberg, 1950, pp. 62–63). Obviously, moreover, the jungle is at their disposal as an area into which they can retreat. Their "unwarlike character," therefore, is the product of many factors and, having come into existence, itself inhibits war; again a Spiraled Explanation.

Treason may originate in part from an absence of patriotism: the traitor identifies his interests with those of the threatening outgroup and hence turns aggressively against his own ingroup. A psychiatric study of three maladjusted American boys who during World War II were pro-German or pro-Japanese suggests that, "feeling unable to inflict pain upon the people in their own environment by their own power, they wished the Nazis or the Japanese to do the job for them" (Escalona, 1946). The status of the outgroup is reversed, but hating brings satisfaction, however psychologically and socially perverse.

### Importance

Certainly, then, the role of the outsider—the enemy—in the establishment, the functioning, and the preservation of nationalism is important. It is, nevertheless, difficult to appraise that role because it clearly fluctuates from nation to nation and, within a nation, from situation to situation. A single principle, however, is incontestable: the greater the threat which the outgroup seems to pose, the more significant does that group become in facilitating both patriotism and nationalism.

On an anecdotal level, for example, reference can be made to peasant costumes in the South Tyrol. Before World War I, according to competent informants there, native dress was slowly disappearing and was being replaced, as is true all over Europe, by the standardized clothes generally prevalent in the West. Then the costumes were banned during the fascist regime. The reaction of many Tyroleans was to hide and then cherish the traditional garb. Since World War II, the custom has been revived and peasant costumes are worn in some areas on all festive occasions, including holy days and ceremonies celebrating Tyrol's nationality.

"I hate to say it," an unusually gifted, intelligent, kindly Tyrolean peasant told this writer, "but each time I hear that an Italian living here in South Tyrol has died I rejoice; Italians are all right in Italy but not here." This man himself had suffered under the Mussolini regime. Even though he is now quite prosperous, he cannot, he will not, forget those experiences in the past. In addition, the presence of Italians in his country, the buildings they are constructing, and the changes in Tyrolean customs he ascribes to them remind him again and again of that past. This hatred, moreover, he is transmitting to his children. He deliberately and repeatedly tells them about the traumas of long ago and he has made it clear that they can in effect show him love and respect only by hating the Italians too. They in turn may never be hurt directly by Italians but their hatred, though vicariously learned, is coming to be very intense.

It is futile to say of those who hate because of what happened to their parents and ancestors that they are being guided by symbols and not by reality. The symbols enable them to express themselves, to show that they are good patriots, to displace their own aggression. The Civil War in the United States, probably every war, has left scars upon the unborn. And those scars are even deeper when some important group of the society has an interest in keeping the hatred alive, which is so often the case.

The threat posed by the outgroup, consequently, may be psychological in nature and hence as dependent upon people's interpretation of a situation as upon reality itself. If they feel generally secure or if they are especially satisfied with their society, they are less likely to feel inclined to take vigorous action either to preserve or expand the power and culture of their nation; they may disregard even hostile outgroups. Under such conditions, their anxiety must first be aroused before they will acknowledge the threat and hence be stirred to nationalistic activity.

The outgroup or the enemy, like every variable affecting nationalism, seldom if ever operates in isolation. When immigrants to the United States cluster together and maintain nationalistic feelings and ties with the country of their birth or origin, for example, the presence of outsiders in their midst promotes cultural unity. But the fact that they are surrounded by strangers with different customs by itself does not determine the strength of their nationalism or the length of time it takes them to become assimilated. Involved is a very complicated interaction between some of the attributes they themselves possess (their skin coloring, native language, religion, education, purpose for emigrating in the first place) and the corresponding attributes of people already living there (Warner and Srole, 1945).

Even during a war the strength of people's convictions concerning the threat offered by an actual enemy fluctuates, of course, from person to person. In addition, if there is more than one enemy, yet another kind of dispersion may appear. Attitude scales, for example, were administered toward the end of World War II to a very restricted group of college students in the Chicago area; their feelings toward Germany were found to vary "much more widely" than those toward Japan (Gilliland and Blum, 1945, p. 392). The outgroup, consequently, is not an unambiguous stimulus pattern.

In time of war, however, patriotic convictions are likely to be strongest; does it follow, then, that the influence of the outgroup is greatest at that time? Once more there is a Spiraled interaction: stronger patriotism can be considered both a consequence and a cause of international conflict, but patriotism can be powerful without conflict. Certainly, let us once more agree, the nation becomes especially precious when it is attacked; and yet patriots such as the Swiss can love their country without seeking war, and nationalistic demands can be vigorously voiced without threatening to fight. While the point has already been made in Chapter 12 that wars, especially modern ones, are much too complicated to be traced to single causes, whether they be economic or nationalistic, still the fact remains that the contribution of patriotism and nationalism can be and has been not inconsiderable. Since the French Revolution the number of wars fought between modern nations has been depressingly large; and most if not all of these conflicts have involved goals associated with peoples' patriotic convictions and their nationalistic demands and actions. Warriors everywhere must be loyal to the regime which commands them; and part of basic training is usually a series of communications and experiences designed to promote that loyalty by increasing patriotism. A distinguished student of war once remarked that "to create a spirit ready to participate in the mass massacre characteristic of the most recent wars, cultural, religious, and political motives have been especially enlisted" (Wright, 1942, p. 290). In his view, then, the contribution of patriotism is noteworthy. After the Soviet Union had been invaded by the German armies, there was a sharp increase in the number of "national" slogans issued each May Day (Yakobsen and Lasswell, 1949, pp. 242–43); since these slogans provide authoritative guides to the regime's information policy, the change can be called symptomatic of the attempt to use patriotism as a psychological device to spur the Russian people to defend not "Communism," "Socialism," "World Revolution," etc., but "Mother Russia." Finally, nationalistic media also sustain the swagger of the victors and the sorrows of the vanquished after each war, with the frequent result that the end of one conflict has been the prelude to the next.

At the conclusion of two chapters seeking to determine the factors facilitating patriotism and nationalism, it would be refreshing to be able to present evidence that some of them are generally more important than others. The present chapter has explicitly espoused the view that the presence of an outgroup which appears hostile is extremely important in achieving national solidarity and hence in promoting both patriotism and nationalism; but is it always or usually more important than a common language, a common culture, or infallible leaders? The possibility of a definitive reply has already been eliminated in the introductory and concluding pages of the previous chapter: we do not know, we do not know.

Still let us keep human hopes alive by referring calmly to a rough model of how the problem might conceivably be attacked. Years ago, one investigator first selected a half dozen "elements" of nationalism as the basis for his analysis. He himself then ranked seven modern nations on a scale of "possession or non-possesion" of these elements. Thus for one of them, "internal communications," which he determined largely by consulting figures on railroad traffic, he emerged with this ranking: Switzerland, Germany, France, Italy, Spain, and the United States—the seventh country, Great Britain, he did not include in this particular series. Next he obtained ratings from 42 social scientists, editors, and writers in various countries concerning the degree to which the seven countries exhibited what he called "defensive" nationalism; other data simultaneously received from them are not relevant here. Finally, he calculated for the seven countries rank-order correlations between such nationalism on the one hand and the possession or non-possession of the six elements on the other. For two of them, "internal communications" and "historical tradition," the correlations were negligible; but for the remaining four—"geography," "literary tradition," "religion," and "language"—they were statistically significant. In brief, the latter four appeared more closely related to his definition of nationalism than the former two.

The investigator himself, however, is skeptical concerning his own results. He recognizes, for example, that the data from which he derived his index for internal communications are "extremely fragmentary" and that his statistical measures, being based on only seven nations, can be markedly affected by a change in the rank of a single country (King, 1935, pp. 23–37). In addition, two other defects of the procedure appear in the light of methodological developments since his original analysis. His own rating of the countries with respect to the elements was quite subjective and not submitted to a test of reliability and objectivity. The ratings of the "experts" were not only equally subjective but also most variable. Obviously, therefore, what is needed in order to weight the factors associated with patriotism and nationalism is the application of the same procedure in a more objective manner to a much, much larger number of representative nations: both the relevant elements and the nationalism of the nations must be more explicitly rated or ranked. In spite of the study's admitted weaknesses and of the time that has elapsed since its inception and publication, nevertheless, the final conclusion of the author seems to be as valid a statement as can be made even now concerning the essential bases for nationalism:

> Where all our elements of nationalism are present in a nation to a high degree, the national solidarity of that nation will be high. Where all or a majority of these elements are present to a small degree, the national solidarity is likely to be weak. Nationalism is thus the resultant of various historical, economic, and social forces of which the six here analyzed are by no means the only ones. These forces have worked with varying degrees of intensity in different nations. Where all or most of them have been strong, nationalism is likely to be strong; where all or a majority have been weak, nationalism is likely to be weak [King, 1935, p. 37].

## 15. Internationalism

It is only a short step from a discussion of the enemy or the foreigner to internationalism. Just as members of local groups within
a country tend to forget their own personal rivalries when faced
with a common threat, so nationals may overlook their differences when confronted with a common enemy. But do they? No,
such an explanation appears far too simple the moment a specific
instance is examined. The five North American Indian societies,
and later a sixth, which formed the powerful Iroquois League,
probably at the start of the seventeenth century, for example, did
indeed have common enemies and they united, too, in order to extend their own power. But these primarily hunting societies also
had important cultural traits in common: mutually intelligible
languages, similar religions, the same two mythological heroes,
and matrilineal descent. "The analogy of the maternal house-
hold," in fact, "was projected to the League" (Fenton, 1951, p.
51); hence the basic organization of the alliance sprang from an
institution with which all six tribes had already been acquainted.
In addition, the efficiency of the League itself depended not only
on the common enemy but also on its own political structure, a
set of symbols, various customs that evolved, and certain devices
(such as wampum) to record its achievements (Morgan, 1904;
Wallace, 1946).

The psychological factors facilitating internationalism, then, are
the concern of the present chapter. How, the question is being
asked, can internationalism be achieved? The problem is phrased
in this fashion for three reasons. First, internationalism at the present time is virtually nonexistent; hence even an objective analysis
is concerned with a contingency or a possibility rather than with a
set of circumstances of a reality which can be empirically examined. Then, more or less faithful to his chosen approach, the writer

concentrates not on international agreements, treaties, or organizations but on the psychological climates which can promote international cooperation in general. Lastly, the wording of the question suggests that internationalism is a desirable goal, a bias herewith admitted.

## Nationalistic Hindrances

The analysis begins by considering some of the psychological impediments to internationalism that are inherent within nationalism. Throughout this book, it has often been emphasized again and again that patriotism and nationalism serve, and serve well, numerous psychological functions. Otherwise, it should now be clear, millions of people would not be extremely patriotic and nationalistic: psychological equipment is retained only when it continues to be rewarding. Patriotism may be, in Samuel Johnson's famous phrase, "the last refuge of a scoundrel" during a British tea-time conversation or an American political campaign; more significantly, it is an inevitable concomitant of social life and of many generous human impulses. Through nationalism people are provided with a sense of belonging to some local group and to the nation itself: they come to appreciate the goals they are seeking jointly and to be aware of their membership. They feel less alone, they are part of a vital organization. At another extreme, as suggested in the last chapter, their patriotic predispositions and their nationalistic tendencies enable them to displace some or many aggressive impulses onto an outside enemy or outgroup.

· The displacement involved in nationalism, like all displacement, results from a combination of circumstances. A well-known fact, which has been previously emphasized, is that people, when frustrated, usually have many or certainly a number of channels through which they have at least the theoretical opportunity to express themselves. The expression of aggression directed toward the nation's outgroups is facilitated by the social circumstance that its release in such a manner is considered socially respectable. The choice of this mode of expression, it must now be strongly emphasized, is not inevitable. Thus the ways in which Negroes in the United States have released their aggressive impulses are numerous, and have varied from self-reproach to overt hostility against white people (Dollard, 1939). Only relatively rarely has nationalism developed as a protest; both the Garvey Back-to-Africa movement and the Black Muslims of the present day must be viewed in this light. These militant movements have been difficult to bring into existence for many reasons: Negroes lack land on which to build their own nation, and Africa as a possible site they consider either remote or unattractive, or both; they know that Negro culture in the United States has not been sufficiently or distinctively different from the rest of American culture and so they have not wished to abandon or alter radically the country of their birth; and they have been able to express their demands through many other kinds of organizations, especially recently. Aggressiveness, in general, need not inevitably give rise to nationalism.

In addition, the amount of aggression to be displaced through nationalism or some other institution depends in part upon the severity of the frustration. If people's basic problems are reasonably well resolved and, moreover, resolved from their standpoint, they are less likely to turn to any kind of scapegoat. It follows, therefore, that nationalism is likely to give way to a permanent rather than an expedient form of internationalism only under propitious economic, political, social, and hence psychological conditions.

There are more particular aspects of patriotism which hinder the growth of internationalism. People's distinctive feelings toward themselves, their land, and their culture are usually accompanied, as previously indicated, by a conviction of superiority. It is easy to say that distinctiveness need not give rise to superiority and that even superiority may not lead to gloating or to anxiety, but in fact both consequences are usually unavoidable. In this respect internationalism may well depend upon the ability to minimize, ignore, or discredit the distinctive attributes of one's own nation and instead to emphasize the universal similarities transcending national boundaries.

The core of patriotism, furthermore, is probably the strongest hindrance to internationalism, viz. the conviction that one's personal welfare is a function of the nation's general traditions and way of life and of its particular policies at a given moment in history. People with such a conviction are loath to diminish their loyalty to the nation for fear that, in effect, they will jeopardize themselves. Somehow they must be convinced, if the political goal is to weaken nationalism, that their welfare is or can be linked more strongly to some form of internationalism.

In America prejudiced children, adolescents, and adults, as already stated on two occasions in this book and as has been empirically established again and again (e.g. Kutner, 1958), differ more or less markedly from their unprejudiced counterparts with respect to needs, personality traits, and modes of apprehending and coping with the external world. Under these circumstances, prejudice is more than a frivolous, dangerous, or nasty component that is added to the personality; its roots are deep and it is often a symptom as well as a cause of the individual's basic approach to people and the milieu. Such prejudices, consequently, cannot be easily altered. Here the crucial issue for internationalism is whether patriotism and nationalism anywhere resemble prejudice: do they play a similar psychological role in the lives of patriots and nationalists? The question is answerable in two ways. On the one hand, the studies on prejudice just cited include national groups and hence their findings with respect to aggressiveness are applicable to nationalism: Mexicans or Japanese are usually paraded alongside Jews and Negroes on paper-and-pencil tests. On the other hand, the really meaningful prejudice for most Americans is concentrated upon groups which live in the neighborhood and can be perceived; whereas the significant groups for internationalism are far off. Your neighbor may be a Negro, a Jew, or an Italian; he is not likely to be a Russian or a Chinese. In most places of the world, however, the important foreigners may be less remote. Although the issue must be left unresolved, then, it seems probable that a difference exists between straight bias or prejudice and the hostility associated with patriotism or nationalism.

Unquestionably, the general conclusion must be, patriotism and nationalism are strong. All their forms and features cannot ever or easily be altered, no more than family loyalty can be expected to disappear. From this standpoint, there is no magic prescription for attaining internationalism, rather prospects appear dim though not impossible.

## The Possibility of Change

If patriotism is so deeply rooted in people and if nationalism is almost inevitable in the modern world, the question opening this chapter recurs: how can internationalism be facilitated or achieved? A dash of optimism must immediately be added to the discussion: change is possible, or rather most change is. That proposition receives almost universal assent and is itself a factor helping to produce change. Such change, moreover, is not inexorable; it can come in large part from the deliberate decision to adopt measures which will make the future differ from the past.

First, there must be a sombre glance at current popular theories of social change related to internationalism. They presumably summarize man's knowledge, and also they guide and reflect the beliefs of leaders who produce or hinder change. To shorten the discussion, attention is focused only on extreme views, that of Marxism and its opponents.

At a quick, superficial glance it looks as though Marxism excludes the possibility that change can result from men's decision to change. The Communist Manifesto of 1848 remains the most convenient and authoritative source to cite because it provides a key to most Marxist thinking. Therein it is stated that the significant impetus to internationalism is an economic fact: "the need of a constantly expanding market for its products chases the bourgeoisie over the whole surface of the globe." As a result, nations engage in international trade: "in place of the old wants, satisfied by the production of the country, we find new wants, requiring for their satisfaction the products of distant lands and climes." All spheres of human activity are subsequently affected: "national one-sidedness and narrow-mindedness become more and more impossible, and from the numerous national and local literatures there arises a world literature." In short, it can be said that "in place of the old and national seclusion and self-sufficiency, we have intercourse in every direction, universal interdependence of nations" (Marx and Engels, 1930). Here, then, is a one-way sequence from economic expansion to alterations in patriotic predispositions; and indeed many shifts of people in the direction of internationalism have probably resulted from such economic change. At the same time all Marxists, including Marx, have also stressed the element of voluntarism in human affairs in spite of the doctrine of economic determinism; for otherwise propaganda, agitation, subversion, diplomacy, etc., would be futile epiphenomena. In practice, too, communist countries actively engage in what is now called political socialization and to which Lenin referred when he discussed the gradual "withering away of the state" after the revolution (Lenin, 1919). In the sections just quoted from the Manifesto, there is acknowledgment of Spiraled psychological changes which, though they follow an initial economic change, themselves then accelerate the economic trend; the "new wants," for example, require the further expansion of international trade. Internationalism, in short, is feasible from the Marxist standpoint; and hence good Marxists do no violence to their doctrine if they strive to move forward to this type of utopia.

Marxism has always had theoretical opponents, the most impressive of whom have denied or deprecated the importance of economic factors and have turned instead to psychological ones. Early in this century, for example, it was suggested that some of the tenets of the Protestant Reformation encouraged convictions and behavior which set the stage for the developments of capitalism. Many of Benjamin Franklin's aphorisms—"time is money," "save and have"—aimed to promote the kind of hard work and investment on which industrialism was subsequently to depend (Weber, 1930, pp. 48–51). A much later non-Marxist panacea refers not to religion but to what is called the "need for achievement": innumerable relations between some measure of that need on the one hand and economic growth or nationalism on the other hand have been demonstrated. It is then asserted that such a psychological factor is always present before important economic changes occur; for example, "achievement motivation is in part responsible for economic growth" (McClelland, 1961, p. 36). In fact, however, the data are all correlations, so that the analyst has not proven his contention, although the number of instances he has deliberately collected is impressive. The concept of achievement, be it noted, is so broad that it is able to include convictions concerning national and nationalistic goals; hence this theory also supports the view that people can determine to some extent the course of their own society.

A more flamboyant splash in recent times has been created by a theory of economic development which has been deliberately proposed and then hailed as an alternative to Marxism. According to this view, patriotism and nationalism rather than economic factors explain the conditions under which a "traditional society" is able and eager to "take off" and head toward the goal of being an economically "mature" society:

> A reactive nationalism—reacting against intrusion from more advanced nations—has been a most important and powerful motive force in the transition from traditional to modern societies, at least as important as the profit motive. Men holding effective authority or influence have been willing to uproot traditional societies not, primarily, to make money but because the traditional society failed—or threatened to fail—to protect them from humiliation from foreigners [Rostow, 1961, pp. 26–27].

Once more the element of voluntarism in human affairs is brought forward to the center of the stage. Fine, but a word of caution seems in order: noneconomic theories may be pushing the pendulum a trifle too far. Certainly *some* economic changes are needed before people's attitudes change.

If internationalism can be partially planned, then the initiative must come from the leaders in the society. In Chapter 13 their importance in creating and perpetuating nationalism has been underscored. They could perform many of the same functions in behalf of internationalism, provided of course that they themselves have been initially converted. There are, in fact, spotty bits of evidence indicating that people's belief in the possibility of change is related to their desire to change. In a poll conducted in nine Western countries during 1948, for example, to which reference has previously been made, the following question was included: "Some people say that there should be a world government able to control the laws made by each country. Do you agree or disagree?" Education, socio-economic status, sex, and age apparently did not affect the replies to this question. Instead, those favoring world government tended to believe that "human nature" could be changed and that "world peace is possible." Two incidental findings from this study indicate, in addition, that the inclination toward internationalism is linked to other predispositions and to cultural factors. First, the respondents supporting internationalism came in greater numbers from among those with left rather than right political orientations. Then there was considerable variability from country to country: the percentages agreeing with the quoted question ranged from a high of 56 for Italy and 48 for Norway to a low of 35 for Australia and 19 for urban Mexico, with the remaining countries all in the middle 40s (Buchanan and Cantril, 1953, pp. 64–66).

## Indoctrination

What are the psychological changes which people must sanction and which must come to pass for greater internationalism to be achieved? It is impossible even to describe them objectively or semi-objectively without sounding pious, but maybe such piety should cause no embarrassment. More tolerance, for example, is needed: tolerance of differences, tolerance of foreigners. How, the question must be instantly posed, how can such tolerance be achieved? It must be achieved by changing people's attitudes in these respects from unfavorable to favorable or at least to neutral; they must come to feel not fearful but confident when confronted with differences or foreigners. But how?

On the level of interpersonal contact, it is often assumed that increased knowledge resulting from increased contact is likely to promote such friendliness. Perhaps or maybe most of the time; yet there are exceptions of course. Generalizations on this score ought to be more readily obtainable from the field of race relations because people prejudiced against one another usually share a common territory and hence can meet, and also because research on prejudice has been extensive. As good a summary as exists concerning the effects of social contacts upon prejudice reads as follows:

Prejudice (unless deeply rooted in the character structure of the individual) may be reduced by equal status contact between majority and minority groups in the pursuit of common goals. The effect is greatly enhanced if this contact is sanctioned by institutional supports (i.e., by law, custom, or local atmosphere), and provided it is of a sort that leads to the perception of common interests and common humanity between members of the two groups [Allport, 1954, p. 281].

Noteworthy in this statement is the number of qualifications. Contact as such does not reduce prejudice: it is contact occurring under certain prescribed conditions, having the indicated consequences, and indeed only involving people with certain previously established personality inclinations. Presumably any generalization about contact and internationalism must be similarly qualified. In addition, the shift from nationalism to internationalism may be more complicated than from prejudice to sweetness and light. For prejudice as a social reality diminishes as people's individual prejudices diminish; whereas corresponding changes in patriotism and feelings about outgroupers do not necessarily alter the country's nationalistic policies and activities if the nation's leaders remain unaffected.

The fact remains, though, that internationalism ultimately requires people to reorient their thinking and mode of evaluating. In almost a literal sense they must be converted to a religion which, in preaching universal brotherhood, is able to transcend the loyalties engendered by nationalism. Such a religious conviction is not easy to come by, largely because so far even the religions organized on an international basis, such as Roman Catholicism and Islam, have proven sufficiently elastic to be fitted into national frameworks. "Social reforms," a philosopher states with reference to internationalism, "have not always waited on a religious change of heart in the past, nor, therefore, should we expect them to do so in the future" (Cohen, 1954, p. 99). The contention may be correct, but small changes can set the Spiral in motion: the heart helps the society change, the society changes the heart, etc.

Now one certain, general way of changing the heart is through love, as all women and most men are supposed to know; hence it

may very well be that genuine internationalism will be ultimately and deeply achieved through intermarriage of people
of different nationalities. Intermarriage as such is probably feared
and disparaged by racists and strongly inclined nationalists more
than any other change. For they realize correctly that false ideas
must largely vanish and be replaced by new ones if a marriage in
the Western sense is to be successful. It is a little difficult if not
impossible to be blindly patriotic concerning one's own country
when one's beloved comes from a different land. Most people,
however, have neither the inclination nor the opportunity to
marry outside their own group, and so it can hardly be anticipated that the United Nations or any other international organization will derive much of its strength from miscegenation. Still
with increasing travel, intermarriage is likely to play a more important role in the future, especially among intellectuals and leaders.

A final attempt to phrase the necessary psychological changes:
somehow people must become convinced that their welfare is
no longer linked only to the nation. It has been suggested several
times in this book that national loyalty results from a verbal leap
out of a smaller but meaningful unit such as the neighborhood
and the region. It ought to be possible to jump farther and land
upon an international organization whose outlines are really no
more directly or meaningfully perceivable to individuals than are
those of the nation. The orientation must be much, much broader;
if a late eighteenth-century phrase may be quoted out of context, each man must become "a steady Patriot of the World
alone" (Canning, 1802, p. 189). Here, in fact, is the view of
many thinkers—"narrow circles can, without conflict, be supple-
mented by larger circles of loyalty"—but they then quickly admit
that this is a "happy condition . . . not often achieved" (Allport,
1954, p. 46). One final reference to the Tyrolean study: to attain
nationalism, the boundaries of what is called the *Heimat* must
be made to disappear.

## Thin Rays of Hope

Visible, if one looks carefully and patiently, are scattered signs
indicating trends toward internationalism. In the present day,

more and more international organizations are coming into existence, and more and more international contacts are occurring, at
least within if not between the great blocs into which the world is
now divided. Above the international organizations of the East
and the West is the United Nations, with its specific subdivisions
such as UNESCO and the World Health Organization, which operate across boundaries and in spheres likely to have direct impact upon people. There are international scholarly and educational associations which publish journals and whose members
come together at conferences. "Cultural exchanges" between countries include students, professors, artists, scientists, and sometimes
technicians and engineers. Most modern nations broadcast internationally by shortwave, and their regular radio and television
programs cross borders freely with or without international hook-
ups. Mail, transportation, and certain industries (such as whaling
and fishing) function within a set of international regulations.
Having less scope and still operating on an international level
are the European Economic Community and the Council for Mutual Economic Assistance in Europe. Everywhere nations have re-
ciprocal tariff agreements. In fact, when a broad survey of international, peaceful activity is digested (e.g. Blum, 1963), it is
impossible to avoid the impression that nobody anywhere is safe
from this international barrage, maybe even those who live on
mountains either actually or symbolically.

Many Risky Stimulus Inferences, however, must be made concerning the effects of such activities upon men's evaluations and
beliefs. In some countries only a small proportion of the inhabitants are affected by international contacts and communication or
are even aware of international activities. Radio programs and
press releases can boomerang: or they go unperceived because
prospective audiences are not interested or are prevented by
their own governments or social pressure from tuning in. An organization such as the Peace Corps is not always an unqualified
success; but who indeed would expect any vast enterprise to be?

When the European Economic Community causes Italians to
see more German motor cars and likewise Germans to see more
Italian cars in their respective countries, how long will the names
of the cars continue to remind them of the foreign origins of these

products? Will such a reminder make them more aware of the Common Market itself? Even if they become conscious of that Community, will their patriotic feelings be correspondingly altered or will they simply be grateful to this international organization for providing them with better cars at cheaper prices? Will they, in brief, simply buy more foreign cars without growing more international in their outlook?

It is much too early to offer any definitive account of the factors that are producing this United States of Europe on a limited scale. A few tentative hypotheses, however, may be quickly suggested. In the first place, the results of nationalism are patently and pathetically clear to many Europeans. Even young adults and children who were too young or not yet born at the time can be made to appreciate the chaos and tragedy resulting from World War II; there is almost universal agreement that this catastrophe occurred in a Europe divided by national rivalries. Then, secondly, immediate benefits accrue from membership in the Common Market: foreign products become available without an increase in cost, and national economies have prospered. Thirdly, and sadly, the presence of an important competitor, the Soviet bloc, has given people—at least their leaders—a sense of urgency, and so they favor limited forms of international cooperation as a result of this external threat. Then, finally, old difficulties remain, such as national rivalries and suspicions from the past and the economic dislocation usually resulting from the revision of tariffs.

There are, moreover, a number of nonfactual but very compelling a priori reasons for anticipating that internationalism is not impossible. It has become quite trite to point out that the solution of any problem which is important to people reduces their tensions somewhat. The platitude, however, is very helpful: in spite of vast increases in the population, considerable progress is being made everywhere in preventing and fighting disease and often, too, in raising the general standard of living. To some degree, therefore, people are possibly becoming a little less prone to displace aggression upon foreigners or to feel dependent upon their own nation for survival.

Perhaps it is useless to state—but sheer conscientiousness prevents censorship—that some tensions could be reduced if diverse peoples were not to inhabit the same territory. Differences do create friction, and tolerance and even appreciation of the strange and the exotic can be easier and pleasanter at a distance when, consequently, no cultural threat looms. Here is no plea for apartheid in South Africa or against regions, such as Jamaica or Hawaii, where diverse groups already live quite peacefully together. Rather a factual reminder is expressed that some forms of amicability can be more easily cultivated from afar. What can be said in this context and in conclusion about the German-speaking South Tyroleans whose views and attitudes have so frequently appeared in the pages of this book? Certainly, they would be overjoyed if the Italians were to leave and if their country were to attain a vaguely defined "autonomy" under Italy or to be returned to Austria. That solution, aside from considerations of justice and legality, however, is utterly unrealistic: the Italians are now too deeply committed to, and embedded in, the Alto Adige; no political party or leader in Italy who might advocate a significant diminution of Italian rights there could possibly survive. No, this writer thinks, the conflict can be resolved only when the patriotism and nationalism of the two cultures function more firmly within a united Europe; when both groups of nationals consider themselves Europeans primarily and Tyroleans and Italians only secondarily with respect to the essential goals of existence. Actually, as direct citations in Chapter 9 demonstrate, the most ardent Austrian and Italian groups are in essential agreement with this prognosis. Until the millennium arrives, consequently, it is well to realize that friction is unavoidable and that for decades ahead changes and concessions can be, at the most, only gratifying palliatives.

In passing the prospect of nuclear warfare must be mentioned as a negative incentive for peoples everywhere to weaken national sovereignty and to participate in international organizations. Why do nationals continue to show concern for the connection between personal or social welfare and the nation when everyone could be virtually eliminated by such a war? The question is not rhetorical. And yet for most people atomic and hydrogen bombs are abstractions, remote terrors which are less pressing than the concrete, meaningful demands of the moment. The need to reduce and eventually to eliminate the possibility of another full-scale war, however, is one which the leaders of a nation are at least in a position to appreciate: they have immediate access to relevant facts and plans. Perhaps, perhaps they can become superhuman to give higher priority to that need.

Another wisp of hope for internationalism is also so depressing, if from another standpoint, that it ought to be suppressed: to the extent that nations adopt uniform ways of behaving, people will feel that their own countries are less distinctive and hence, since distinctiveness is an important component, will lose some of their patriotism. Clearly there are dreary trends in the direction of such uniformity: clothes, cosmetics, popular music, transportation, sports, motion pictures now vary less from country to country than formerly. You feel at home in a foreign country, or at least you think you are a little less conspicuous than you used to be— the world is becoming, as the barbaric neologism would have it, more internationalized.

A question-begging bit of encouragement for internationalism comes from the apparent fact that significant social changes occur, at least more readily, when the people who are changing are surrounded by others in a similar situation: supporting groups are most helpful (Doob, 1960a, pp. 129–34). Most aspects of patriotism and nationalism are related to conformity. A study of South African college students, for example, reveals a significant connection between scores on an anti-African scale and those on a conformity scale—in correlational terms, .42 for Afrikaners and .46 for English-speaking South Africans. "It's better to go along with the crowd than to be a martyr": 35 per cent of the relatively unprejudiced but 53 per cent of the relatively prejudiced agreed with this single item from the conformity scale (Pettigrew, 1958, pp. 32–33). When conformity requires not quite so much patriotism and nationalism but more internationalism, the atmosphere facilitating change will have been altered. Somehow, though, the process must begin, and it can begin most easily after the conversion of a few leaders with prestige. Many small changes may eventually have a profound, cumulative influence. Such a bandwagon, however, seems far off.

Finally, it may very well be that a snowball in some other field of social change can produce an avalanche. Students at Princeton University, for example, were asked in 1932 and again in 1950, to indicate which of 84 traits they thought characterized 10 different ethnic groups. During the second investigation, "there were many expressions of concern by students who felt that the task was a somewhat unreasonable one"; and in general far fewer of the students subscribed to any of the same stereotypes eighteen years later (Gilbert, 1951). The investigator himself indicates that these differences have been due to the greater popularity of social science among undergraduates, to the changing composition of the student body, and to "the gradual disappearance of stereotyped characterizations in our entertainment and communication media." In any case, such a decrease in the readiness to apply glib labels to other nations is an invasion of the patriotic disposition; it may eventually lead to really significant shifts in patriotism and nationalism.

For the sake of exposition and, more importantly, in behalf of what is believed to be a good social value, this chapter has deliberately argued for internationalism, hopefully in an objective way. The same points could have been made without taking sides by asking: if one favors internationalism, what obstacles must be overcome? Such phrasing would have been a not very clever ruse to conceal the underlying motivation. In this final paragraph, it seems desirable to continue in the same vein and to face judiciously and straightforwardly another question of value. Aside from their perilously close connection with war, the greatest evil of all, are patriotism and nationalism good or bad? Psychologically it is clear that much of patriotism, like any strong emotion, and much of nationalism as we know it today, like any profound human urge, restrict the choices confronting each person: some of mankind's best thoughts, institutions, and devices are not encouraged to enter the nation from the outside. For often nationalists consider the acceptance of ideas and products from the outside to be signs of a weak character or to contribute to the development of such a character, unless somehow the innovations can be absorbed or engulfed by the nation's own culture. The narrowness resulting from nationalism, however, is also a psychological asset: nationalistic convictions are relatively few, and those few can be simplified; and the culture in which nationalism thrives and which it promotes usually is relatively unified, with the consequence that in some, in many, respects both the society and its aims are intelligible to people. Internationalism, on the other hand, provides diversity; without prejudice one is able more easily to select from the riches of the world. Diversity, however, can produce the dreadful feeling of complexity and lead to the horror and the privilege of being free to accept certain alternatives and to reject others. Nationalism creates the kind of security which induces insecurity and war in the modern world. Internationalism gives rise to insecurity which may be converted into security by people unafraid of coping with diversity. A challenging, puzzling choice for those able or willing to choose.

# REFERENCES

Adorno, T. W.; Frenkel-Brunswik, Else; Levinson, David J.; and Sanford, R. Nevitt. *The authoritarian personality.* New York: Harper, 1950.

Allport, Gordon W. *The nature of prejudice.* Cambridge: Addison-Wesley, 1954.

Almond, Gabriel A. and Verba, Sidney. *The civic culture.* Princeton: Princeton Univ. Press, 1963.

Amman, Hektor. Die Grundlagen des Sprachenfriedens in der Schweiz. *In* F. H. Riedl (ed.), *Südtirol: Land europäischer Bewährung.* Innsbruck: Universitätsverlag Wagner, 1955, pp. 181–87.

Anonymous. The Basque government in exile. *Basques* (Bulletin of the Basque Delegation in the U. S. A.), 1943, no. 1, pp. 3–5.

Baier, Kurt. *The moral point of view: a rational basis of ethics.* Ithaca: Cornell Univ. Press, 1958.

Ballis, William Belcher. *The legal position of war: changes in its practice and theory from Plato to Vattel.* The Hague: Martinus Nijhoff, 1937.

Barker, Roger G. and Wright, Herbert. *Midwest and its children.* Evanston: Row, Peterson, 1955.

Bauer, Johannes. *Volksfrommes Brauchtum Südtirols.* Innsbruck: Universitätsverlag Wagner, 1959.

Berelson, Bernard R.; Lazarsfeld, Paul F.; and McPhee, William N. *Voting: a study of opinion formation in a presidential campaign.* Chicago: Univ. of Chicago Press, 1954.

Berger, Morroe. *The Arab world today.* Garden City: Doubleday, 1962.

Blum, Robert (ed.). *Cultural affairs and foreign relations.* Englewood Cliffs: Prentice-Hall, 1963.

Bogardus, Emory S. *Immigration and race attitudes.* Boston: Heath, 1928.

BOVERI, Margret. *Treason in the twentieth century*. New York: Putnam, 1963.

BRANDT, Richard N. *Hopi ethics: a theoretical analysis*. Chicago: Univ. of Chicago Press, 1954.

BRUNER, Jerome S. and PERLMUTTER, Howard V. Compatriot and foreigner: a study of impression formation in three countries. *J. Abnormal and Social Psychol.*, 1957, 55, 253–60.

BUCHANAN, William and CANTRIL, Hadley. *How nations see each other*. Urbana: Univ. of Illinois Press, 1953.

BÜHLER, Charlotte. National differences in "world test" projection patterns. *J. Projective Techniques*, 1952, 16, 42–55.


CAHNMAN, Werner J. Religion and nationality. *Amer. J. Sociol.*, 1944, 49, 524–29.

CANNING, George. New morality. *In* Anonymous, *The school for satire*. London: Jacques and Co., 1802, pp. 181–208.

CANTRIL, Hadley and STRUNK, Mildred. *Public opinion 1935–1946*. Princeton: Princeton Univ. Press, 1951.

CATTELL, Raymond B. The dimensions of culture patterns by factorization of national characters. *J. Abnormal and Social Psychol.*, 1949, 44, 443–69.

—— The principal cultural patterns discoverable in the syntal dimensions of existing nations. *J. Social Psychol.*, 1950, 32, 215–53.

CHADWICK, H. Munro. *The nationalities of Europe and the growth of national ideologies*. Cambridge: Cambridge Univ. Press, 1945.

CHILD, Irvin L. *Italian or American?* New Haven: Yale Univ. Press, 1943.

—— and DOOB, Leonard W. Factors determining national stereotypes. *J. Social Psychol.*, 1943, 13, pp. 475–87.

——; POTTER, Elmer H.; and LEVINE, Estelle M. Children's textbooks and personality development. *Psychol. Monog.*, 1946, 60, no. 279.

——; STORM, Thomas; and VEROFF, Joseph. Achievement themes in folk tales related to socialization practice. *In* John W. Atkinson (ed.), *Motives in fantasy, action, and society*. Princeton: van Nostrand, 1958, pp. 479–92.

COHEN, L. Jonathan. *The principles of world citizenship*. Oxford: Basil Blackwell, 1954.


DAVIS, Allison; GARDNER, Burleigh B.; and GARDNER, Mary R. *Deep south*. Chicago: Univ. of Chicago Press, 1941.

DELAISI, Francis. *Political myths and economic realities*. London: Noel Douglas, 1925.

DETMOLD, Christian E. (trans.). *The historical, political, and diplomatic writings of Niccolo Machiavelli.* Boston: Houghton, Mifflin, 1891.

DEUTSCH, Karl W. *Nationalism and social communication.* New York: Wiley, 1953.

DINGWALL, Eric John. *Racial pride and prejudice.* London: Watts and Co., 1946.

DOLLARD, John. *Caste and class in a southern town.* New Haven: Yale Univ. Press, 1939.

—— *Fear in battle.* New Haven: Inst. of Human Relations, 1943.

DOOB, Leonard W. *Becoming more civilized.* New Haven: Yale Univ. Press, 1960a

—— The effect of codability upon the afferent and efferent functioning of language. *J. Social Psychol.,* 1960b, *52,* 3–15.

—— *Communication in Africa.* New Haven: Yale Univ. Press, 1961.

—— South Tyrol: an introduction to the psychological syndrome of nationalism. *Public Opinion Quart.,* 1962, *26,* 172–84.

DURBIN, E. F. M. and BOWLEY, John. *Personal aggressiveness and war.* New York: Columbia Univ. Press, 1939.

EMERSON, Rupert. *From empire to nation.* Cambridge: Harvard Univ. Press, 1960.

ENGELBRECHT, H. C. *Revolt against war.* New York: Dodd, Mead, 1937.

ESCALONA, Sybil. Overt sympathy with the enemy in maladjusted children. *Amer. J. Orthopsychiatry,* 1946, *16,* 333–40.

EYSENCK, H. J. *The psychology of politics.* London: Routledge and Kegan Paul, 1954.

FALLERS, Lloyd A. Ideology and culture in Uganda nationalism. *Amer. Anthrop.,* 1961, *63,* 677–86.

FELS, J. *Begriff und Wesen der Nation: eine soziologische Untersuchung und Kritik.* Münster: Aschendorffsche Verlagsbuchhandlung, 1927.

FENTON, William. Locality as a basic factor in the development of Iroquois social structure. *Bureau of Amer. Ethnology Bull.,* 1951, no. 149, 39–54.

FESTINGER, Leon. *A theory of cognitive dissonance.* Evanston: Row, Patterson, 1957.

FIELD, M. J. *Search for security: an ethno-psychiatric study of rural Ghana.* Evanston: Northwestern Univ. Press, 1960.

FIGGIS, Darrell. *AE (George W. Russell): a study of a man and a nation.* Dublin: Maunsel, 1916.

FLORSTEDT, Friedrich and STIEBER, Willi. *Neue deutsche Sprachlehre.* Frankfurt: Moritz Diesterweg, 1943.

Foreign Affairs Association of Japan. *The Japan Year Book: 1943–44.* Tokyo: Foreign Affairs Assoc. of Japan, 1943.

FRENCH, David. The exploration of Wasco ethnoscience. *Year Book, Amer. Philosophical Society,* 1956, pp. 224–26.

FRENKEL-BRUNSWIK, E. A. A study of prejudice in children. *Human Relations,* 1948, *1,* 295–306.

FREUD, Sigmund. *Group psychology and the analysis of the ego.* London: International Psycho-Analytical Press, 1922.

GESS, Karol N. The vanished glory: a problem in international psychology. *Psychoanalytic Rev.,* 1950, *37,* 345–50.

GILBERT, G. M. Stereotype persistence and change among college students. *J. Abnormal and Social Psychol.,* 1951, *46,* 245–54.

GILLILAND, A. R. and BLUM, R. A. Favorable and unfavorable attitudes toward certain enemy and allied countries. *J. Psychol.,* 1945, *20,* 391–99.

GINSBERG, M. National character. *Brit. J. Psychol.,* 1942, *32,* 183–205.

GOODRICH, Leland M. *Documents on American Foreign Relations: July 1941–June 1942.* Boston: World Peace Foundation, 1942.

GRAHAM, Milton D. The effectiveness of photographs as a projective device in an international attitudes survey. *J. Social Psychol.,* 1954, *40,* 93–120.

GRINKER, Roy and SPIEGEL, John P. *Men under stress.* Philadelphia: Blakiston, 1945.

GSCHNITZER, Franz. *Tirol: geschichtliche Einheit.* Vienna: Bergland Verlag, 1958.

—— (ed.). *SID,* a fortnightly bulletin published by the Südtirol Information Dokumentation, Innsbruck, Austria, 1963.

HALLECK, H. W. *International law.* San Francisco: H. H. Bancroft, 1861.

HARTLEY, Eugene L.; ROSENBAUM, Max; and SCHWARTZ, Shepard. Children's use of ethnic frames of reference; children's perceptions of ethnic group membership. *J. Psychol.,* 1948, *26,* 367–98.

HAYES, Carlton J. H. *France, a nation of patriots.* New York: Columbia Univ. Press, 1930.

——. *Essays on nationalism.* New York: Macmillan, 1937.

HERTZ, Frederick T. *Nationality in history and politics.* London: Routledge and Kegan Paul, 1944.

HERZOG, George. *Jabo proverbs from Liberia.* London: Oxford Univ. Press, 1936.

HODGKIN, Thomas. *Nationalism in colonial Africa.* London: Frederick Muller, 1956.

HOLMBERG, Allan. Nomads of the long bow: the Siriono of Eastern Bolivia. *Smithsonian Inst., Institute of Social Anthropology,* 1950, no. 10.

HUDSON, Manley O. (ed.). *International legislation.* Washington: Carnegie Endowment for International Peace, 1950.

HUNTER, Earle L. *A sociological analysis of certain types of patriotism.* New York: Paul Maisel, 1932.

HYMAN, Herbert H. *Political socialization.* Glencoe: Free Press, 1959.

ILG, Karl. Die rote Farbe in der Tiroler Tracht. *In* F. H. Riedel (ed.), *Südtirol: Land europäischer Bewährung.* Innsbruck: Universitätsverlag Wagner, 1955, pp. 211–20.

ISOTTI, Bruno (ed.). *Alto Adige,* a fortnightly bulletin published by Centro Nazionale Studi Alto Adige, Rome, 1961.

JAHODA, Gustav. Development of Scottish children's ideas and attitudes about other countries. *J. Social Psychol.,* 1962, *58,* 91–108.

JUNG, C. G. *The archetypes and the collective unconscious.* New York: Pantheon, 1959.

KATZ, Elihu and LAZARSFELD, Paul F. *Personal influence.* Glencoe: Free Press, 1955.

KING, James Clement. *Some elements of national solidarity.* Chicago: Univ. of Chicago Libraries, 1935.

KIRSCHWENG, Johannes. Heimat. In *Reimmichls Volkskalender.* Bozen: Athesia, 1953, p. 54.

KLUCKHOHN, Clyde and LEIGHTON, Dorothea. *The Navaho.* Cambridge: Harvard Univ. Press, 1946.

KLUCKHOHN, Florence R. and STRODTBECK, Fred L. *Variations in value orientation.* Evanston: Row, Peterson, 1961.

KOHN, Hans. *The age of nationalism.* New York: Harpers, 1962.

KUTNER, Bernard. Patterns of mental functioning associated with prejudice in children. *Psychol. Monog.,* 1958, *72,* no. 460.

LAIDLAW, W. A. *A history of Delos.* Oxford: Basil Blackwell, 1933.

LAMBERT, Wallace E. and KLINEBERG, Otto. A pilot study of the origin and development of national stereotypes. *Internat. Soc. Sci. J.,* 1959, *11,* 221–38.

LASSWELL, Harold D. and KAPLAN, Abraham. *Power and society.* New Haven: Yale Univ. Press, 1950.

LAWSON, Edwin D. Development of patriotism in children—a second look. *J. Psychol.*, 1963, *55*, 279–86.

LEE, S. G. *Manual of a thematic apperception test for African subjects.* Pietermaritzburg: University of Natal Press, 1953.

LEHMAN, Harvey C. National differences in creativity. *Amer. J. Sociol.*, 1947, *52*, 475–88.

LENIN, N. *The state and revolution.* London: Allen and Unwin, 1919.

—— and ZINOVIEV, G. *Socialism and war.* London: Martin Lawrence, 1931.

LERNER, Daniel. *The passing of traditional society.* Glencoe: Free Press, 1958.

LEROI-GOURHAN, André. *Ethnologie de l'union française: Afrique la Somalie française.* Paris: Pays d'Outre-mer, 1953.

LEWIN, Kurt. *Principles of topological psychology.* New York: McGraw-Hill, 1936.

McCLELLAND, David C. *The achieving society.* Princeton: Van Nostrand, 1961.

McDOUGAL, Myres S. and FELICIANO, Florentino P. *Law and minimum world public order.* New Haven: Yale Univ. Press, 1961.

McDOUGALL, William. *The group mind.* New York: Putnam's, 1920.

MANDELBAUM, Maurice. *The phenomenology of moral experience.* Glencoe: Free Press, 1955.

MANNHEIM, Karl. *Ideology and utopia.* New York: Harcourt, Brace, 1936.

MARX, Karl and ENGELS, Friedrich. *The communist manifesto.* New York: International Publishers, 1930.

MAY, Mark A. *A social psychology of war and peace.* New Haven: Yale Univ. Press, 1943.

MAYER, Kurt. Cultural pluralism and linguistic equilibrium in Switzerland. *Amer. Sociol. Rev.*, 1951, *16*, 157–63.

MELTZER, H. Children's thinking about nations and races. *J. Genetic Psychol.*, 1941, *58*, 181–99.

MINER, Horace M. *St. Denis: a French-Canadian parish.* Chicago: Univ. of Chicago Press, 1939.

MOELLENHOFF, Fritz. The price of individuality: speculations about German national characteristics. *Amer. Imago*, 1947, *4*, 33–60.

MORGAN, Lewis H. *League of the Ho-de-no-sau-nee or Iroquois.* New York: Dodd, Mead, 1904.

MORGENTHAU, Hans J. *Politics among nations.* New York: Knopf, 1948.

MUIR, Ramsay. *Nationalism and internationalism*. London: Constable, 1916.

MURDOCK, George P. *Our primitive contemporaries*. New York: Macmillan, 1934.

———. The common denominator of cultures. *In* Ralph Linton (ed.), *The science of man in the world crisis*. New York: Columbia Univ. Press, 1945, pp. 123–42.

———. *Social structure*. New York: Macmillan, 1949.

———; FORD, Clelland S.; HUDSON, Alfred E.; KENNEDY, Raymond; SIMMONS, Leo W.; and WHITING, John W. M. *Outline of cultural materials* (4th edition). New Haven: Human Relations Area Files, 1961.

MUSSEN, Paul Henry; CONGER, John Janeway; and KAGAN, Jerome. *Child development and personality* (2nd edition). New York: Harper and Row, 1963.

MYRDAL, Gunnar. *An American dilemma*. New York: Harpers, 1944.

NUSEIBEH, Hazem Zaki. *The ideas of Arab nationalism*. Ithaca: Cornell Univ. Press, 1956.

OAKESMITH, John. *Race and nationality*. London: Frederick A. Stokes, 1919.

PARTRIDGE, G. E. *The psychology of nations*. New York: Macmillan, 1919.

PATAI, Raphael. *Israel between East and West*. Philadelphia: Jewish Publication Society of America, 1953.

PETTIGREW, Thomas F. Personality and sociocultural factors in intergroup attitudes: a cross-national comparison. *Conflict Resolution*, 1958, 2, 29–42.

PEYRE, Henri. *Literature and sincerity*. New Haven: Yale Univ. Press, 1963.

PIAGET, J. *Judgment and reasoning in the child*. Paterson, N.J.: Littlefield, Adams, 1959.

PILLSBURY, W. B. *The psychology of nationality and internationalism*. New York: Appleton, 1919.

POTTER, David M. *People of plenty*. Chicago: Univ. of Chicago Press, 1954.

PYE, Lucian W. *Politics, personality, and nation building*. New Haven: Yale Univ. Press, 1962.

RAGLAN, Lord. *The hero*. London: Methuen, 1936.

RASMUSSEN, K. *The people of the polar north*. London: Kegan Paul, Trench, Trübner, 1908.

———. *Greenland by the polar sea*. London: William Heinemann, 1921.

RITSCHEL, Karl Heinz. *Südtirol: ein europäisches Unrecht*. Graz: Styria, 1959.

RÓHEIM, Géza. The psychology of patriotism. *Amer. Imago*, 1959, 7, 3–19.

ROSCOE, John. *The Baganda*. London: Macmillan, 1911.

ROSEGGER, Peter. Vom Edelweiss. *In* Anonymous, *Lies und Lerne!* Bozen: Athesia, 1960, p. 161.

ROSTOW, W. W. *The stages of economic growth*. Cambridge: Cambridge Univ. Press, 1961.

Royal Institute of International Affairs. *Nationalism*. London: Oxford Univ. Press, 1939.

———. *Documents on International Affairs 1939–1946*. London: Oxford Univ. Press, 1951, v. 1.

———. *Documents on International Affairs 1947–1948*. London: Oxford Univ. Press, 1952.

———. *Documents on International Affairs 1949–1950*. London: Oxford Univ. Press, 1953.


SARBIN, Theodore R. Role theory. *In* Gardner Lindzey (ed.), *Handbook of social psychology*. Cambridge: Addison-Wesley, 1954, vol. I, pp. 223–58.

SHAFER, Boyd C. *Nationalism: myth and reality*. New York: Harcourt, Brace, 1955.

SHAW, Albert (ed.). *The messages and papers of Woodrow Wilson*. New York: George H. Doran, 1924, vol. I.

SMITH, Cleveland H. and TAYLOR, Gertrude R. *Flags of all nations*. New York: Crowell, 1946.

SMITH, John E. *Value convictions and higher education*. New Haven: Edward W. Hazen Foundation, 1958.

SNYDER, Louis L. *The meaning of nationalism*. New Brunswick: Rutgers Univ. Press, 1954.

STAGNER, Ross and OSGOOD, C. E. An experimental analysis of a nationalistic frame of reference. *J. Social Psychol.*, 1941, *14*, 389–401.

STERLING, Richard W. *Ethics in a world of power: the political ideas of Friedrich Meinecke*. Princeton: Princeton Univ. Press, 1958.

STOUFFER, Samuel A., LUMSDAINE, Arthur A., et al. *The American soldier: combat and its aftermath.* Princeton: Princeton Univ. Press, 1949.

SUMNER, William Graham. *Folkways.* Boston: Ginn, 1906.

SWANSON, Guy E. *The birth of the gods.* Ann Arbor: Univ. of Michigan Press, 1960.

TEGNAEUS, Harry. *Le héros civilisateur.* Stockholm: Victor Pettersons Bokindustri, 1950.

TRAGER, Helen G. and RADKE, Marian. Early childhood airs its views. *Educational Leadership,* 1947, 5, 16–24.

TUCKER, Robert W. *The just war.* Baltimore: Johns Hopkins Press, 1960.

VATTEL, E. de. *The law of nations.* Philadelphia: Johnson and Co., 1865.

VON FIEANDT, Kai. Ueber den finnischen "Volkscharakter." *Schweizerische Zeitschrift für Psychologie,* 1953, 12, 199–210.

WALLACE, Ernest and HOEBEL, E. Adamson. *The Comanches.* Norman: Univ. of Oklahoma Press, 1952.

WALLACE, Paul A. W. *The white roots of peace.* Philadelphia: Univ. of Pennsylvania, 1946.

WALLERSTEIN, Immanuel. *Africa: the politics of independence.* New York: Vintage Books, 1961.

WARD, Barbara. *Five ideas that change the world.* New York: Norton, 1959.

WARNER, W. Lloyd. *The living and the dead.* New Haven: Yale Univ. Press, 1959.

—— and SROLE, Leo. *The social systems of American ethnic groups.* New Haven: Yale Univ. Press, 1945.

——; MEEKER, Marchia; and EELLS, Kenneth. *Social class in America.* Chicago: Science Research Associates, 1949.

WEBER, Max. *The Protestant ethic and the spirit of capitalism.* New York: Scribner's, 1930.

WECTER, Dixon. *The hero in America.* New York: Scribner's, 1941.

WEILENMANN, Hermann. *Pax Helvetica.* Erlenbach-Zürich: Eugen Rentsch Verlag, 1951.

WELLS, H. G. *A modern utopia.* New York: Scribner's, 1905.

WILSON, Godfrey and Monica. *The analysis of change.* Cambridge: Cambridge Univ. Press, 1945.

WRIGHT, Quincy. *A study of war.* Chicago: Univ. of Chicago Press, 1942.

WYLIE, Laurence. *Village in the Vaucluse*. Cambridge: Harvard Univ. Press, 1958.

YAKOBSON, Sergius and LASSWELL, Harold D. Trend: May day slogans in Soviet Russia, 1918–1943. *In* Harold D. Lasswell, Nathan Leites, et al., *Language of politics*. New York: Stewart, 1949, pp. 233–97.

ZANGWILL, Israel. *The principle of nationalities*. London: Watts, 1917.

ZNANIECKI, Florian. *Modern nationalities*. Urbana: Univ. of Illinois Press, 1952.

# INDEX